MW01687276

MÉTIS SOLDIERS OF SASKATCHEWAN: 1914-1953

Cathy Littlejohn

Library and Archives Canada Cataloguing in Publication Information

Littlejohn, Catherine
Métis soldiers of Saskatchewan, 1914-1953 / Catherine Littlejohn.

Includes bibliographical references.
ISBN 978-1-926795-10-2

1. Soldiers--Saskatchewan--Biography. 2. Métis--Wars--History--20th century. 3. Métis veterans--Saskatchewan--Biography. 4. Métis--Saskatchewan--Biography. 5. Saskatchewan--Biography. I. Gabriel Dumont Institute of Native Studies and Applied Research II. Title.

FC109.1.A1L54 2012 **971.24004'97** **C2012-907485-3**

Gabriel Dumont Institute Project Team:

Darren R. Préfontaine, Project Leader and Editor
David Morin, Graphic Designer and Copyeditor
Amaranta Sokol Como, Editor
Karon Shmon, Publishing Director
Murray Lindsay, Icon Designer
Don Ward, Editor
Globe Printers, Saskatoon, Printer

Gabriel Dumont Institute
2–604 22nd Street West
Saskatoon, SK S7M 5W1
www.gdins.org
www.metismuseum.ca

The Gabriel Dumont Institute acknowledges the financial support of the Office of the Federal Interlocutor for Métis and Non-Status Indians, Aboriginal Affairs and Northern Development Canada for the production and publication of this resource.

MÉTIS SOLDIERS OF SASKATCHEWAN: 1914-1953

Table of Contents

Dedication

This work is dedicated to the Métis military men and women who served Canada,
to those Métis soldiers who lie in graves, and to those who still struggle.
For all those Métis veterans who are in graves all over the world,
Whose voices will be forever silent,
WE MUST SPEAK FOR THEM
Because if the situation were reversed
THEY WOULD HAVE SPOKEN FOR US.
— Claude Adams

Claude Adams wrote this dedication in 2001 for the final report of the National Métis Veterans' Association to Veterans Affairs Canada (VAC). Recently his voice was silenced and his struggle ended. This work is dedicated to him and to all the others who have carried on the soldiers' fight since returning home from the battlefields.

Mother of Canada Statute, Vimy Ridge Memorial.

Author's Acknowledgements and Introduction

This work has been ten years in the making. During this time, a number of people have provided support, guidance, information, and resources. I would like to thank you all for your interest and encouragement.

This book would not have started if it had not been for Bruce Flamont. In 2001, he introduced me to the Métis veterans and their continuing struggles. With a small grant to compile a database on Métis soldiers from across Canada, he and Lynn LaRose oversaw the beginning of this initiative. The six-month project only began this process, as funding was soon suspended. The Gabriel Dumont Institute's previous work formed the core of our first list, and I want to acknowledge the generosity of Michelle Harding in passing on the work of the initial research team.

Then there were the three Claudes who fostered the work and believed in the importance of remembering Métis soldiers: Claude Adams provided inspiration and guidance; the recently deceased Claude Goulet helped me learn how to work with the First World War attestation papers online, and shared the extensive research that he had done on the Cumberland House/The Pas soldiers; and Claude Petit who has been a continuing source of knowledge and assistance. I want to thank each of them.

Individuals who provided research assistance for particular areas of the province include Bev Worsley (Fort Qu'Appelle and area), Martin Aubichon and Lloyd Bishop (Green Lake), the late Edward King and his family (Meadow Lake), Maurice Blondeau (Lestock and the Touchwood Hills), the late Mary Rose Boyer (Estevan and the southeast), and Jimmy Durocher (Île-à-

Claude Goulet (Left) and Unknown Veteran, Batoche.

la-Crosse and area). Nora Cummings and Yvonne Garicpy also provided names of family members as well as images. I would also like to thank Roy Fosseneuve (Cumberland House) for his enthusiastic support. Countless others have contributed stories and pictures over the years, and I want to thank them all.

I also acknowledge the contributions of current and recent Métis soldiers who have put young faces on the military for me. They include Claude Goulet whose health and life changed forever; Felix Merasty who said it was taken for granted that he would join up because he was from Île-à-la-Crosse; Adam Daigneault who found his solace in traditional Métis fiddling; and Michael Rivard who is still in the forces, spent one tour in Afghanistan, and is always on my mind. A special thank you should be extended to the staff of the Saskatchewan Archives Board and the Local History Room, Frances Morrison Library, Saskatoon for their invaluable help.

This book represents a continuation of the work of others who have been finding and documenting the stories of those Saskatchewan Métis who served in the First, Second, and Korean Wars. The book does not tell the whole story, but it is an attempt to tell as many stories as possible to preserve a record of the contribution and sacrifice of the province's Métis people.

This book is an invitation to veterans and families to remember their own stories and offer them to the community as a testament of their courage. It is important that Métis community members understand their veterans' contribution in part by understanding the varied and often dangerous tasks that these service people completed and the conditions in which they had to live. This book tells the story of the battles in which the men were involved and the context in which those battles took place. Please feel free to critique this book, add stories that should be included, and provide names of other service people so that their contribution can be acknowledged.

I would like to thank the Gabriel Dumont Institute for publishing this book, and in particular, Karon Shmon, Darren Préfontaine, David Morin, and Amaranta Sokol Como for their hard work in putting this book together.

Cathy Littlejohn
Saskatoon, Saskatchewan
Winter 2012

Gabriel Dumont Institute Introduction

On two occasions in the past few years, Cathy Littlejohn went to France and Belgium, and visited several Canadian war cemeteries, including Bény-Sur-Mer. While visiting these vast, well-kept cemeteries, she placed mini Métis sashes on the graves of 15 Métis soldiers from Saskatchewan. By doing this simple action, she brought a bit of home to the graves of our men who fell in Europe so long ago, and demonstated that we shall never forget them. This heartfelt pilgrammage was an integral component leading to the production of this book. Viewing the graves of so many fallen Canadian soldiers and our poignant war memorials brought home the sad and brutal reality of war.

War is an unfortunate reality of the human experience, and Canada, while not particularly warlike, has never been immune to it. Despite the mythmaking of both the right and left, Canada is neither a fully warrior nation nor a peacekeeping one. We are both, having fought in a variety of international wars, including the South African War, WWI, WWII, the Korean War, the first Gulf War, NATO's war against Yugoslavia over Kosovo, the US-led invasion of Afghanistan following the 9/11 attacks, and more recently in Libya, and in innumerable peacemaking and peacekeeping missions throughout the world. Within the territory of present-day Canada, there have also been numerous wars and battles. Among the First Nations, tribal warfare has occurred since time immemorial and continued into the mid-to-late 1800s as the Métis and other Plains Aboriginal groups, including the Lakota, Nakota, Dakota, Cree, Ojibway, and Blackfoot fought over bison-hunting grounds. There were also a myriad of wars to sustain or conquer New France, the Americans invaded Canada during the American Revolutionary War and during the War of 1812, and there were popular uprisings in Upper and Lower Canada, in Red River and in present-day central Saskatchewan in 1885.

Some of our wars have been overtly imperialistic, such as the Red River Expedition in which the Dominion government suppressed the Métis following the Red River Resistance, and the *fin-de-siècle* South African (Boer) War, which matched the British Empire against the Afrikaners who were fighting to protect their homes. Other wars that Canada has fought have been more altruistic, such as WWII. While Canada has participated in dozens of wars in various scales, three wars in the 20th century have provided the largest contributions in terms of enlistments and military activity. These are WWI, WWII, and the Korean War, which taken together are the focus of Cathy Littlejohn's book, *Métis Soldiers of Saskatchewan.*

The kind of Canada that took part in these three wars, fought between

August 1914 and July 1953, was different than today. The country had a small population (7.8-14.8 million), which was overwhelmingly of British and French-Canadian ancestry, with a smattering of "new" Canadians on the Prairies and in the country's larger cities. Aboriginal peoples, decimated by disease, neglect, and government policy, had not yet recovered from the disastrous nineteenth century, in which thousands perished; they were a blip on the demographic radar and collectively had no say in the direction of Canada's foreign or defence policy.

For a sparsely-populated country, Canada's war efforts in 1914-18 and in 1939-45 were profound. In these two wars, 1.8 million Canadians and Newfoundlanders enlisted to fight a faraway enemy. During WWI, the Canadian Corps (along with the Australians) were the British Empire's shock troops. In the last two years of the war, the Canadians won a series of bloody battles, including Vimy Ridge (on Easter weekend, April 1917), which culminated in a series of fast-paced battles known collectively as "Canada's Hundred Days." These battles — which smashed the German Army, put it in retreat and won the war — focused on the capture of Amiens in early August 1918 and of Cambrai on October 9, 1918. All told, more than 60,000 Canadians died in the "war to end all wars."

A generation later, Canada was a major player in the victory against fascism. By the end of WWII, Canada had raised the largest volunteer military in a total war situation, had the third largest navy in the world, and the fourth largest air force. 1.1 million, the vast majority of them volunteers, served Canada in the 1939-45 war; over 42,000 of them died for our freedom. 50,000 Canadian women served in auxiliary non-combat roles, such as nursing or transporting supplies and materiel.[1] Canada hosted and trained thousands of Commonwealth and allied airmen through the Commonwealth Air Training Program. The Royal Canadian Navy and Canadian Merchant Marine convoys shouldered much of the responsibility for transporting troops, foodstuffs, and war matériel across the North Atlantic. Our war industries churned out, thanks to the tireless efforts of thousands of women factory workers, vast amounts of war matériel. Our farms produced invaluable foodstuffs such as wheat, cheese, and beef, which fed the allied armies. By war's end, Canada's industrial output grew exponentially to the point where, on a per capita basis, we out-produced the US.[2] In Sicily, Italy, Normandy, the Falaise Pocket, Belgium, in the Netherlands and into northwest Germany, the Canadian Army made short work of the Wehrmact and its armed SS adjuncts — the world's most formidable army.[3] It was a staggering achievement for a country of 11 million people.

The Korean War has not been an area of great interest to Canadians, likely since it happened so close to the end of WWII. After WWII, Canadians wanted to forget about war and get on with postwar reconstruction. Nonetheless, 26,000 Canadians served in the war and more than 500 died. In April 1951, the Canadian Army (and the Australian Army) defeated a much larger Chinese and North Korean force at Kap'yong, thus preventing a Communist victory. For this action, the 2nd Princess Patricia's Canadian Light Infantry received the United States Presidential Citation. The war ended in a stalemate and harkened back, in many respects, to the trench warfare of WWI.

Aboriginal Canadians answered the call in these wars in great number, despite the fact that they existed on the fringes of society. After the 1885 Resistance, more First Nations people were put on reserves and Indian Agents, who used the "Pass System" to keep people on their reserves, closely monitored their every movement. The Métis largely became landless people and squatted on the approaches of Crown Land or road allowances; hence, they became known as the "Road Allowance People." Poverty, a lack of educational opportunities (since the Métis largely did not own property, they paid no property taxes — a prerequisite to sending children to school in Saskatchewan prior to the election of the CCF government in 1944), and societal racism ensured that the Métis would remain a marginalized, colonized people.

Nonetheless, the Métis volunteered during WWI, WWII, and the Korean War in large numbers. Unfortunately, we don't have exact enlistment figures for the Métis, as we do for Status First Nations or Euro-Canadians, but we can deduce that their enlistments in proportion in WWI and WWII were as high as the English-Canadian average of forty-two to fifty 50 per cent for men between eighteen and forty-five.[4] The only thing holding back Métis enlistment would have been poor health: many had suffered from tuberculosis or had been malnourished while living on road allowances. For instance, men with missing teeth were turned away. Nonetheless, units such as the Canadiens-Français du Nord-Ouest, Princess Patricia's Canadian Light Infantry, the Loyal Edmonton Regiment, the Regina Rifle Regiment, the Royal Winnipeg Rifles, the Saskatoon Light Infantry, the Saskatchewan Light Horse, the Saskatchewan Regiment, the South Saskatchewan Regiment, and the Winnipeg Grenadiers had scores of Métis soldiers during the two world wars.

Cumberland House, Green Lake, Lebret, Duck Lake, and many other Métis communities sent hundreds of young men into combat. While their men went to war, many Métis women manned trap lines to support their families. The fact that the Métis enlisted and fought for a country that had, through implicit and explicit government policy, marginalized and often oppressed them, speaks to their fundamental generosity of character.

Every Métis family and community has its own war stories. In 1997, the Gabriel Dumont Institute chronicled Métis war stories in *Remembrances: Interviews with Métis Veterans*. Here is a very important war story from that book: Joseph McGillivary, a Métis trapper from Cumberland House, claimed to have captured SS Obersturmbannführer Kurt Meyer, the man responsible for the murder of more than 150 Canadian servicemen. However, history credits the capture to partisans[5] or to the Americans. There is a story related to this one, which is not in the book, but one that nevertheless touched one Métis family. The teenage fanatics of the 12th Armoured SS, Hitler Jugend, which were led by the very same Kurt Meyer, murdered Cumberland House's Napoleon Morin.

In another Métis war story, Frank Tomkins, and every male in his extended family from Girouard, Alberta, enlisted during WWII. His brother Charles Tomkins was attached to the US 8th Air Force Bomber Command and because of his fluency in Cree was one of the first Code Talkers.[6] The Americans used the Code Talkers to confuse the enemy by sending orders in an unintelligible language. After briefly using Canadian Métis and Cree as Code Talkers, the US military began using their own Native-American servicemen, largely Navajos, to fill this vital role. Other family members served in the infantry. Nevertheless, despite their service to their country, Frank and his family were unable to receive veterans' benefits![7]

Memories such as these, which focus on individuals or small communities, are more tangible and personal than the larger picture that outlines our national achievement and sacrifice. As individuals, as communities, and as a nation, we should never forget our war stories. They instill in us the horror of war, and the necessity of always looking for a peaceful solution to resolve international conflict; however, they also demonstrate that when all we hold dear is under assault, sometimes we have no choice but to fight. We should never forget these stories and the role played by our brave soldiers, sailors, and airmen and women who fought for our freedom. They willingly fought for a country which, despite its many injustices, remains a favoured place. Collectively, we can only hope to live up to this legacy by properly remembering and honouring their sacrifice, while building a country that is respectful to all our peoples.

For *Métis Soldiers of Saskatchewan*, Cathy Littlejohn has spent a great deal of time developing a detailed list of more than 1,700 Métis soldiers from Saskatchewan who fought in two World Wars and in the Korean War. This book, moreover, is important because our Great War veterans have passed on and those from WWII and the Korean War will soon leave us too. *Métis Soldiers of Saskatchewan* keeps the stories of Métis veterans in our memories and ensures that we will remember them and never forget their sacrifices.

Painstakingly, and over the course of several years, Cathy has collected the stories of Métis soldiers through published remembrances, oral histories, newspaper accounts, local histories, academic studies, and popular history books, as well as photographs. By reading this book and perusing through her soldiers list, you will see that more Saskatchewan Métis died during the D-Day landings than during the 1885 Resistance, and that most Métis volunteered in the two World Wars and very few were conscripted. Cathy's research also demonstrates that in WWI, Métis enlistees were primarily privates and were in other lower ranks, but during WWII and the Korean War, the Métis started to become non-commissioned officers and in some instances, officers. No doubt, Métis enlistees in the present-day Canadian Forces would now include various ranks in all three services: the Army, the Royal Canadian Navy, and the Royal Canadian Air Force.

This important commemorative book will greatly contribute to our collective knowledge of the role played by Saskatchewan's Métis during Canada's various war efforts, and complements a similar book by Bryan Cyr about Métis veterans from Manitoba.[8] It will also be a wonderful companion volume to the Gabriel Dumont Institute-sponsored national Métis Veterans' Memorial Monument[9] that will eventually be installed at Batoche.

Darren Préfontaine
Gabriel Dumont Institute Publishing Department
July 2012

Métis Go To War

... today there are no more staunch upholders of the rights of Canada than the Metis, and many are those of the younger generation who have laid down their lives for King and Country during the late war [World War I].[10]

— Patrice Fleury, Captain of the Métis Scouts, Northwest Resistance, who lost his son in the First World War

A disproportionate number of Saskatchewan Métis people participated in the wars of the twentieth century. The impact on our families and small communities was enormous. The story of these Métis soldiers is part of Saskatchewan's story.

We, the Métis people, know the contribution that our people made in service to Canada. Our grandfathers, fathers, sons, brothers, mothers, sisters, and daughters have protected this land. Many were in Canada's military forces. We made sacrifices. We did our duty.

Métis soldiers fought for the British Crown during the War of 1812. Métis voyageurs helped British officers take Fort Mackinac from the Americans in July 1812, and defended it against recapture in 1814. We were there to capture the American warships, the *Tigress* and the *Scorpion*. Métis fighters defended Lake Huron and helped to preserve the Northwest for Britain.

Métis Scouts attached to the International Boundary Commission.

In 1816, Cuthbert Grant led Métis cavalrymen at the Battle of Seven Oaks. Métis horsemen became the backbone of the supply system for the Red River colony and the fur trade. With discipline and organization, we pursued bison. As military historian Stewart Mien has written,

> *Equipped with rifle and horse, they* [the Métis] *became efficient buffalo hunters, often the main suppliers of meat and other bison products to the forts and trading posts. These hunters established an impressive military organization based on a ten man unit with a captain at its head. The origins of this unit lay in the annual hunting parties which rode onto the plains after the buffalo. The Métis were excellent light cavalrymen.*[11]

Patrice Fleury, Métis captain of scouts during the 1885 Resistance.

According to Mien, our greatest fame came in 1851 at the Battle of the Grand Coteau, where we defeated the Sioux, then the fiercest and most respected fighters on the Plains. In Mien's words, "Thereafter, the Métis were an important military force in the West."[12] Our grandfathers told of fighting with First Nations people and acting as mediators between different First Nations. The Métis *Law of the Prairie* was enforced in Rupert's Land and later in the North-West Territories in the time between the cessation of the Hudson's Bay Company regulations and the imposition of laws by the new absentee landlord, the Dominion of Canada.

Métis guides, interpreters, freighters, and soldiers travelled with all major exploration, missionary, tourist, and trade caravans crossing Western Canada in the nineteenth century. We protected travellers going through First Nations territory. Our reputation, gained at the Grand Coteau, guaranteed those travelling with us safe passage.

The Boundary Commission and the North-West Mounted Police (NWMP) depended on our support to conduct their work. After the Battle of the Little Big Horn, not only 4,000 Sioux, but also over 100 Nez Percé, a number of Bannock (Northern Paiute) and numerous other First Nation groups congregated at Wood Mountain and Fort Walsh seeking the Queen's protection. The NWMP used our experience and our ability to speak many languages to protect the force and the First Nations people as well. For our efforts, the American Army hunted us down when we crossed the border to hunt bison to feed the American Indians who could not cross the border to hunt for themselves. Our Métis cavalry was critical in maintaining peace and stability among Native Americans, Canadian First Nations, the US Army, and the NWMP.

In 1885 and after, we protected the US/Canada border. We provided a home guard in communities such as St. Albert, in present-day Alberta, where Métis men made up the largest portion of the St. Albert Mounted Rifles. Some Métis men were part of the Nile Voyageurs who went to Africa to help the British liberate Khartoum. Our superb cavalrymen were sought after as troops in the South African (Boer) War and in the First World War.

Surveyors (Scout) Corps during the 1885 Rebellion, probably at Qu'Appelle, SK.

The First World War

For the descendants of proud, fearless voyageurs and buffalo hunters, 1885 ushered in a period of suffering and despair. A rebellion, a railway and a scrip program were to have dramatic and long-lasting effects. Only with the onset of World War One were some Métis able to break the bonds of poverty and prejudice.

— Julia Harrison
Metis: People Between Two Worlds[13]

Saskatchewan Métis men went to war because German troops invaded Belgium in August 1914. In 1839, Britain had signed a treaty with Belgium and other European powers, promising to declare war on any country that invaded Belgium. Britain declared war on Germany on August 4, 1914. As a consequence, all British colonies and dominions, including Canada, were automatically at war with Germany too. This European treaty plunged our country into war.

Canada did not have a professional military force when war was declared. It raised a citizen's army — an army of volunteers. By the end of the war, more than 600,000 Canadians had enlisted out of a population of approximately 8,000,000. More than 60,000 would be killed and 220,000 wounded. The tremendous response to the call for volunteers was in part due to the method of recruitment. Recruiters went across the country, visiting communities and signing up volunteers. They visited many Saskatchewan Métis communities, and many of our men volunteered to fight in the Belgian and French countryside.

Opposite Page:
Left: “D” Squadron, 22nd Saskatchewan Light Horse Officers, Battleford, Saskatchewan, 1911.
Right: Twenty-seventh Light Horse, Camp Sewell?, Manitoba. [ca. 1911].

This Page:
Top to bottom:
22nd Saskatchewan Light Horse, Training at Camp Sewell, Manitoba, May 1912.
Military Parade, Battleford, Saskatchewan, 1914.
Military Parade, Battleford, Saskatchewan, 1914.
Voluntary Expedition Force, Battleford, Saskatchewan, August 16, 1914.

Some non-Aboriginal people in Saskatchewan were surprised at the huge number of Saskatchewan Métis who enlisted in the First World War. After all, it was less than thirty years since the Métis had stood against the North-West Field Force during the 1885 Resistance. In a September 1916 letter to the editor of the Saskatoon *Phoenix*, entitled "Why are so many Metis Enlisting?" Métis leader Joe Z. LaRocque explained that it should be no surprise that we were answering the call to fight for Britain because our people had "defended their sovereign in days gone by."[14] Recruiters aggressively sought Métis soldiers, signing up men on the spot. Compared to the recruits that were coming from the towns

George Loyie.

Robert Guthrie Sr.

Joseph Victor Daniels, France, 1914.

and cities, our men had skills, abilities, and experience that suited them for military service. The Métis were skilled horsemen, they could live off the land, they were comfortable handling guns, they were excellent marksmen, and were fearless in battle, as the government well knew. Métis soldiers were respected for their bravery, tenacity, and marksmanship.

Men from every Métis community went to be soldiers. Métis men who had been in the militias before the war were some of the first volunteers. By the time conscription was introduced, in early 1918, many young Métis men had joined the Canadian Corps, many underage. The response was phenomenal. John Klyne of Estevan, for example, had 32 direct descendants serve in the First World War.[15]

Recruiters are remembered in our communities. Pierre Vandale, a Métis from the Duck Lake area, wrote a poem about them:

Going to War

There was one fellow
going round to dances
and things like that
and he'd tell them:
I'LL HIRE YOU
And they'd sign up
or whatever
and then ask him:
WHAT FOR?
And he said:
FOR DOING NOTHING
And naturally
he'd … get them all
to sign these papers
So a lot got involved
in going to war
And they didn't know
why they were going
or where they were going.[16]

Many of our communities were stripped of men. Enlistment records show that Métis men in their forties enlisted along with boys as young as fifteen and sixteen years of age. Many who initially signed up were men with connections to the 1885 Resistance. In 1885, William Vandale fought beside Gabriel Dumont and Louis Riel to protect his family and community. In the

First World War, he and his sons were brothers in arms in the Canadian military that so recently had been the enemy. Another Métis soldier, Arthur Tourond, was born in Fish Creek and was a two-year-old when the Resistance took place. Louis Riel had carried Tourond — the tall, fair-haired, blue-eyed Métis who enlisted in 1916 — to safety after the Battle of Batoche.[17] In 1918, he was sent to France to fight for Canada. Dumont and Riel were among the names on the enlistment rosters for Canadian soldiers serving in the First World War.

Opposite Page: Top: Joe McGillis, Métis [ca.1914-1918]. Bottom: Army Training, Western Canada [ca.1914-1918]. This page: Officers of 28th Battalion. Canadian Expeditionary Force [ca.1914-1918].

Many Métis men from the Batoche and Duck Lake areas signed up, including Ernest, Pierre, and Alfred Petit; Ernest Joseph, James, and William John Arcand; Harry Badger; Fred and John Bourassa; Edmond Joseph, Ernest, and John-Baptiste Boyer; John Caplette; Robert Caron; August, Gabriel, Harris, John Louis, and Martin Dumont; François Fayant; George Ferguson; Jules Fisher; Clément Fleury; Peter Ledoux; Edward LaFramboise; Pierre Lafontaine; Gabriel LaPlante; Joseph Larivière; Isadore Richard and Napoleon Ledoux; Henry, John, and William John Letendre; Pascal Montour; Gabriel, James, and Israël Ouellette; Gustav, Joseph, Michael, Samuel Parenteau, and Joseph Paul Parenteau; Jean Marie, Israël, William, and Robert Paul; Zacharie Racette; Joe Trottier; and Norbert Vandal.

Alfred Petit.

Clément Fleury.

Jean-Marie Paul.

Jules Fisher.

Patrick Lejour.

S. Dumont.

Thomas Samuel Sr.

William Jensen.

Robert Caron.

Top Left: Tom Ouellette (Right) and R. Joseph Ferguson (Duck Lake). Top Right: Napoléon Ledoux. Middle Left: Ralph Morin, Oscar Roy, Charles McCallum, and George Villebrun. Middle Right: Peter Sandy (1889-1956) and Louis Chatelaine (1898-1986). Bottom Left: George and William Montour. Bottom Right: Joseph Robert Paul and Unknown.

Meadow Lake and Green Lake sent Métis men to the First World War, including Alfred, Clarence, and Norbert Arnault; James and John Ballendine; Joseph, Louisant, and William Bourassa; Albert, J.-B., Ambroise, and Nick Boyer; Louis and Peter Chatelaine; Antoine Collins; Charles Daniel; Antoine and John Deguerre; Étienne and Louis DeLaronde; Owen Jeanor Fleury; John Lesard; Jules Haggerty; Samuel Halcro; Fred Kennedy; Ambroise Marion; Norbert andVital Morin; Napoleon Nault; Ambroise Laboucane; Alex Sinclair; and Ernest and William Ross.

Top Left to Right: William John Bourassa. Alexander Sinclair. Bottom Row Left to Right: Baptiste Gerard, Peter Morin, Paul Morin, and Norbert Morin. Frederick Kennedy. Opposite Page Top Row: Norbert and Ralph Morin. Norbert Morin. Peter Hyacinthe Morin. Opposite Page Bottom Row: William Bourassa.

Many of our young men signed up for service as soon as they could. Walter Peter Sayers, son of Emma Sayers (Bresaylor), was a teamster who could both read and write. Shortly after his eighteenth birthday in January 1917, he tried to get in the Army. Barely five months later, in June 1917, this 5' 7" fair complexioned, grey-eyed and brown-haired Métis was declared fit. He became a member of the 77th Depot Battery, Canadian Field Artillery, Canadian Corps and was on his way to the front.[18]

Île-à-la-Crosse sent its men to war too. Joe Maurice remembered:

Soldiers from Île-à-La Crosse

And he says he remembers the First World War.
Lots of people left from here he said.
But most of them are not living now
from the First World War.

They never told the people, what they were fighting for,
And he says most of you know lots
of people from around here
got killed at the war.

— Joe Maurice (translated)[19]

The Great War reached Cumberland House too. This small Métis community in northeastern Saskatchewan sent thirty-five soldiers to the First World War. These were Private (Pte.) Gordon Adam Buck, Pte. Francis Buck, Pte. Louis-Pierre Cadotte, Pte. Charlie Canada, Pte. Jonas Carriere, Lance (L)/Corporal (Cpl.) Alexandre Chaboyer, Pte. Charlie Chaboyer, Sapper (Spr.) Patrick Chaboyer, Spr. Alfred Cook, Pte. Colin Cook, Pte. Daniel Cook, Pte. Joseph Henry Deschambeault, Pte. Jean-Baptiste Dorion, Pte. John Gregory Dorion, Pte. Alexander Fosseneuve, Pte. Felix A. Fosseneuve, William Greenleaf, Pte. George Cypron Halcrow, Pte. William David Thompson Jones, Pte. Eric Thomas Keddie, Pte. Oswald Victor Keddie, Pte. Joseph Richard McAuley, Pte. John McKay, Pte. Frank Paul, Pte. Edward Pelly, Pte. Isaac Pelly, Pte. Joseph Adam Pelly, Pte. Jean-Baptiste Richard, Pte. Edward T. Sayhes, Pte. Henry Settee, Chief Thomas Settee, Pte. Horace W. Umpherville, Pte. Charlie Wilson, and Pte. Zacchaeus Young.

Henry Settee (Centre), Angus Sayese (Left) and Henry Sayese (Right), 1918.

In the spring of 1916, as soon as the ice had gone from the rivers, a group of young men left Cumberland House by canoe to enlist at The Pas. These included a trapper, Charlie Canada, son of Jacob Canada; Jean-Baptiste Dorion, another trapper, not yet 18; and Horace Walter Umpherville, from Glen Mary, who was living at Cumberland House. They enlisted together. Charles Canada died before the end of the year. Cumberland House's Private Oswald Keddie and Jean-Baptiste Dorion were either killed in action or died of their wounds.[20]

Our Métis community provided French-speaking soldiers in a time when it was politically expedient to show the Canadian public that French Canadians were enlisting. One recruitment team targeted French Canadians in Alberta, Saskatchewan, and Manitoba. On many attestation forms, Métis enlistees became part of the 233rd Battalion, Canadien-Français du Nord-Ouest based in Edmonton, which began recruiting in early 1916 throughout Western Canada. This battalion was absorbed into the 178th (Canadien-Français) Battalion, Canadian Corps on March 1917. Others enlisted in the 232nd Battalion, called the "French-Canadian Brigade," which was recruited

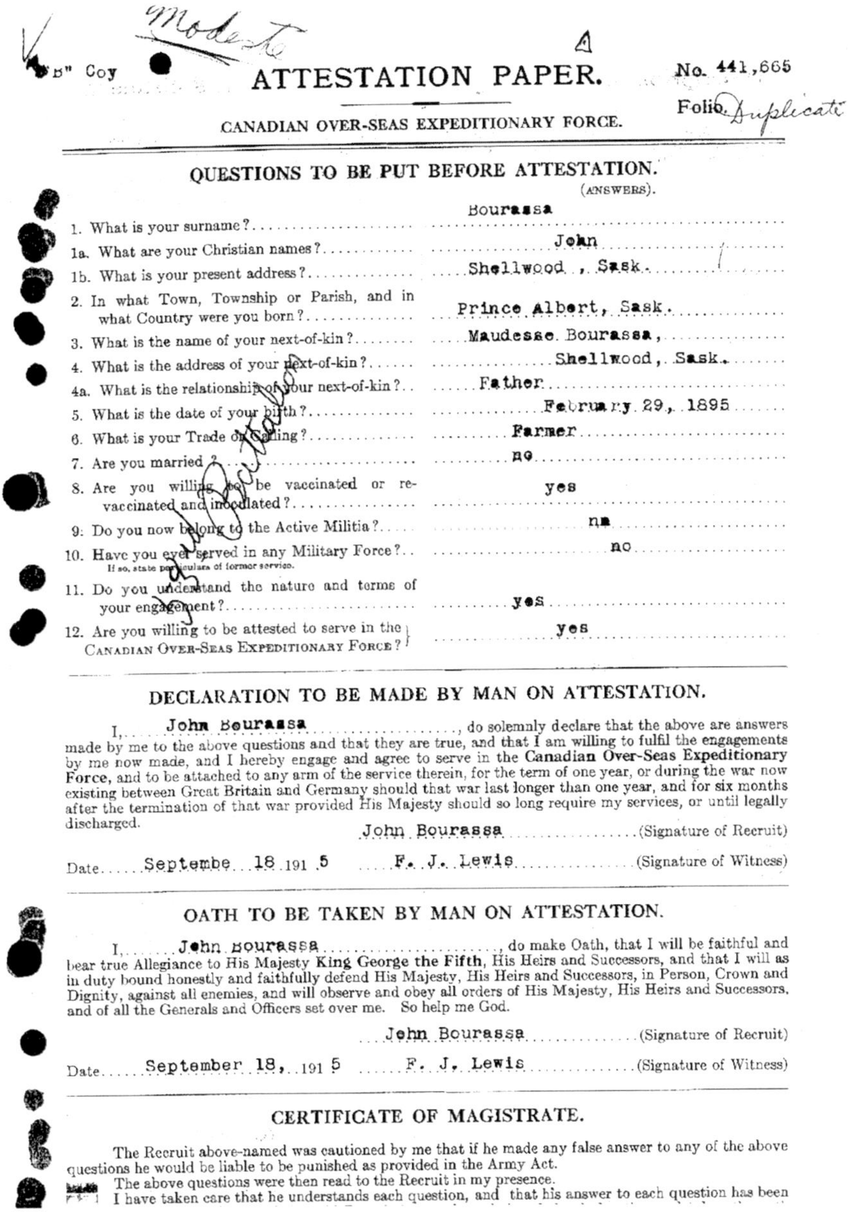

"B" Coy — Modeste

ATTESTATION PAPER.

No. 441,665

Folio. Duplicate

CANADIAN OVER-SEAS EXPEDITIONARY FORCE.

QUESTIONS TO BE PUT BEFORE ATTESTATION.

	(ANSWERS).
1. What is your surname?	Bourassa
1a. What are your Christian names?	John
1b. What is your present address?	Shellwood, Sask.
2. In what Town, Township or Parish, and in what Country were you born?	Prince Albert, Sask.
3. What is the name of your next-of-kin?	Maudesse Bourassa,
4. What is the address of your next-of-kin?	Shellwood, Sask.
4a. What is the relationship of your next-of-kin?	Father
5. What is the date of your birth?	February 29, 1895
6. What is your Trade or Calling?	Farmer
7. Are you married?	no
8. Are you willing to be vaccinated or re-vaccinated and inoculated?	yes
9. Do you now belong to the Active Militia?	no
10. Have you ever served in any Military Force? If so, state particulars of former service.	no
11. Do you understand the nature and terms of your engagement?	yes
12. Are you willing to be attested to serve in the Canadian Over-Seas Expeditionary Force?	yes

DECLARATION TO BE MADE BY MAN ON ATTESTATION.

I, John Bourassa, do solemnly declare that the above are answers made by me to the above questions and that they are true, and that I am willing to fulfil the engagements by me now made, and I hereby engage and agree to serve in the **Canadian Over-Seas Expeditionary Force**, and to be attached to any arm of the service therein, for the term of one year, or during the war now existing between Great Britain and Germany should that war last longer than one year, and for six months after the termination of that war provided His Majesty should so long require my services, or until legally discharged.

John Bourassa (Signature of Recruit)

Date September 18 1915 F. J. Lewis (Signature of Witness)

OATH TO BE TAKEN BY MAN ON ATTESTATION.

I, John Bourassa, do make Oath, that I will be faithful and bear true Allegiance to His Majesty **King George the Fifth**, His Heirs and Successors, and that I will as in duty bound honestly and faithfully defend His Majesty, His Heirs and Successors, in Person, Crown and Dignity, against all enemies, and will observe and obey all orders of His Majesty, His Heirs and Successors, and of all the Generals and Officers set over me. So help me God.

John Bourassa (Signature of Recruit)

Date September 18, 1915 F. J. Lewis (Signature of Witness)

CERTIFICATE OF MAGISTRATE.

The Recruit above-named was cautioned by me that if he made any false answer to any of the above questions he would be liable to be punished as provided in the Army Act.

The above questions were then read to the Recruit in my presence.

I have taken care that he understands each question, and that his answer to each question has been

William John Bourassa, WWI Attestation Papers.

Joseph Victor Laliberte.

Julius Haggerty, Gaudry, and Chartrand, Willow Bunch.

primarily in Manitoba in early 1917. Many of our soldiers ended up in Québec regiments like the Vingt-Deuxième (the "Vandoos" to English-speaking Canadians). The linguistic abilities of our men were a great asset in France.

Recruiters sought our hunters for their knowledge of and ability to handle firearms. They were valued for being able to see and distinguish shapes on the landscape in the dark. These were exactly the skills needed to survive on the front lines during the First World War. John Gregory Dorion (Cumberland House), John Ducharme (Meadow Lake), Henry Settee (Cumberland House), and Walter (Horace) Umpherville were some of the Métis hunters who enlisted.

Top to Bottom: Tenth battalion, Canadian Expeditionary Force, Valcartier, Quebec, 1914.
Army camp, Regina, Saskatchewan, 1918.
Men on the troop ship "Olympia", sailing to England during the First World War. [ca.1917-1918].
Soldiers travelling in box car in France, during the First World War [ca. 1917-1918].
Opposite Page Bottom: 232nd Battalion, Canadian Expeditionary Force recruits, North Battleford, Saskatchewan, 1916.

After a preliminary introduction to drilling, learning discipline, and following military protocol, our men were sent to England to get battle ready for the task ahead in France and Belgium. The men were a little better prepared than they had been when they joined up, but just a little. They did have their kits — their uniforms and the notorious Ross Rifle, which became the snipers' favourite weapon for its accuracy, but the infantryman's curse for its unreliability. It is hard to imagine what the young Métis boys must have experienced, travelling across the ocean. They must have been thinking of what lay ahead with a certain sense of excitement obscured by a fear of the unknown, as much as their fear of the enemy. The transport ships carrying the troops demonstrated that the First World War was a war which combined old methods of warfare with modern technology: in the holds of the ships were horses.

The 1st Canadian Division moved to the front lines in April 1915. Fresh from training in Britain, our soldiers inherited part of the old French trenches, south of the Ypres-Poelkapelle road abandoned by the French Army after the First Battle of Ypres (October-November 1914).

Our soldiers strengthened the trenches, as the walls were falling in, then buried the fallen French soldiers, and built latrines. Since this area was considered "quiet," the inexperienced Canadian soldiers and French Colonial troops were assigned here.

The First World War lasted four years. There were few large, decisive battles. For the most part, soldiers fought over a few metres of territory, and these small victories were often followed by the territory being lost again. The front lines moved by inches, and the men waited for orders to attack.

Village of St. Julien, France, 1915.

Joseph LaRose and Sons: Wilfrid (Joseph's Left), Ramie (Uniform), William John, Albert George (Moustache), Pool Room, Tantallion, SK.

The fact that the battles were few did not mean that the soldiers at the front were safe from death and injury. The randomness of the fighting, particularly the fear of death, led to anxiety, challenging the soldiers' mental security. In the words of historian Norm Christie, "Poison gas, flame-throwers, massive underground explosions, bullets and constant artillery fire were the weapons used to tear both men and land apart."[21]

Our soldiers were introduced immediately to life in the trenches. In the words of Métis soldier Owen Sanderson,

> *Trench life was vulgar. We slept in the wet and cold, and we were only a few hundred yards from the German lines. We would hear them holler and fire, and then the bullets whistle. I smelt the powder and heard the bullets whistling, and that was all I wanted to see.*[22]

Owen Sanderson.

The soldiers dug the trenches themselves when they moved to a new location on the front line. This is where the men lived and died. The trenches afforded what little protection the soldiers had from the elements and enemy fire. The men ate, slept, and worked in the trenches. Trenches were narrow passages that met and turned in different directions creating a maze of walkways with street names to allow the soldiers to keep track of where they were.

Shell bursting in a trench, injuring an unidentified member of the 5th Battalion, C. E. F.

Trenches were just a little deeper than the height of an average man. If a soldier forgot himself and stuck his head above the trench, he was a perfect target for an enemy sniper waiting for just such a target. The most dangerous trench duty was at the Observation Post where a soldier had to stand high enough to watch what the enemy was doing. The observers provided the sniper with a great shot because the Observation Posts were placed as close to enemy positions as possible.

Essex Farm, Flanders Fields. Inside of Canadian Trench.

"No Man's Land" was what the soldiers called the space between the opposing trenches. No Man's Land was by no means empty space. It was a horrible, dangerous place. Snipers from both sides watched for signs of movement. Shells from both sides burst all around. Barbed wire protected trenches from attack by opposing forces. The incessant bombardments had stripped trees and other signs of life from the landscape.

German shell bursting near advanced dressing station [ca.1914-1918].

Métis soldiers faced this dismal reality. There were rats, and the constant stench of wet clothes and bodies. Keeping dry was a persistent problem. As part of their defence against the German advance, the Belgian people opened the canals at night and flooded the land. By the time our men arrived to defend Belgium, the fields were mud lakes. As if that was not enough, it rained day after day. One result of soldiers always having wet feet was "trench foot," a condition that literally caused feet to rot.

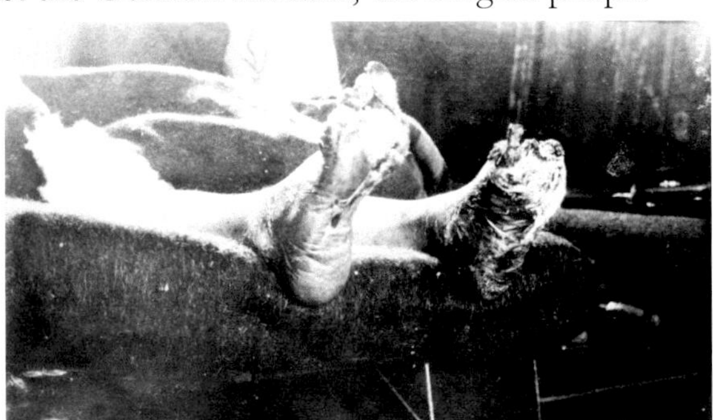

Case of trench feet suffered by unidentified soldier, 1917.

Top Left: A trench on the Canadian front showing "funk holes." Top Right: Canadian Pioneers laying trench mats over mud. Battle of Passchendaele. November 1917. Bottom: Draining Trenches. 22nd Infantry Battalion (French Canadian). July 1916.

Amidst this, Métis soldiers performed essential jobs. Gaspar Morin (Shell River), Alexander Settee (Cumberland House/The Pas), Joseph Edward Corrigal (Prince Albert), Célestin Lafond (Green Lake), John Baptiste Morin (Green Lake), George Alexander Villebrun (Jack Fish Lake), and Zacchaeus Young (Cumberland House) were members of the Canadian Forestry Corps. This special forestry battalion provided materials to make duckboards, which allowed soldiers to walk on the bottom of the trenches while keeping their feet out of the mud. The foresters also found wood to shore up the trenches and tunnels.

Some Métis hunters became snipers. Sniping was a significant job in the Great War. On the battlefield, where enemy lines were only a few hundred metres apart, a sniper could be a very effective weapon. "Sniper fire was usually fatal and, therefore, more greatly feared than shrapnel, T.M. shells, and bombs … the rifle bullet struck like an invisible bolt, without warning or any chance of seeking cover."[23] Edward Klyne and A. N. Fidler

Scouts and snipers (8th infantry Battalion), June 1916.

— who would later become recognized leaders among our people — were snipers in the First World War.[24]

One of the most celebrated Métis snipers in the First World War was Henry Norwest. He was one of 90 people in the Canadian Expeditionary Force/Canadian Corps to earn the Military Medal with Bar, the equivalent to earning two Military Medals. Before joining the forces, Norwest was a cowboy. Although he is considered to be from Alberta, his father lived in northern Saskatchewan. He initially enlisted under the name "Henry Louie." However, Henry Louie was discharged for disorderly conduct and drunkenness after only three months in the Army. This did not deter Henry. He signed up again under the name Henry Louis Norwest. On his new attestation papers, he listed his employment as a saddler working for the Royal North-West Mounted Police (RNWMP). He was immediately assigned to the 50th Battalion.

Victor Wheeler, regimental historian for the 50th, wrote of Henry Norwest:

> *Our famous sniper no doubt understood better than most of us the cost of life and the price of death. Norwest carried out his terrible duty superbly because he believed his special skills gave him no choice but to fulfill his indispensable*

mission. Our 50th [Battalion] *sniper went about his work with passionate dedication and showed complete detachment from everything while he was on the line … Yet when we had the rare opportunity to see our comrade at close quarters, we found him pleasant and kindly, quite naturally one of us, and always an inspiration.*[25]

For the men living day after day in the front line's atrocious conditions, anxiously waiting for something to happen, trench raiding became an activity introduced by the Canadian troops. Providing a diversion, it fit nicely with ways of battle familiar to Aboriginal soldiers. It required bravery and stealth. At first, the British commanders rejected trench raiding, but it soon became a standard part of trench warfare. It was a form of harassment and intelligence gathering, and it gave the soldiers a way of taking on a challenge and building morale. Métis veteran Paul Pelletier won a Military Medal in a trench raid. He described the circumstances:

I saw some Germans coming over the trenches carrying a jug. I told my partner to keep an eye on them, and I crawled down into their trenches and stole the jug. My officer asked where I got the jug. I told him that I had got it off the Germans in the frontline. He said that I had risked my life and they gave me a medal.[26]

April 22, 1915, just weeks after our troops had established themselves on the front, the way of waging war suddenly changed. Our soldiers were in the middle of this change, which Norm Christie explains:

The Second Battle of Ypres was a turning point in the history of warfare. It was the dawn of "Total War." Until April 1915, wars had been fought within certain gentleman's rules of what was acceptable and what was not. The use of gas had been strictly forbidden. On April 22, 1915, all that changed. After this violation, war would know no rules.[27]

April 22, 1915 was a beautiful spring day in Belgium. The Germans had been waiting since mid-February to use the chlorine gas cylinders that they brought to the front. Until this fateful day in April, the winds had not favoured a gas attack against the Allied Powers. April 22, 1915 was different. The wind was blowing from the German lines. One who was there described the scene:

… I saw these Germans and I thought that they were, I wondered what they were doing, just one here and one a little further along. It looked like tin cans they

had put over and the smoke from them boiled up and it didn't rise, you know, the atmosphere kept it down and the wind blew it towards us, you see. I thought it was smoke and they were going to come up behind so we started firing at them to prevent them from following up this smoke. Then when it came along towards us, it turned green, a greeny yellow colour, chlorine gas, it was. It came up and went over the trenches and it stayed, not as high as a person, all the way across.[28]

Dan Pelletier was there. In an interview, he described how the gas felt:

Daniel Pelletier.

> *It hit you hard, once you were in contact with it; it took effect just like that. Some boys couldn't talk. Some went crazy over the pain. What a terrible thing. Of course, they'd strike when you didn't expect it. You'd never know* [when] *the gas was coming and suddenly it was all around; in the dark you could feel it. It shut out the sun. That gas business was pretty tough. It was the worst part of the war for me.*[29]

The Germans used 6,000 cylinders loaded with 160 tonnes of chlorine that day.[30] Professor Fritz Haber, director of the Kaiser Wilhelm Institute for Physical Chemistry in Berlin, had proposed the use of chlorine gas for war. Chlorine was readily available in large quantities for use in German industries. It could be packed in cylinders for easy transport, and when it was released from the cylinders, the liquid turned to gas. It was an extreme lung irritant, which damaged lung tissues. Death came when the lungs filled with fluid from the person's body.[31] By the end of the weekend, 2,000 Canadian soldiers had died this terrible way.[32]

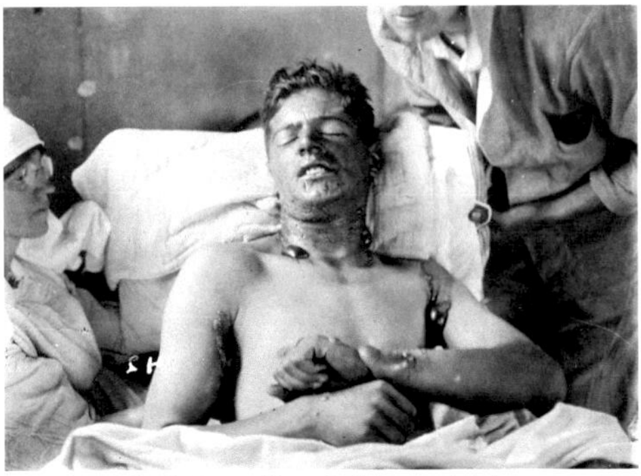

Unidentified Canadian Soldier with burns caused by mustard gas, ca. 1916-1918.

It was during the Second Battle of Ypres that Canadian soldiers gained a reputation for courage. When they were faced with gas attacks, they stood their ground. In this first experience with gas, the Canadian men had no protection. They had no way to defend themselves. They had witnessed the French colonial troops in front of them dying in agony. Still, they held their ground. Christie has written, "Through blind courage, they withstood the poisonous gas, the massive artillery bombardments and, although outnumbered [they withstood] the frontal assaults of the German infantry."[33] According to British General Sir John French, our Canadian soldiers "undoubtedly saved the situation."[34]

Some Métis soldiers suffered devastating effects from gas attacks, including Walter McKay, Alex Primeau, and John-Baptiste Dorion. Clarence (Peter) Arnault was gassed and would die on his return to Meadow Lake in 1918. We have no record of how many of our young men died from being gassed on the battlefield or how many came home with lung damage. As the war ground on and gas attacks continued, gas masks and suits were developed, and soldiers themselves found ways of stopping the gas from getting into their lungs. One method reported was urinating on a handkerchief and holding the material over the nose and mouth.[35] Such ingenious approaches must have saved many soldiers.

Nurses en route overseas, Winnipeg, Manitoba, 1915.

The sacrifice of the Canadian soldiers who lost their lives in the Great War's first gas attacks is commemorated at what is known as "Vancouver Corner" at St. Julien, France. Here a single soldier, with his arms crossed, rises on a column. "The Brooding Soldier" represents the Canadians who fell in the April 22-24, 1915 gas attacks. Its somber grandeur is symbolic of the grim yet courageous approach of the soldiers, including young Métis soldiers, as they faced the new and hideous kind of war — war for which no amount of training could have prepared them. Despite the dangers, they fought on, and closed the gap in the lines and prevented the German Army's advance.

St. Julien Memorial, Brooding Soldier.

Some Métis soldiers served as scouts. The Canadian Army's battalion scouts were known for their initiative and individual bravery. According to Lieutenant-General R. E. W. Turner, Chief of the General Staff, Canadian Corps, "It can be truthfully said that the Canadians on their front owned 'No Man's Land.' "[36] Canadian commanders employed scouts who gained knowledge of the enemy's terrain, location, and strength.

The scouts did not recklessly throw themselves into areas of danger between the enemy and the Allied lines, but the ones chosen for their superior intellect and resourcefulness had specific training to hone their natural talents. The scouts' instructors made it clear that the most important thing about being a scout was not good eyesight, good hearing, a good physique, being a good shot, or having knowledge of map reading, but rather, "a scout's honour is the most important thing of all":[37]

> *It was to develop this sense of honour that was the chief end and aim of our training. For no matter how clever or expert a scout might be, if he could not be trusted to carry out his commission, then he was no good as a scout … The importance of having scouts who, no matter what difficulties or dangers were involved would carry out orders and return with the information required can easily be understood.*[38]

Scouts were part of a battalion's intelligence section, that included observers, scouts, and snipers. They lived together and ate together. They trained during rest periods. Scouts' training included "map reading, the use of a prismatic compass; marching on compass bearings by day and night; sketching and making reports; signaling (Semaphore and Morse); methods of crawling; practice in bomb-throwing; and revolver practice."[39] The soldiers practiced in old trenches or in the territory behind the Allied trenches.

Gas helmet drill, 92nd Highlanders, August 15, 1916.

The scouts' patrols into enemy territory were invaluable. Patrols obtained information about the enemy, including the location of enemy outposts or the strength of enemy defences, such as the condition of strategically placed barbed wire in front of trenches that protected against infiltration. The scouts had to constantly survey No Man's Land because — with the rain, mud, bombardment, and battles — the land's contours were always changing. Most of the scout's work was done at night because, with the trenches being so close together, it was impossible to approach the enemy positions undetected in daylight. But even in darkness, No Man's Land was a dangerous place.

In addition to patrolling enemy trenches, scouts guided the relief troops into the front line trenches as well as the troops being relieved. Doing this required that the scouts had to intimately know the area's routes. This knowledge was gained through "diligent and painstaking reconnaissance work."[40] The scouts investigated what would lie ahead in upcoming battles before the regular troops attacked the enemy lines.

François-Xavier Cardinal was a Métis scout who earned the Military Medal for his valour in the Battle of the Drocourt-Quéant Line in September 1918. This battle was a turning point in the war, as the Canadian Corps broke through the Hindenburg Line and forced the German Army into retreat. Cardinal was one of the few conscripts to receive a medal. This Métis farmhand from Ituna was born in Lebret, the son of William and Caroline Cardinal. He served with the bilingual Royal Montreal Regiment, arriving in France in mid-August 1918. He was one of three scouts who entered the village of Cagnicourt in advance of the Canadian Corps' 1st Division. They encountered hundreds of Germans peering out of doorways and windows. The scouts pretended that their troops were right behind them and the Germans gave themselves up. The three Canadians captured 150 German troops. The unit's war diary states that Cardinal got the Military Medal "for going over the top."[41]

According to Michel Gravel, Cardinal refused to be evacuated,

> *Along with 40 other wounded men of the Royal Montreal Regiment who were inspired by their officers, many of whom were themselves wounded — he continued fighting for two days. He engaged the enemy during the main attack on September 2, 1918, during which time he participated in the capture of the village of Cagnicourt, a fortified village just behind the Drocourt-Quéant Line. On September 3, 1918, after only two hard-fought days at the front, he was evacuated, never to return to battle.*[42]

Spring 1916 was a time of difficulty for the Canadian Corps. The fighting took place in a series of craters left from underground explosions set off by the belligerents' mining operations. Joined by the Canadian 3rd Division, Canadian soldiers on the front were tasked with holding the line from Hooge to Mount Sorrel. The battlefield on which our men were asked to fight was a place so inhumane that it was hard for the soldiers to describe it. The men who were there found it difficult to write about in their diaries, and would rarely they speak of it when they returned home. Everything for miles around had been destroyed. The battlefield was strewn with dead men and horses. Broken pieces of equipment, shells, barbed wire, guns, and wagons were everywhere. One Canadian soldier wrote, "They speak of a place called Hell. If they can beat this they have to show me."[43] Historian Tim Cook refers to this battleground as an "open graveyard."[44]

Daniel Pelletier and Toby MacKenzie.

In the old history books, the war, as it was fought from trenches, was called a "war of attrition." The armies wore each other down with shellfire, night patrols, and the anxiety of not knowing when death might come. They waited for something to happen. When an encounter between the combatants occurred, victory meant that one army moved the line a few metres one way or the other. There would be no all-out victory, which would move the soldiers out of their horrible conditions. Through it all, the numbers of casualties continued to climb. The battalions had to be constantly rebuilt with reinforcements brought in while veterans were maintained in reserve to ensure that the battalion's "corporate knowledge" was passed down to the reconstituted unit.

As these dangerous and indecisive skirmishes took place, the number of Métis casualties mounted. Frederick William Boyer was killed May 1, 1916.

Mount Sorrel was one of the most important points on the line. The Germans were interested in capturing the heights. On June 2, 1916, German guns of all calibres were unleashed on the Canadian lines.[45] As the fighting continued, German engineers exploded underground mines and German soldiers

attacked with flamethrowers. The Canadian lines were decimated. Early in the Battle of Mont Sorrel, Saskatchewan Métis soldier, Pte. Roderick James Pocha, with the 9th Reserve Battalion, was killed. Mount Sorrel changed hands a couple of times before a counterattack on June 13, which returned the territory to the Canadians. The Germans did not attack again.

The Allied commanders decided that September 26, 1916 would be the day that they would battle the Germans for Thiepval Ridge. The three-day battle was a series of attacks and counterattacks. Wave after wave of Canadian infantrymen tried to reach the top of the ridge. The Allied Powers could claim partial victory, at best, with the loss of more than 10,000 men during September. The 5th Battalion was in the middle of this fierce battle which left many dead, including those whose bodies could not be identified. The 5th Battalion alone recorded 122 missing. Among the missing at Thiepval Ridge was Lebret's Pte. Joseph Réne Boileau. His name is inscribed on the Vimy Memorial with

Top to Bottom: A Scene on the battlefield near Coucelette. October, 1916.
"No Man's Land" in front of Canadian lines, Courcelette, France, October 1916.
Canadian soldiers returning from trenches during the Battle of the Somme, France, Nov. 1916.

others whose bodies have never been found. In addition, David Whitford, 1st Canadian Mounted Rifles, died September 20, 1916, and one of the tunnellers, Angus Halcrow (Pelican Narrows) was killed on Christmas Day, 1916.

The skirmishes continued, and in the early days of February 1917, on one day alone, two Saskatchewan Aboriginal soldiers, Alexander Bigman of Battleford and Frederick Bloomfield of Fir Ridge, met their death. Then, on February 13, 1917, a violent engagement started, which included a combined offensive by the Canadian Corps' 44th, 46th, 47th, and 50th Battalions. Under an intense bombardment of artillery and trench mortars, a Canadian raiding company helped meet the Corps' objectives by capturing German prisoners, gaining invaluable information on the enemy's activities.[46] During this engagement, Green Lake's John Gerard was wounded, and W. A. Vandale, son of William Vandale who had served with Riel in 1885, died from his wounds.

The Allied High Command was determined to remove the Germans from Vimy Ridge, which they had occupied since October 1914. The Allied forces had attacked three times and were repelled each time. So many French and British soldiers had been killed on the western slope that one Canadian infantryman described it as an "immense graveyard."[47] From their perch on the top of the ridge, the Germans could view all the activity below, including the amassing of weapons, ammunition, supplies, and troops in preparation for an assault on their position. They bombarded these activities, and snipers took aim at the soldiers working in the open.

The Allied commanders chose the Canadian Corps to seize the ridge from the Germans. Canadian commanders consulted with the French and British officers to avoid the mistakes they had made. The planning phase began months ahead of the attack. All the knowledge, skill, and expertise of the Canadian citizen army was brought to bear on the problem. The scouts performed essential service in obtaining the intelligence necessary to

Left: A machine gun emplacement on the crest of Vimy Ridge and the men who drove the Germans from it during the Battle of Vimy Ridge, April 1917. Right: Canadian machine gunner dug in shell holes in Vimy advance. April 1917.

plan the attack. Trench raids were carried out against the Germans to create confusion and to retrieve information on the German Army's intentions.

Canadian historians eulogize the Battle of Vimy Ridge as a symbol of Canadian nationhood "— a symbol of what Canadians could do together — a symbol that epitomized the sacrifice of the young Dominion."[48] According to Cook, "The victory at Vimy had been achieved by all four divisions, which drew men from across the country."[49] This Canadian force included Saskatchewan Métis men. When the artillery attack began on March 20, 1917, Dan Pelletier was part of a Lewis machine gun crew. The machine guns were used "to harass the enemy behind the lines, targeting communication trenches, road interchanges and the like, in hope of catching ration and working parties or the movement of trench supplies."[50]

Dan Pelletier described the effectiveness of the machine gunners.

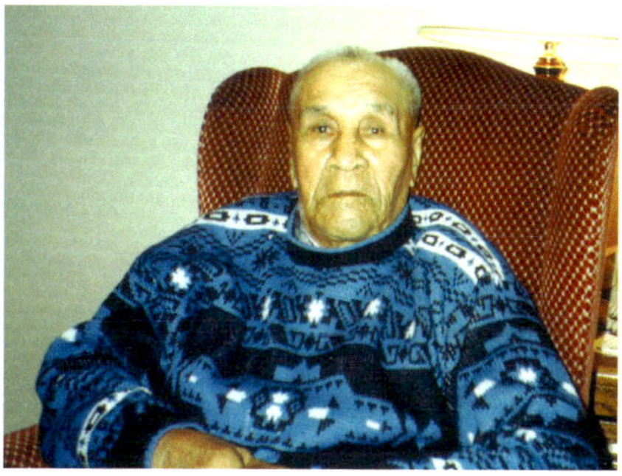
Dan Pelletier.

> *Yeah, we had the Lewis gun that we used. The good one. Machine gun. A lot of damage and a lot of casualties too. If you're good at that machine gun, like the Lewis Gun, you don't miss you know. You just shoot at something you know. You hit the ground and the darn dirt like flies up in the air, eh. Just like it was big. That Lewis gun was bad. It was a good rifle. Only take about a couple of seconds to load up … We used to go to targets, often, you know. We don't miss anybody.*[51]

Wounded prisoners [ca.1914-1918].

The men of the Canadian Engineer Corps (RCE) were invaluable in determining where the big Germans guns were located so that aerial attacks and the gunners could disable them at the appropriate time. As well, they were responsible for constructing defences, sanitation systems, and bridging, obtaining water supplies, and assisting in trench raids.

Replicas of the German trenches and fortifications were made. Soldiers were drilled; they were asked to study the location of the German trenches and any obstacles in the way. They practiced their marching in order to follow the creeping artillery barrage as

Bringing Canadian wounded to the Field Dressing Station. Vimy Ridge. April 1917.

the dust created by the big guns obscured their movement from the snipers above. The guns blasted the terrain just in front of the infantry at three-minute intervals. While making progress toward their objective, the soldiers paced their advance to 90 metres every three minutes to avoid being hit by their own fire.

Tim Cook states that "the logistical planning that sustained the Canadians verged on the unbelievable."[52] Food, water, ammunition, and all other supplies had to be transported to the front. Every night, convoys of an estimated 1,800 vehicles brought the necessary commodities, returning to where they began before dawn. This activity took place night after night. Essential to the movement of supplies in the Canadian sector were the small gauge railways built through the territory by railway troops. Alfred Cook, Colin Cook, and Patrick Chaboyer (Cumberland House) and Edward Collins (Meadow Lake) were railway troops.

Canadian soldiers lived and worked in tunnels 35 metres under the surface. Miners were recruited for tunneling. John Louis Blondeau and Joseph Clément Blondeau (Shand) were among the miners, and Angus

Top: 29th Infantry Battalion advancing over "No Man's Land" through the German barbed wire and heavy fire during the Battle of Vimy Ridge, April 1917. Bottom Left and Right: Vimy Ridge Canadian Trenches.

Vimy Ridge Canadian Trenches.

Halcrow (Pelican Narrows) was with the Canadian Corps' tunnellers. Living areas were dug out by the tunnellers. There were passageways wide enough for men in their kit to move around, with places to pass. During the winter of 1916-1917, 11,000 troops were sheltered in underground barracks with ventilation, lighting, water, and latrines.[53] The tunnels provided places of security and some comfort to the troops compared to the cold wet exposed life in the trenches. In the days leading up to the Battle of Vimy Ridge, the tunnellers were asked to build tunnels to protect the relief troops moving to the front and to No Man's Land.[54]

Today, visitors can tour the tunnel that was known as "Grange Subway." To enter the tunnel is to enter a different world. The passageways are narrow and the chalk walls, now covered with different coloured moulds, would have been more eerily white when they were formed. The tunnels are lighted now, but during

Vimy Ridge, Grange Subway.

the First World War, the soldiers would have been working in a gloomy electrical twilight. Within the tunnel, two alcoves provided quarters for the couriers and the officers. The couriers' cots were in a small area cut out of the tunnel. Here the couriers rested between their assignments, which took them above and out into No Man's Land. The life expectancy of a courier was five days.

Another tunnel system was dug 35 metres below the main tunnel. Although the chalk was easy to dig, it also carried sound a great distance. Tunnel digging was done in silence. Thousands of tonnes of material dug out to make the tunnels were carried out in sandbags, and were hidden from the sight of the Germans. The lower tunnels were used to transport explosives to plant under the German positions. Evidence of these activities still exists above ground: craters still pock the area. The tunnels for the explosives often had foul air, which meant that air had to be pumped in for the miners while water was pumped out of the deeper tunnel into the higher tunnel. Engineers, members of the labour corps, tunnellers, and infantrymen all worked through the night to complete the necessary underground facilities. According to Nigel Cave, the tunnellers "played an invaluable part in the victorious attack on Vimy Ridge."[55]

Part of the preparation for the battle involved trench raids to harass the German soldiers, capture prisoners to gain intelligence about the location and strength of their forces, and to disable guns and fortifications. On February 19, 1917, at 5:30 p.m., the 46th Canadian Infantry Battalion carried out a minor raid. The raiding party consisted of three officers and ninety-three men from other ranks divided into three parties further subdivided into sections of one non-commissioned officer and six men each with additional snipers and two-man Lewis Automatic Machine Gun crews. Sappers, stretcher-bearers, and signalers completed the raiding team. The party advanced under cover of an artillery barrage:

Shrapnel bursting over our troops in the act of digging themselves in at Vimy Ridge. April, 1917.

> *The line was found to be thinly held but few live Germans were encountered. Two came to the door of the dugout but refused to come further; they were dealt with. At a second dugout in rear of the Triangle where the fight took place during*

the last raid, a party of 12 came out, 4 escaped. Several dead Germans were encountered in the trench, having been killed by the artillery and Stokes barrage.[56]

The trench raid resulted in no prisoners taken, twelve dugouts bombed and destroyed, four sniper posts eliminated, one machine gun placement smashed, and another machine gun nest found that had been destroyed by artillery.[57] As a result of this successful operation, five men were recommended for decorations. Private Patrick (Patrice) Lejour, a Métis soldier from Duck Lake, was one of the three enlisted men to receive an award. He received a Military Medal for brave conduct and devotion to duty.[58] Gabriel Laplante lost his life on March 12, 1917 while trench raiding and preparing for an assault.

Patrice (and Alexandrine) Lejour.

When all the practice and preparations for the attack on Vimy Ridge were completed, Dan Pelletier indicated that "a military band played and I remember we prayed for the guys going to the front."[59] April 9, 1917, the 10th Brigade, which included many Saskatchewan battalions, was in reserve for the 4th Division attacking Hill 145. Hill 145 was the main objective because it was the point on the ridge that afforded clear views of the Allied lines below. If it could be taken, the Allied Powers would be able to see German positions around Lens and beyond.

5:30 a.m., April 9, 1917:

Zero Hour: Intense artillery bombardment — one continuous roar. The ground trembled and shook and mingled with the roar of the guns, the swishing and screeching of the shells filled the air covering our own advance forming a rolling barrage. Smoke and debris thrown up by the bursting shells gave the appearance of a solid wall.[60]

The Canadian Light Horse going into action at Vimy Ridge. April 1917.

The battle for Hill 145 was fierce not only because of the Germans' superior position, but because of the German tunnels and dugouts which formed a defensive network. "April 9, 1917 was the single bloodiest day of the entire war for the Canadian Corps and [the] bloodiest in all of Canadian military history."[61] Despite the terrible losses, our soldiers took the ridge.

Tank advancing with Infantry at Vimy. April 1917.

Vimy was an amazing victory. It was the first time that all our Canadian soldiers fought together. They did what the British and French armies had not been able to do. The word "Vimy" itself became synonymous with Canada's contribution to the First World War.

The capture of Vimy Ridge did not end the war, however. More danger would await the Canadians. The Germans held another hill, the "Pimple" as the soldiers called it. The 10th Brigade launched an attack on this objective on April 12, 1917. Again, the artillery blasted the hill in advance of the attack in an effort to dislodge the enemy from the reserve positions and destroy their communication trenches. The Canadian attack fittingly was accompanied by a snowstorm and a favourable wind. The Germans could not see their targets for a clear shot. The 46th (South Saskatchewan) Battalion put up an effective resistance, and by 7:00 a.m., two hours after the assault on the Pimple (Hill 119), it was in Canadian hands.

Top: Happy Canadians who captured Vimy Ridge returning to rest billets on motor lorries. May 1917. Bottom: View over the crest of Vimy Ridge showing the village of Vimy, which was captured by Canadian troops. May 1917.

The 46th Battalion, commemorating the names of the men killed on April 9 and 12, 1917, erected two crosses on the Pimple. No trace of them remains today.[62] On the crosses would have been the names of Saskatchewan Métis who gave their lives in the battle, which, in the eyes of many Canadians, forged Canada's nationhood. Private Francis (Frank) Brabant (Lestock) was killed on April 9, 1917 during the fight for Vimy Ridge. Private Samuel Halcrow (Île-à-la-Crosse) and William Charles Sanderson (Prince Albert) were killed in the fighting over the next days.

Left: Vimy Ridge, Canadian Cemetery No. 2.
Right: Vimy Ridge, Canadian Cemetery No. 2. Unknown Canadian Soldier Grave.

As our Canadian soldiers advanced on the German positions, the Germans bombed the area with high explosive shells and unleashed the most horrible weapon they had yet used. Mustard gas "was a slow-acting agent that killed the nerve cells so that the victim would only start to feel the effects hours after being poisoned."[63] According to war diaries, gas was used against our troops almost every day in late April and early May, 1917. Every obstacle was put in the way of the Canadian advance. However, by maintaining night patrols, gathering intelligence, and continually rebuilding lines of communication and transport, our forces moved relentlessly forward. The Germans vacated the front.

On April 26, 1917, Canadian assault troops moved to take possession of the territory to mount an attack on Arleux-en-Gohelle. Despite a creeping barrage for cover, the German guns caught dozens of marching Canadian soldiers by surprise. Private Peter Andrew Cromartie (Halcro) died that day. Even with 1,255 casualties, the Canadian troops won the day and the Germans retreated to Fresnoy.[64]

Ambroise Louis Marion (Duck Lake) died on May 16, 1917. This tall, dark-haired, dark-skinned Métis was a recipient of the Military Medal. On

Top to Bottom: Mud and barbed wire though which the Canadians advanced during the Battle of Passchendaele. November 1917. Personnel of the 16th Canadian Machine Gun Company holding the line in shell holes during the Battle of Passchendaele. November 1917. A Canadian sleeping in the front line. February, 1918.

May 24, 1917, Pte. Leo Gardiner (Battleford) was killed. He was buried in England.

Our soldiers were drawn into the Third Battle of Ypres, more commonly called the Battle of Passchendaele. This meant returning to the Ypres Salient and the horrific conditions that they had encountered in the Second Battle of Ypres earlier in the war. The August battles came at the cost of almost 16,000 Canadian casualties. At least one Saskatchewan Métis soldier gave his life at Passchendaele. Private Alexander Decoteau (Battleford), who was twenty-eight when he was killed, is buried in Passchendaele New British Cemetery. Jean-Baptiste Dorion (Cumberland House) died of wounds received there.

The Battle of Amiens — fought on August 8-11, 1918 — took the life of Percy William Ducharme, Military Medal (MM). Ducharme had enlisted as J. W. Morin (Midnight Lake) at Battleford, on August 6, 1915 and then, again under his alias on January 29, 1916. On his attestation paper completed in 1916, he named his next of kin as Antoine Morin of Meadow Lake. In his Last Will and Testament, written in June, 1916, he bequeathed the whole of his property to "my father, William Ducharme, Midnight Lake." After having served as a sniper with the 42nd Battalion under the name of Joseph William Morin, a notation was made on his official record on July 25, 1918 "[t]hat having declared his true name to be Ducharme,

Percy William, [he] will be known as such in future." On August 4, it was announced in the Divisional Orders that he was to receive the Military Medal for his service on July 17-20, 1918. He was killed in action on August 8, 1918. His medal was forwarded to his father. Dying with him in the Battle of Amiens were Ptes. Edward J. Baptiste (Battleford), Joseph Bourassa (Prince Albert), and Edward J. Collins (Meadow Lake).

Between the end of the Battle of Amiens and the capture of Mons on November 10-11, 1918, the Allied Powers engaged the Germans in a series of quick, bloody battles, including the Battle of the Drocourt-Quéant Line. In Canada, France, and Belgium, these battles, which won the war, are known as "Canada's Hundred Days." During this forceful push by the Allied Powers, the Canadian Corps eradicated the German lines and pursued the fleeing Germans. As a result of this intense and bloody fighting, a number of our soldiers were killed. In the capture of Monchy-le-Preux, Frank Klyne (Estevan) died. Killed on August 15 was Private Antoine Collins (Meadow Lake). John Letendre (Lestock) died September 2, 1918. In the Battle of Canal du Nord, fought on September 27, 1918, Frederick Kennedy (Beauval and Green Lake) was killed. On October 5, 1918, John Deguerre (Battleford) was killed, and Roger Victor Richard died on October 14, 1918. In the last month of the war, Private Louis Klyne (Qu'Appelle) died from wounds, and Private Charles Daniels (South Battleford) was killed.

The First World War took over our lives in Saskatchewan. We all knew someone who was there. Although just a youngster at the time, Médéric McDougall was part of it:

Grandfather and Grandmother

So it was during war time
The war of '14 to '18
and of course we heard
A lot about the war

And because I could read a bit
I used to go down there
with the newspaper
And read to them

And they were very interested
They used to get me down there
and like to hear me read the news
About the war especially . . .[65]

Cumberland House men made a unique contribution to the war effort. They moved copper from the mines in Flin Flon to the railhead at The Pas. Copper was essential in manufacturing the bullets which the Allied forces needed to fight overseas. Métis men were teamsters and worked the boats in this vital service for the war effort. One of them, John Gregory Dorion, told how the copper was transported from the mine:

> *It was about one hundred miles from Flin Flon, Manitoba to The Pas, Manitoba, the closest railroad. They then shipped the ore to Montreal.*
>
> *Charlie Morgan … was using ninety teams of mules; he hauled the ore as far as Sturgeon Landing, or Namew Lake in Saskatchewan. They stockpiled it there; that was a winter operation. From Flin Flon to Sturgeon Landing was forty-five miles. So they had to have a swing man by camp number two, during the summer.*
>
> *Ross Navigation hauled material for Mandy Mine for Flin Flon during the winter. The mule teams would haul the ore to Sturgeon Landing. The first swing was as far as camp number two. The first operation had four swings, from Mandy to camp #2, then to Sturgeon Landing, then to Morgan's camp, then finally The Pas, Manitoba … They had a river sternwheeler named City of Prince Albert.*[66]

Ruben Blondeau.

Pat St. Denis.

Then there was conscription. Our men were called up. This obligatory service affected even older, married Métis men like Henry James Umpherville, a twenty-six year old farmer from Glen Mary. Many families were split on their reaction to the war and conscription. There are stories of those who left the country to be with relatives in the United States, who were having their own debate about joining the war. Others were hidden by their families. These families were strongly opposed to fighting in a foreign war. Young men who did not register for the draft were labelled as defaulters and were subject to being arrested.

Some young men responded to the draft; however, they often did not return to their regiment after a leave. Their files listed them as deserters. The

RNWMP watched for them at their parents' homes, and the police had the authority to arrest them and return them to the Army. Parents or other relatives could be jailed for aiding and abetting the conscripted recruit. On the other hand, there were men who were discharged from the Army for dishonourable conduct only to re-enlist under an alias. Underage soldiers could not be sent overseas, and therefore many were kept in Canada until their nineteenth birthday. Those underage soldiers who went overseas usually had their families inform the Army about this matter. They were gathered up and sent back to Canada. If no one alerted the Army or drew attention to the error in the men's age, nothing happened to stop the underage soldier from fighting on the front line with his comrades. By the time conscription was imposed, every man willing to fight was needed on the front. Few questions were asked.

Graves of Unknown Canadian Soldiers.

The loss of so many young able-bodied men was devastating in those communities where our people lived off the land. We lost those who hunted for food, harvested resources, and brought goods and income into our homes. Food became scarce. Materials to make clothing and summer shelter were in short supply. Many older people, who had relied on their sons and grandsons to hunt, gather wood, and carry water for them, had to be cared for by others in the community. It was no wonder that some young men, such as Alfred Cook (Cumberland House), waited to be conscripted. He was called up and joined the Army in Winnipeg on May 30, 1918. Some of our men may have deliberately stayed home to look after those who could not look after themselves. Unfortunately, the work of our men, which sustained our communities, was not designated an essential service.

The First World War was tragic in that many of the soldiers who lost their lives were never found. In the relentless bombardment of the battlefields, soldiers' bodies, which had been buried by their friends where they had fallen, were often blown up and their remains never identified. These soldiers remain unknown, but not forgotten.

The Menin Gate Memorial to the Missing, the Thiepval Memorial to the Missing of the Somme, and the Canadian National Vimy Memorial all stand as reminders of the sacrifices of these men who never received a proper burial and have no individual grave site. The Menin Gate in Ieper (known during the war as "Ypres"), Belgium is one of the memorials to the missing. The British government decided that the Menin Gate would be an appropriate place for remembrance because, between 1914 and 1918, hundreds of thousands of Allied soldiers travelled through the gate when going to the battlefields. One hundred and sixty panels remember the names of 54,986 young men who left home to fight for freedom and have never been found. Among the names on the Memorial is Napoleon Nault, a Métis soldier from Cochin, Saskatchewan.

Menin Gate, Last Post Ceremony.

We lost many of our young men. Most of them were buried in France. We can only name those who died in Europe:

Pte. Alexander Bigman (Battleford)
Pte. Frederick Bloomfield (Fir Ridge)
Pte. Frederick William Boyer
Pte. Harry (Hormidas) Boyer (Duck Lake)
Pte. Wilfrid Boyer (Lorenzo)
Pte. Frank Brabant (Lestock)
Pte. Charles Canada (Cumberland House)
Pte. Edward J. Collins (Meadow Lake)
Pte. Peter Andrew Cromartie (Halcro)
Pte. Joseph Crow (Kamsack)
Pte. Charles Daniels (South Battleford)
Pte. Alexander Decoteau (Battleford)
Pte. James Deegan (Fort Qu'Appelle)
Pte. John Deguerre (Battleford)
Pte. Percy William Ducharme (MM) (Meadow Lake)
Pte. Peter William Ducharme (Midnight Lake)
Pte. Clément Fleury (Duck Lake)
Pte. Leo Gardiner (Battleford)
Pte. John Gerard (Green Lake)
Pte. Malcolm Grey (Sintaluta)

Pte. Angus Halcrow (Pelican Narrows)
Pte. Samuel Halcrow (Île-à-la-Crosse)
Pte. Philip Jackson (Balcarres)
Pte. Oswald Victor Keddie (Cumberland House)
Pte. Frederick Kennedy (Beauval)
Pte. Herbert Bruce Kennedy (Duck Lake)
Pte. Frank Klyne (Estevan)
Pte. Louis Klyne (Fort Qu'Appelle)
Pte. Gabriel Laplante (Duck Lake)
Pte. John Letendre (Batoche/Lestock)
Pte. Ambroise Louis Marion (Duck Lake)
Pte. Napoleon Nault (Stony Lake/Jackfish Lake)
Sergeant (Sgt.) John James Norris (Regina)
Pte. Henry Louis Norwest (MM and Bar) (Prince Albert)
Pte. Roderick J. Pocha (Prince Albert)
Pte. Roger Victor Richard
Pte. William Charles Sanderson (Prince Albert)
Pte. William Sinclair (Weyburn)
Pte. William Alfred Vandale (Nutana)
Pte. Louis White (Battleford)
Pte. David Whitford (Piapot)
Pte. Alfred Whitford (Birch Hills)
Pte. Wilfrid Whitford (Birch Hills)

The ones who came back were glad just to be alive. As one veteran said, "I joined the bloody Army in 1914. I went overseas in 1918. Germany, France, Belgium. I got hit three times. Got wounded three times. I'm still alive."[67] Some of those who survived the battlefield did not live long. Some came back with Shell Shock (now classified as Post-Traumatic Stress Disorder, or Combat Stress Reaction). Some came back with lung problems caused by gas attacks. Some who came back brought sickness with them. The Spanish Flu, the first pandemic in recent times, followed the soldiers home in 1919. The young soldiers who returned to a joyous reunion in their communities were not aware that they were bringing more misery with them.

Grave of C. Cunningham.

There was a Sickness

That's the First World War
I remember it now
the people was dying too
there was lots of them

There was a sickness
going around here that year
the first year
I was over there in school

I'm remembering how
my Mum used to write me that
how many people died in the South
where they were hungry
and everything was dry

Was the flu
some kind of
and there was no doctor
just the Indian's doctors
some Indians
but they were really good though.
—Mary Jacobson[68]

The Spanish Flu came to all our communities. Cumberland House was hit very hard. William Sayese remembered:

> *… there were people dying by families and there was a Provincial Police here with the name of Paquette. When he heard someone died, they used to take them straight out of the house, straight down to the Anglican Church. And then there were so many dead bodies there you know that some of the seats fell down. They were too heavy loaded.*
>
> *It was during March when the sickness was over. They had men dig graves: they just made a big trench and they buried them there.*
>
> *It was, oh, pretty near half of the Cumberland; the whole reserve died here. The whole reserve.*
>
> *Yes, it was the Spanish Flu they call it. They thought it was just a common cold you know; but just as soon as they step outside and they come in, you know, they died.*[69]

William Dorion returned to an epidemic in Cumberland House.

> *I was away at the time of the Flu which took most of the people. When I came home I found mostly everyone sick. Most of the people didn't have water or wood. So I started hauling and cutting wood for them. Everyone helped those who were not sick. The dead weren't buried till in the Spring. The bodies were stacked in one house until they could be buried. Some of them were buried together.*[70]

Another account states:

> *… influenza swept through this small community. It struck in the brunt of winter taking many lives with it. All it left in the minds of the surviving was the dreadful thought of the influenza's deadly blow. So many were sick that no gravediggers could be found. All the corpses were kept in a warehouse at the mission until spring … Coffins were made from lumber obtained from dismantled porches. Mr. Dougald Mackenzie made a very good hunt of caribou during the crisis and went from house to house to feed the sick and starving with milk and fresh meat.* [71]

Alex Bishop remembered the Spanish Flu in Green Lake. He said, "Whole families [died]: all the children, man and wife."[72]

For Métis families, life returned very much as it had been before the war. Except that now, families and communities had to deal with the pain and suffering of those who came home. Some of our men (a small minority) benefited from the Soldiers' Settlement Board. In 1923, the Board awarded land on the south corner of Murray Lake to J.-B. Boyer. Most returned soldiers put their new skills and knowledge to use in rebuilding their lives and communities.

The Second World War

The late Edward King recalled:

> *On September 10, 1939 the Second World War started. I was working for John Dahl when the news came. For me the war was far away. I saw one or two soldiers in 1939 and they wore their uniforms from the First World War. My stepfather Jules Haggarty had been in World War I and was wounded, so he knew what war was about. He said, "This war will last a long time." He also said, "You will be in the army before this war is over."*[73]

Edward King, 1943.

Recruitment of Métis People

During the Second World War, the Métis were actively recruited by the Canadian military. There is evidence that the Saskatchewan Métis Society (SMS) was directly involved in the recruitment of Métis service members. Former premier of Saskatchewan, James G. Gardiner, now federal Minister of the Department of National War Services, knew the province's Métis community, including the SMS leadership. He had used our leadership to "bring out the vote" in Métis communities as early as 1934.[74] Once again, our leadership was asked to bring the community out to support the government. Our leaders provided role models for our people. In July 1940, Z. M. Hamilton wrote a letter of introduction for Edward Klyne and A. N. Fidler to Flying Officer Stewart, Royal Canadian Air Force (RCAF) Recruitment Headquarters. He described Klyne as having been SMS Secretary for many years and Fidler as belonging "to one of the most historic families of the

Second World War recruitment poster, Canada [ca. 1940-1945].

Second World War recruitment poster, Canada.

mixed blood of the west." Hamilton informed Stewart that the two men were "recognized leaders among the Métis people, and if they could pass your tests and be enlisted, it would have a good effect upon the native population."[75]

Hamilton, who was also involved in the Saskatchewan Historical Society, was one of the people used by the government to identify and recommend Métis recruits. In a letter dated May 6, 1941, Minister Gardiner thanked Hamilton for "the work you have done among the Métis in the Qu'Appelle Valley." He wrote that he was sending the letter to the Defence Department, "asking them to consider the possibility of using your services in connection with recruiting."[76]

For the first time in the history of the Canadian military, women were involved. The Canadian government realized that the armed forces had to

Top Left to Right: Personnel of the Canadian Women's Army Corps (C. W. A. C) disembarking from a troopship at Naples, Italy, 22 June 1944. Window display promoting Canadian Women's Army Corps [ca. 1943]. Bottom Left to Right: Dorothy Trotchie (Askwith). Edith Hilda Merrifield. Alice Petit.

be expanded, but the supply of men was becoming depleted. Many tasks had to be done to maintain the military's services. The government had to consider the possibility of employing women in non-combat duty and free up the men for combat. On August 13, 1941, permission was given for the establishment of the Canadian Women's Army Corps (CWAC)s.[77] Métis women volunteered for duty in various branches of the Canadian military as well. They included Dorothy Trotchie (later Askwith) who joined the RCAF at 17 years of age, Loretta Boyer (Cochin), Gertrude Clara Fraser who joined the Women's Royal Canadian Naval Service (WRCNS), and Annie, Ada, and Jean Lewis, sisters, who all joined the CWAC, and Alice Rainville who enlisted in the RCAF Women's Corps.

By 1942, the Regina *Leader-Post* received reports from the SMS on the number of Métis recruits from their different areas. The March 6, 1942 edition observed:

> *A rather remarkable response to the call for volunteers during the present war, is to be found in the official records of the Touchwood branch, Saskatchewan Metis Society, with 89 persons out of a total registration of about 500 souls, either serving, discharged or rejected or waiting call.*[78]

By 1942, the following Métis from Touchwood were in the service: Albert Bellrose; Frank Boivin; George and Ernest Desjarlais; Charles and Mike Dufour; Harvey Fiddler; Arthur Emile, George, and Stanley Fisher; Charles and Stanley Folstrum; Albert and Joe Lafontaine; Albert Lajour; Fortune Lamontagne; John William, Thomas, and Alfred Loftus; Alex, Lawrence, Walter, and Claude McKay; J. G. Nickelson; William Nofield; John, William, Paul, and Antonie Pelletier; Maurice and John Poitras; Edward, Maurice, and Leonard Robillard; David Sabiston; William Ferguson; Ernest Adolphe; Fred, Floyd, and Burns Anderson; Thomas and John Champagne; Harry Favel; James Isbister; John, Harry, Raymond, and A. Laplante; Burns Morris, Earl, and Glen Pratt; Glen Robinson; John, Peter, Douglas, Edward and Raymond Sinclair; William Stone; Glen Wady; and Ed Brass. As noted above, three sisters — Annie, Jean and Ada Lewis — joined the CWAC.[79]

While most of the Touchwood service members were in the infantry and service corps, George Anderson, Glen Pratt, William Stone, William Nofield, and Ernest Adolphe either were already in the RCAF or were awaiting the call to serve. George Bellrose, Paul Lafontaine, and Vern Pratt had served and been discharged.[80]

On March 9, 1942, the Regina *Leader-Post* printed the list of Métis enlistees provided by the SMS in Regina. Those in the armed forces included

Norman, William Patrick, and Oliver Anderson; Allan and George Brabant; Alex and Robert LaRocque; George Terry; John, Norman, Vincent, Alfred, Frederick, Stanley, and Albert Parisien; Edward and John St. Germain; Harry McKenzie, James, John, Alex, and Edmond Klyne; and Alex Harrington.[81]

The SMS provided the newspaper with the names of seventy-one Métis from the Qu'Appelle Valley serving in the armed forces as of September 1942. Those already in the services were Alex Beaulieu; Edward and Peter Blondeau; Lance Corporal (L/Cpl.) Paul, Frank, and John Amyotte; Leo and Henry Brabant; Allan Blyne; Cpl. Ed Charrette; Leading Aircraftman (LAC) Thomas Delorme; Ernest, Rifleman (Rfn.) Matthew, J. W., Louis, and Alex Desjarlais; Cpl. Albert Dazé; Eddie, Ray, and William Fisher; Jack Foster; Joe Jeannotte; William Kelly; Flying Officer (F/O) Bill Johnnie, Maurice, and Leo LaRocque; Tom LaPlante; Cpl. Robert, Sgt. Alex, and Edwin LaRocque; Edmond and Tommie Major; John and Louis Morin; Ted Ouelette; Ernest and Cecilia Pagé; Fred, Albert, and Morris Parisien; Peter Peletier; Charles, Jimmie, George, George M., Mike, and Joe Pelletier; Jim C. and Johnnie Peltier; Fred, Joe, Modeste, Norman, Leo, and Edward Poitras; Fred Roberts; Peter, Allan, Stan, and Cpl. Norman Racette; August Robillard; Roman Ross; Elie Sinclair; Alex Swan; and Joe Welsh.[82]

Top: John Amyotte.
Bottom: James G. and Edward Poitras, South Saskatchewan Regiment, Winnipeg, 1941.

Green Lake sent Charlie and Edward Arnault; Ernest, Gabe, Joe R., Martin, and Robert Aubichon; Joe A. Bishop; Fred Lafleur; Jimmy LaFond; Leon, Moïse, Peter, Peter, Peter (three different men), and Stanley Laliberte; Norbert Lesset; Bernard, Charlie, Eugene, George, John James, Napoleon, and Ralph Morin; and Dan Ross.[83]

In June 1940, Norman McAuley and two companions walked from La Ronge to enlist in the Canadian Army.[84]

Cumberland House sent thirty-nine soldiers to the Second World War. Of these, seven were killed in action, thirteen were injured or wounded, and

Top Left: Charles Arnault.
Middle Left: Peter Laliberte.
Bottom Left: Fred Merasty, Unknown, and Dan Ross.
Above: New Recruits, Meadow Lake, June 25, 1940. The men in the back row are: Rfn. A.E. Speer (L-27877), Rfn. G. Landry (L-27886), E.A. Nault (L-27868), Rfn. W.M. Nault (L-27869), Rfn. A. Hein (L-27830), F. Gladue (L-27866), Rfn. P. Lariviere (L-27675), Rfn. W.J. Shaw (L-27883), H. Lang (L-278__), and Rfn. Cullen (L-278__). The men in the front row are: Rfn. J.O. Beaudry (L-27867), Rfn. A. Spenst (L-27873), J.B. Morin (L-27831), Rfn. J.J. Marion (L-27871), Rfn. C.L. Merasty (L-27892), D.T. Moloney (L-27828), Rfn. E. Frisky (L-278__), Rfn. C.R. Fleury (L-27865), J.T. Fiddler (L-27829), Rfn. A. Falcon (L-27236), and Rfn. G. Whelan (L-27876). The Métis men were Landry, both Naults, Gladue, Lariviere, Beaudry, Morin, Marion, Merasty, Fleury, Fiddler, and Falcon.

two were prisoners of war (POW)s. Those who went were Pte. George Lloyd Budd; Pte. Simeon Bloomfield; Pte. Moïse Canada; Pte. Alphonse, Sgt. Pierre, Cpl. James E. Sr., Pte. Victor Vernon, and Trooper (Tpr.) William J. Carriere; L/Cpl. Cyril and L/Cpl. Frank Emile Chaboyer; Pte. John Henry and Cpl. Lawrence Cook; Spr. Gabriel Dorion; Gunner (Gnr.) Charles, Gnr. John Frank and Gnr. Pierre Gordon Fosseneuve; Lance Sergeant (L/Sgt.) Solomon Goulet; L/Cpl. Joseph McGillivary Sr., Pte. George and Spr. Rod E. McKay; Rfn. Percival E. McKenzie; Pte. Alexander and Pte. W. Napoleon Morin, Pte. Louis Nabess; Tpr. Russell J. Robertson; Spr. Baptiste Sayies; Pte. Edward T. Sayhes; Cpl.

William Sayese; Fusilier (Fus.) Alexander, Pte. Jean-Baptiste, Fus. Nathan, and Rfn. Thomas Settee; Cpl. Angus Thomas; Pte. Stanley and Pte. Zaacheus Young; and Mike Zebreski.

Sturgeon Landing sent Lance Bombardier (L/Bmdr.) John Dionne, Tpr. Philip Dionne, and Spr. Charles Morin. Trooper Dionne was killed in action.

Cochin provided many Métis soldiers as well. We know that four sons of Henry and Jane (née Delorme) Pruden joined up. Larry, Denis, Wallace, and Allen Nault went. Alex and Edward Nolin were soldiers. Tony, Harold, George, and Charles Mitchell enlisted. John Mannix, Julien LeHeureux, Leo Lavallée, Peter Gervais, and Albert, Tony, Loretta, Jean-Baptiste, Claude, Emile, and Mick Boyer were all from the small community. Also serving were Frank and Serve Villeneuve, Ambroise Laboucane, and Leo Lavalle.

Fort Pitt Métis veterans included Joe McGillivary; Napoleon Morin; James, Louis (WWI), Robert, Tom, Victor, and Wilfred Parenteau; Edward Sayhese; Thomas Settee; Charles and Edwin Slater; and Charles Wills.

Top: Bill (William) Sayese.
Middle: Lawrence Sayese.
Bottom Left: Stanley Bear, Lawrence Quinney, and Charlie Umpherville.
Bottom Right: Unknown, Lawrence and Joe Fiddler, and Unknown.

Métis soldiers from Bresaylor included Cecil, Clayton, Doug, Edgar, Gordon, Harris, Henry, Henry Peter, Joseph, Leonard, Sidney, Stanley, and Walter G. Sayers.

Battleford sent the following Métis men to war: Angus, Harvey, James, and Willie Falcon; Ambroise, Jean-Baptiste, Louis, and Wallace Ouellette; Lawrence Martell; Rylie Isbister; and August Sansregret.

Glen Mary/Horseshoe Bend was a small Métis community that contributed many men to the military. Roderick and Stanley Bear; Tom and Joe Fiddler; Max and Ben Lucie; Lawrence Sayese; Hilmer, Colin, John, and Bud Oliver; and Henry, William, Gordon, Walter, Roderick, Robert, Angus, and Jerry Umpherville all went.

Duck Lake's Second World War Métis soldiers included Charles Dumais; Allen, David, J. Louis, George, Lawrence, and Prosper Dumont; Leon, R. Joseph, and Walter Ferguson; Eugene, Joseph, Marie James, William, and Ernest Fisher; Charles, Nelson, Rémi, and Romuald Gariépy; William LaPlante; Golds Laviolet; Henry Ledoux; Dennis, Gilbert, Louis, and Wilfred Montour; Xavier Ouellette; Alfred, Jean Marie, and Marcel Petit; Ambroise, Arthur, Bernard, Emile, Donald, Henri, James, Israël, and Joe Robert Paul; Joe and J. B. Sauvé; Ernest St. Denis; and Frank and William Vandale.

Top Left to Right: Donat (Don) Petit. Israël Paul. Bottom: 20th Field Brigade, Royal Canadian Artillery, Edmonton, Alberta, June 1939.

Top Row: Leon and R. Joseph Ferguson. Hermond and Edgar Pilon.
Middle Row: Marcel Petit. James Paul. Arthur Paul. Bernard Paul and Marie-Rose Sauvé.
Bottom Row: Ambroise and Donald Paul. Alice (Petit) Samuels and Jean-Marie Petit.

Signing Up

Edward King, 1946.

For many Métis, enlisting was a disappointing and disillusioning process. Those willing to give their lives for their country wanted Canada to recognize that they were Métis people. Even after recruiters had singled out Métis men and women for service, there was no place on the Canadian Active Service Force Attestation Paper for people to signify that they were Métis. To this day, our veterans resent the fact that on these documents they were listed by their distant European ethnicity. With a pen stroke, they became "Scottish" or "French," or whatever ethnicity suited the recruiter.

Edward King, of Meadow Lake, recalled his experience: "When I had enlisted they wouldn't accept Métis as a nationality. 'There's no such thing' they told me. I was disappointed not to be recognized."[85]

He described the conversation he had with the Canadian Army official:

> *I couldn't say I was an Indian because you had to have a number to be a Treaty Indian. So they said, 'What are you?' 'What part European?' 'What nationality of European?' 'Well, French,' I said. So they wrote French and nothing else. But I don't write in French. I just speak it. Later on in England when they gave me French papers to fill out to join the French outfit, I couldn't understand the forms.*[86]

According to Eugene Desjarlais, "When I signed up, I had been told that I had been baptized a French-Canadian and not as a Métis and so they put me down as a French-Canadian."[87]

For the late Claude Adams, formally of MacDowall, this was a betrayal of his grandfather who had taken him to Batoche as a young boy and reminded him that the men in the mass grave were his ancestors, and that they were heroes. He knew from that day that he had to always remember that he was Métis. Claude was forced to peel potatoes for his first day in the Army after daring to insist that he was Métis.[88]

Army Platoon, North Bay, ON, Basic Training.

Left: E Troop, A Battery at AL Canadian Artillery Training Centre.
Right: Mounting Guard, Saskatchewan Horse, A Coy, Ottawa, Sept. 1941.

There were many reasons why our people enlisted in the Canadian military. Some are expressed in the following poems of Métis people:

Friends

They all volunteered to go.
Of course when one wanted to go
all wanted to go.
Because they had friends.

And not only that I guess —
you know among friends —
they get together:
Well I'm going.

So the other one says:
Well I'll go too.
So they all go like that.
And they all volunteered.
— Rose Fleury [89]

Away we Go

You know how the young is, eh?
They want to talk together,
And they say: away we go —

Just like this. They are
not obliged to go, you see?
They did not know why they were fighting.

You know how young people are.
They just get things in their head
and then they go.
— Adelaide Ranger[90]

Obliged to Go

The Second World War wasn't
like the first one.
They didn't feel like going
not like the first one
where they wanted to go
just for adventure.

They were obliged to go.
She said the police
would come and pick them up.

She said they seemed
to treat them quite well
as far as food and clothing.

But she said
they trained them pretty hard.

Oh, I asked her why this time
they didn't want to go.

And she said I guess
they were scared they'd get killed
and besides that
many left
their woman
or girlfriends behind.
— Adelaide Ranger[91]

The women who were left had to carry on and provide for their families. They did the work of men.

All the Work

It was quite hard for us.
Because the women
had to do all the work
and things like that.

So we even stooked.
I was old enough.
I was only I guess thirteen —
fourteen at the time —

And I was helping Mom
stook for the farmers.
Because they didn't have no men
to do anything like that.
— Rose Fleury[92]

For other women in our communities, their lives were on hold, waiting for their loved ones to come home.

She Waited for Him

That's the reason she got married older
because she had been going with him
before the war.

And she waited for him.

And she said all the time
that he was out there
he would write to her
She's got his papers — his discharges.
— Adelaide Ranger[93]

For many Métis people, it was family tradition that helped them make the decision to join the military during the Second World War. Many young men fighting in World War II were the sons, brothers, or nephews of men who had fought in World War I. It was not unusual for more than one soldier to come from a single family. Henry and Mary Jane (née Delorme) Pruden from Cochin had four sons join the armed forces during the Second World War.[94] Elloue (Larry) Nault (Jackfish Lake) served in World War I. He was

45-years-old when the Second World War broke out. He lied about his age and served with his sons, Dan, Richard, and Lawrence Wallace in Europe.[95]

Some came from military traditions that went even farther back, as with Edward King:

> *I served overseas and I was with the Winnipeg Rifles. I was wounded in Calais, France the first time in 1944 and then again in Germany, in Holland. I should say after we crossed the German border and then I also went back into the service after in the Korean conflict. That was part of my military service and now I am a member of the Royal Canadian Legion of my hometown.*
>
> *I guess going further back to the Batoche battles. I lost my great — I don't know how far back, my great-grandfather, Joseph Ouellette. He is known by the people who make history as the man over ninety years of age who was killed in the Battle of Batoche. There was three generations of Ouellettes in the Battle of Batoche.*[96]

For Métis veterans like Wilfred John Henry, the decision to enlist was characterized by "poverty and alienation."[97] Many who signed up came from situations where work was hard to find and money scarce. William Sayese (Cumberland House) explained his reason for enlisting:

Wilfred John Henry.

> *I was in the Second World War. I asked my wife. I says, "I'm going to join the army." Do you know what we had for breakfast? We had just a cup of tea for breakfast and a little bit of sugar: that's what we had for breakfast. Now that is enough of that," I said to my wife, "I'm going to join the army. The government can look after you better than I can. So if I do get killed you will be well looked after."*
>
> *"No," she says, "You're not going to leave me." "I gotta go," I said, "We've got to do something or we'll starve here."*[98]

The men from Duck Lake had their reasons too:

Why Duck Lake Went to War

No! no! They didn't have to go.
But they went.
Money was scarce.
No jobs.
— Charles Pilon[99]

So did the people from Batoche and St. Louis.

Why his People Went to War

There were a lot of our people,
the half-breed people,
that were living under
pretty poor conditions
and of course a lot of people
think that anything is better
than living under poor conditions.
— Médéric McDougall[100]

It was the same in Glen Mary, according to Roderick Bear:

We were hard up for jobs. There was no jobs then either. I think that was most of the guys joined up for that. There was no work. Like he said we were working for $1 a day or $2. I know my uncle had no job and he went there, Stanley Bear. Just getting odd jobs stoking and that.[101]

Chitek Lake was no better. In the words of Euclide Boyer:

I moved to Chitek Lake in 1941 from a homestead where my dad had homesteaded in 1929 and in those days it was pretty rough. You had no work, well there was work, but there was no money to pay you with. So I had to work for fifty cents a day, cutting brush mind you. We had to cut brush from daylight 'till dark for 50 cents.[102]

So I went and joined up. And no way of getting rejected. I passed A-1, and there I was stuck for 3 years. I was 20 years old. When I joined the army, first of all, I didn't want to be called in.[103]

Generally, the men from our communities went in groups to enlist, as the Regina *Leader-Post* reported in 1941:

Nine robust backwoodsmen from the hardy north country threw pioneering into reverse this week by forsaking the echoing call of the woods for the more urgent call for manpower to build up the Canadian army.

Quitting the freedom of the northern wilds they left the old trading post of Cumberland House, west of The Pas, to help to maintain the freedom of the Empire.

By canoe and portage Russell J. Robertson, George Budd, Edward Sahyes, James Carriere, William Carriere, Alphonse Carriere, Gabriel Dorian [sic], *Napoleon Morin and Louis Nahbess travelled to The Pas for a medical examination, were found fit and are now on their way to* [the] *Saskatoon army depot.*

Keen to join up and anxious to stalk the enemy, these iron-nerved sons of the north approached F. Reid of Cumberland House, who completed arrangements for their enlistment.

Military district officers were pleased to hear of their most recent recruits and said they should serve as an example to those young, able-bodied men in the cities and towns of Saskatchewan who have so much to lose if they do not do something about the present issue.[104]

The province's newspapers were impressed by our contribution to the war. A reporter for the Regina *Leader-Post* wrote, in a special dispatch from Lebret on September 18, 1943,

Tradition enjoins on the descendants of those brave pioneers of the western plains, a devotion to religion and patriotism, and particularly the faith of their fathers. The majority of the men enlisted are all descendants of men who took no active part on the Metis Rebellion of 1870 and 1885, although their sympathies were with their leader, Louis Riel. Through the teaching and spreading of the principles of British Liberty these men are today in the ranks of the great patriots, and have donned the garb of the fighter for liberty and justice.[105]

Leaving Home

For the Cumberland House men, leaving home came when they decided to enlist. Vital Morin left home in Île-à-la-Crosse for a three-day trek to Meadow Lake. He didn't go home for four years.

On the main street [of Meadow Lake], *he ran into two cousins, who were both wearing well-creased, snappy uniforms. He asked them why they were dressed that way, and they informed them that they had joined the army because of the war … Seeing an army uniform and a trip across the world as enticing, Vital Morin signed up that day. He was packed off to Regina, then to Ontario, and finally to England.*[106]

For many of our men, going to war meant leaving their wives and children, as William Sayese did:

> *I had five children; it was kind of hard to leave them, you know. When I volunteered for overseas and they let me go: "Well, you can go if you want to," so, they gave me the embarkation leave to live with my family for 24 hours … So I came to The Pas and lived for 24 hours with my children. The hardest part I felt, you know, was when they come to see me off at the train. And I looked out the window of the train; they were crying and waving at me; so I waved too.*
>
> *And then when I was sitting down, there must have been an awful nice guy on that train too — someone tapped me on the shoulder and said, "Cheer up soldier, you'll be coming back again. Just a minute," he says. He went back in the train and brought his briefcase, and he says, "Here's $10.00 for you — spending money; use it in case you want to eat." Then he pulled out a bottle of whiskey. He says, "Forget your troubles; here have a good, big drink." So I took it.*[107]

Training

Our men were sent to different parts of the country for their basic military training. Euclide Boyer told of his experience:

> *I took my basic training in Camrose, Alberta. And I was a bad boy for awhile. I didn't like discipline coming off the homestead and work in the bush and stuff like that, being your own boss, and young fellow from the homestead, you don't have too much discipline. So I couldn't understand discipline. I ran away a few times from the army, but just to let them know that I wanted to do what I wanted to do. And they punish you for it. They put you in detention, and that didn't prove to be much good either. So when I decided to soldier, I just went right ahead.*
>
> *I always wanted to drive trucks. So I joined the army service corps. I wanted to be a truck driver. But after awhile I learned that it was kind of a gimmick. They go by category. If you were A-1 you didn't get a chance to drive truck. You went right with the rifles and machine guns. We took advance training at Currie barracks in Calgary.*
>
> *Lots of parade square. Lots of it. You had to understand the basic rules of regimental life. "Boyer, if we can't break you, we'll break your mother's heart." And I guess they would do that.*[108]

William Carriere took his initial training in Saskatoon:

> *I can remember when we were in Saskatoon there was ladies that were joining up in the services. So we stayed in that same building and I said to the boys, "Let's*

go look at the ladies there …" So we went over there and stood around and looked at them. They had wonderful drills. They have already been in the service for quite a while but they were teaching other new recruits. Then an officer came board, the captain, and he gave us hell. He told us to get out of there and I will always remember that. But we weren't doing wrong. We were just looking at them ladies. We were so surprised to see them — how they marched, and how they did the drills. It was so nice, but our officer came and kicked us out of there. "You're not supposed to be here!" and all that. He was

Top: Privates James G. and Edward Poitras, South Saskatchewan Regiment, Winnipeg, Manitoba [ca. 1941]. Bottom Left: Private J.P. Flammond, Private James G. Poitras, Winnipeg, Manitoba [ca. 1940-1945]. Bottom Right: John Howse, Métis, while attending basic camp, Grande Prairie, Alberta, 1943.

calling us down. That's the way the army was. You have to have discipline, to do things properly. Anyway, then we start. One by one we went in. My brother [Pierre] *got in first, and the next guy was my other brother Alphonse. Next day I got in. James got in and other guys got in. So we made it and I always remember that marching. We were with George Buck and they marched and, by golly marched right in. They turned exactly at the same time. They met one another like that. They bounced back, and then we laughed so darn much, you know, and we, got hell for that too. So they put us in a real stiff march. But once you get used to it, it was easy … We stayed in Saskatoon for about two weeks, I think, and then from there we went to Niagara Falls.*[109]

Joseph McGillivary, of Cumberland House, described how he was trained to be a sniper:

I took my basic training at Fort Osborne Barracks in Winnipeg.

I went to England, it was a place called Stude Park, in Surrey, when I finished my advance training. I left for England on April 1, 1942. I didn't stay long in Fort Osborne. Strude Park is very close to Aldershot, very close. That's when they placed me on that sniper thing.

They taught us map reading and shooting, all about the rifle, night marches, mostly map reading. You had to know where you were. They would take you somewhere in Scotland, take you there blindfolded, leave you there until night and then they would have you find out where you were. You had to be good on a map to pinpoint yourself in Scotland. It was quite hilly there. That makes a difference, the contours of the land. You had to go by the stars, the sun and the moon. That's what we would use later on. Luckily, I was pretty good on the map. I never got lost. It was pretty hard when you had never seen a country before to try and find your way out and you can't ask nobody. In the war that can come in handy … Even when we went back to the unit, we still trained. Still trained with the rifle to be a good shot. I was pretty good.[110]

Home Guard

Yeah, He was a Soldier

Yeah, he was a soldier in the Second World War
but he didn't go overseas. He stayed in Canada —
Saskatoon and Regina.
He'd see his cousins and he'd decide to go too.

Well the Germans wanted to take all the land.
Oh, yeah, he was against them.

Except he became sick
and had to leave the army.

Oh, yeah, he wanted to go overseas —
to go and see the country.
— Aimé Dumont[111]

Although all our men wanted to go overseas, some were forced to remain in Canada to serve in the Home Guard. Corporal William Sayese repeatedly volunteered to go overseas:

> *So I stood before the Colonel: "Sir, what is the matter; I volunteered for overseas and I can't go?"*
>
> *"Because we're making good use of you here in Canada." He says, "You're in the war too, Mr. Sayese; you're in the war too. The whole world is in it. You're doing a very good job — protecting your own country; the country you love to live in. That's the reason why we're keeping you here," he says.*[112]

William Sayese was trained as an instructor, earning the rank of corporal. "That's how I got my education," he said; "they knew I didn't have any education, so they put me into Military School for about six months":

> *It was located in Saskatoon. But it didn't really … it wasn't the kind of education that the kids have now; it was mostly about the war, you know, the weapons and everything … That's how I came to learn English, and writing.*[113]

Some of our men died while serving at home. Corporal James LaRocque died in Regina in 1941. On November 13, 1941, the *Leader-Post* stated that he was "probably the first Métis of the province to die in army service in the war."[114]

Going Overseas

Many of our men did go overseas. Euclide Boyer recalled the trip there.

> *A lot of guys were crying. We had a Negro, well more than one, but we were all mixed up you know. I believe there was a few Americans on there too. Some Negroes on top deck there, they had a recreation area. We were all in there, and we had a piano. And some of those guys got on the piano and sang there. They were playing the blues. I can remember that very clearly like today. And guys were*

breaking down with tears and everything. I never got seasick, but I just about got seasick. I had to go and lay down on my hammock.

We landed at South Hampton, England. The British got along pretty good with Canadians actually, but I don't know. Most guys got along real well with the womenfolk in England, and even the Indians, like the native boys, the English girls weren't scared of them. They didn't know what they were, they thought they were just Canadian, and it was great.[115]

Most of our men served in the Army because there were racial, education, and health restrictions in the Air Force and Navy, which made our men ineligible.[116] However, there were the exceptions. Able Seaman (AB) Raymond Cyr, RCN Veterans' Reserve, son of Frank Cyr (Jackfish Lake), served on the *HMCS Hespeler.*

Service in England

Our men spent the first years of their service overseas training and serving in England. A newspaper article, "Saskatchewan Men Heroes in the Blitz," gives tribute to our men:

Though these men had no chance to meet the Nazis face to face, they return to their homes heroes. They encountered more action in one week battling fires and rescuing blitz victims at a heavily bombed British port than troops in training had experienced in 18 months.

They were waiting at the port for dispatch back to Canada from a Canadian base depot, suffering from stomach, nerve and other disorders when the blitz broke for more than seven days, four hours each evening. Though classed as unfit, they volunteered to fight fires, drive ambulances and rescue victims from wreckage earning the reputation of heroes.[117]

Listed among the heroes was Private J. H. Halcro (Prince Albert).

Our men helped the English farmers to harvest their crops and do all necessary farm work to help feed the country. According to a news report,

Shouldering pitchforks in place of rifles and handling scythes instead of Tommy guns, hundreds of Canadian troops are working in the harvest fields of England.

One Canadian division initiated a farm help scheme sending 50 soldiers every two weeks from a number of Canadian units to farms in many parts of England. In addition to this regular scheme, men from a number of Canadian units aid farmers in their districts where labour is scarce. All work is voluntary.[118]

One of the men specifically mentioned was Private Peter Gaudry,

Top to Bottom: King George VI inspecting 3rd Field Regiment, Royal Canadian Artillery at Aldershot, Hants, February 1940. Troops in action, southern England, March 1940. Unidentified member of the Regina Rifle Regiment, England, September 1941. An unidentified member of the Regina Rifle Regiment, England, 30 March 1943.

originally from Willow Bunch. He had been working as a cowboy on his ranch in the foothills of Alberta when he enlisted. He commented, "It really felt good to be near horses again."[119]

Hong Kong

Canada sent a military force to Hong Kong to help the British defend their colony. Major-General Harry D. G. Crerar, Chief of the Canadian general staff, claimed that this Canadian force adhered to the principle of "territorial representation."[120] He considered it "most desirable that one unit should come from Western Canada and the other from Eastern Canada."[121] Two Class C infantry battalions — designated as "not recommended for operational employment at present, due either to recent employment requiring a period of refresher training or to insufficient training"[122] — were sent as Canada's contribution to Hong Kong's defence against Japan's war-hardened military forces.

Joe Amyotte, a Métis soldier from Balcarres, received word in May 1941 that he was going to Hong Kong. He was given 24 hours to pack

Infantrymen of "C" Company, Royal Rifles of Canada, disembarking from H.M.C.S. Prince Robert, Hong Kong, 16 November 1941.

his gear and go home on an eight-day pass before leaving for the Far East. While he was visiting his family, the authorities sent a different regiment to Hong Kong. Amyotte maintained that by the time the mistake was noticed, the Winnipeg Grenadiers were en route to Hong Kong.[123]

Many of our men were with the "C" Force that was sent to Hong Kong. The following men were part of this dangerous mission: Privates George Charles Badger, Edgar J. Baptiste, K. J. Inkster, Ernest P. and F. Malbeuf, J. P. A. Ouellette, R. F. and W. J. Parenteau, Victor Ross, C. Settee, T. E. St. Germaine, E. H. and U. L. Vermette, and L. E. Young.[124]

Alfred Malbeuf was there:

> *When I got to Winnipeg, they asked for a bunch of volunteers. So, we volunteered. Then I had 4 days leave. When I got back to Winnipeg, we were sent overseas. We went straight to Hong Kong. It was 21 days to go over. We got to Hong Kong November 27, 1941. The war broke out in Hong Kong on December 2, 1941 and it lasted until December 25, 1941.*
>
> *There were 1000 men from Winnipeg and about 50 from Dundurn. There were machine gunners. We had a little better than 2000 men. Then there were combat rifles, another 2000 men. So we had over 4000 men on that boat.*[125]

The inexperienced soldiers who arrived in Hong Kong had no idea what was in store for them. The result was catastrophic:

The Hong Kong tragedy began on Dec. 8, 1941, when the Japanese attacked the southern Chinese port, then held by a British garrison that included almost 2,000 Canadians. After a valiant but hopeless stand, the garrison gave up on Christmas; by then more than a third of the Canadians were dead or wounded. Due to the harsh prison-camp conditions, some 260 more perished in the following years. By one count, our [the Canadian] *final bill for Hong Kong was 567 souls.*[126]

Victor Ross.

Not only were Saskatchewan Métis soldiers at Hong Kong for the fateful battle of December 1941, but some of our people are resting there still, in the Sai Wan War Cemetery. These include Ptes. George Walter Sayers (Bresaylor), Walter Joseph Parenteau, and Victor Ross (Green Lake) who died on Christmas Day, 1941. Privates Lewis Edward Young (Meadow Lake), Ernest P. Malbeuf (Ituna), George Charles Badger (Kamsack), and Robert F. Parenteau (Fort Pitt) were taken prisoner — all are buried in Japan.

The Regina *Leader-Post* published a story about the fight at Hong Kong, and listed Pte. T. E. St. Germaine (Qu'Appelle) as one of the three Regina-area men who were "Hong Kong defenders." T. E. St. Germaine was the son of Pte. J. St. Germaine who was serving overseas, and had joined the Winnipeg Grenadiers on April 5, 1941.[127]

A newspaper article in July 23, 1943 described the conditions of prisoners of war held by their Japanese captors:

The Canadian [Active] *Army listed Thursday night in its 331st casualty list of the war the names of 38 men who have died of illness while prisoners of the Japanese …*

Defence department officials said the records of the deaths showed many of them were due to food deficiency, and stressed that the diet of a Japanese soldier generally was not sufficient for an Occidental.

A Red Cross Convention requires a nation holding prisoners to provide them with the same diet it gives its own soldiers stationed at bases. While Japan has never adhered to this, it has announced it would treat its war prisoners in conformity with it.

The Canadian government is attempting to get concentrated vitamin foods to Canadian soldiers held prisoner by the Japanese.[128]

Since the Japanese lived by trading, and were cut off by a submarine blockade, the country soon ran out of food. The prisoners' rations "usually amounted to one pound [450 grams] of low quality rice per day … The staple vegetable was chrysanthemum tops which were not popular."[129] The only protein the prisoners got was from chopped-up fish heads or the occasional bit of meat:

> *Nutritionists assert that a Caucasian male weighing 70 kg. requires about 2,400 calories a day to maintain his strength and weight. If he is physically active, as those doing camp fatigues (or later those on working parties) were, then the requirement rises to between 3,000 and 3,500 calories.*[130]

Our men suffered from malnutrition. Because of the lack of vitamins and protein, the prisoners contracted photophobia, an extreme sensitivity of the eyes to light, which can lead to impaired vision and eventually blindness. They suffered from neuritic diseases such as pellagra and beriberi, which afflicted nearly eighty per cent of all prisoners at one time or another. This affliction manifested itself in vomiting, diarrhea, swelling, and later patchy numbness of the legs. Others had what was labelled as "electric feet," because the symptoms included sharp, shooting pains in the feet and legs.[131]

Historians argue,

> *It was, and is, impossible to establish the actual caloric value of the prisoners' diet. It has been claimed that it was as low as 900 calories per day … A more normal value probably lay in the 1,000-1,300 range or approximately one half of what is needed to keep a 70 kg. man in sound health.*[132]

The prisoners sometimes found their own food. Alfred Malbeuf told of one of the meals that he "captured":

> *I ate a snake. Skinned it myself. I was that hungry. The boys asked me how it tasted and I told them it tasted like chicken. Simple. The way I killed this snake, the Japanese took off to get some wood, they were four-foot lengths. There was a little creek running there. We always had a rest there. There was a little snake going in the water. Who was going to catch it first? There was more than one trying to catch it. So I caught the darn thing, killed it and put it in my pocket. When I got into camp, I started skinning the thing, from the head first. I showed the Japanese and asked if it was alright for me to cook it. They said yes. When it was cooked, I gave my friend a taste. There were snakes in the camp. Not poisonous. The Englishmen used to tell me that they were good to eat. Great big ones.*[133]

The Canadian POWs were used as slave labour. Maurice Blondeau told the story of a Métis soldier returning to Japan to do a tour of duty who informed him, while approaching Yokohama, that he "spent five years building ships and eating rice and fish heads right in these dock yards."[134]

Dieppe

The August 19, 1942 landing at Dieppe was a catastrophe for our troops. Ross Munroe of the Canadian Press provided an eyewitness account:

> *For eight hours, under intense Nazi fire from dawn into a sweltering afternoon, I watched Canadian troops fight the blazing, bloody battle of Dieppe. I saw them go through the biggest of the war's raiding operations in wild scenes that crowded helter skelter one upon another in crazy sequence. There was a furious attack by German E-boats while the Canadians moved in on Dieppe's beaches, landing by dawn's half-light. When the Canadian battalions stormed through the flashing inferno of Nazi*

Top to Bottom: Maurice Blondeau. Lieutenant-Commander Fred Day and officers of the auxiliary anti-aircraft ship H.M.C.S. Prince Robert with liberated Canadian prisoners-of-war at Shamshuipo Camp, Hong Kong, August 1945. Canadian and British Prisoners in Hong Kong waiting to be liberated by a landing party from HMCS Prince Robert, 30 August 1945.

defences, belching guns of huge tanks rolling into the fight, I spent the grimmest 20 minutes of my life with one unit when a rain of German machine-gun fire wounded half the men in our boat and only a miracle saved us from annihilation.[135]

Landing craft en route to Dieppe France, during Operation Jubilee, 19 August 1942.

According to the Canadian War Museum, the Battle of Dieppe was Canada's worst single-day loss of the war, as 807 died and the German defenders captured 1,946 of our soldiers. Another 100 Canadians died in captivity, many of battle wounds:[136]

> *It had been a massacre that day of August 19, 1942. The Canadians had scrambled from their ungainly landing craft directly into a storm of fire from the German positions dominating the beaches of Dieppe. There had been almost no preliminary naval bombardment to support the attackers nor much preliminary bombing to soften the defences. The Churchill tanks, struggling ashore with enormous difficulty, had found that their treads could not get purchase on the stony shingle. The 27 tanks that made it out of the water could fire their guns, but unable to move well, they could offer only limited fire support to their infantry. Worse was to come as military commanders, offshore and insulated from the chaos by faulty communications and heavy smoke of battle, reinforced failure, sending new battalions from the floating reserve to be cut to pieces on the beaches.*[137]

Left: Canadian Dead litter the Dieppe Beach among Ruined and Abandoned Tanks.
Right: German Soldiers Keep Canadian Prisoners of War under Surveillance as they are led through Dieppe.

Our men were at Dieppe. The South Saskatchewan Regiment (SSR) was one of the regiments sent into the foray. Privates Edward Joseph Poitras, Joseph Pelletier, and Alvin Sayese were killed on the beaches. Those wounded included George Poitras, brother of Edward Poitras, and Pte. Joe Jeannotte, both from the Qu'Appelle Valley, and L/Cpl. Paul Amyotte (Regina).[138] Later, in November 1942 in England, Colin Umpherville, from Glen Mary, died.

Corporal Joseph Jeannotte, of the Qu'Appelle Valley, won a Military Medal for his actions at Dieppe. The *Fort Qu'Appelle Times* reported:

Edward Joseph Poitras.

> *Corporal Jeannotte was with the South Saskatchewan Regiment at Dieppe on August 19, 1942, and during the attack on the village of Pourville and the high ground west of the town, this Non-Commissioned Officer showed the highest degree of courage, and set an example of determination to the men of his section and platoon in pressing forward to the objective, a machine gun position commanding the beach and a low gap in the cliff to the west.*
>
> *His platoon sergeant commanding the platoon became a casualty, and in spite of his own wound, Corporal Jeannotte took over and organized the platoon for the last stage of the attack, which was successful.*
>
> *He then led the post in the face of a determined counter attack by stronger enemy forces until ordered to withdraw.*
>
> *Corporal Jeannotte then withdrew his platoon across ground under heavy fire, and largely due to his coolness, leadership and example, only a few casualties resulted.*[139]

Private Walter Raymond Blondeau (Estevan) became Prisoner 42901 at Stalag IX-C, Arbeitskommando NR 1249, Bad Sulza, Thuringia, Germany.[140]

Paul Delorme from Rocanville was wounded and taken captive. Delorme reported being in a German hospital called Gloster Heina 9 A H Camp for months. He was guarded by German soldiers, and was moved to other camps until his release in 1945.[141] Ironically, he returned to Germany in 1946 as part of the occupation forces.[142]

Pierre Gaudry (Willow Bunch), the son of Amable Gaudry, a First World War veteran and grandson of André Gaudry, NWMP guide, used his family tradition of horsemanship to survive the POW camp. He was captured at Dieppe and placed in wrist irons, but when the German commandant found out that he was a horseman, his bonds were taken off, and he served the next three years grooming the commandant's horses.[143]

Walter Blondeau.

North Africa

In 1943, 201 Canadian officers and 147 non-commissioned officers were sent to British Army units. Corporal James Edward Carriere Sr. (Cumberland House) and Louis Roy (Île-à-la-Crosse) were there. The Canadian contingent arrived in time to take part in the battle for Tunisia.

Sicily

Under pressure from the Canadian government to have Canadian soldiers sent into battle, General Eisenhower, the supreme Allied commander, agreed to let the 1st Canadian Division and 1st Canadian Tank Brigade replace the 3rd British Division in the invasion of Sicily. The infantry brigade was sent to Scotland for intense training in assault landing. Of the exploits of the Canadian Army on the mountainous terrain of Sicily, Farley Mowat has written,

> *Each man who made that climb performed his own private miracle. From ledge to ledge the dark figures made their way, hauling each other up, passing along their weapons and ammunition from hand to hand. A signaller made that climb with a heavy wireless set strapped to his back — a thing that in daylight was seen to be impossible. Yet no man slipped, no man dropped so much as a clip of ammunition. It was just as well, for any sound by one would have been fateful to all.*[144]

According to historian, Terry Copp, "The Sicilian campaign made a significant contribution to the Allied war effort."[145] The pressure on

German troops in Italy resulted in Hitler diverting troops from Russia to the southern front. We had men in Sicily. Private James Paul (Duck Lake), a machine gunner with the Saskatoon Light Infantry (SLI), was "blown out of a bren [gun] carrier" on the second day that he was in Sicily. While two of his crew were killed because of the explosion, he escaped with a fractured nose.[146]

SASKATOON LIGHT INFANTRY (M.G.)

We know that Cpl. William Regan served in Sicily with the SLI and contracted malaria. Sergeant Joseph Martial Poitras (Lebret), Louis Roy (Île-à-la-Crosse), Louis Nabess and Cpl. James Edward Carriere (Cumberland House), Archie Hubert Nicholas (Duck Lake), and Pte. John J. Wheeler, Sr. were also there. We do not know how many more took part in this pivotal but bloody campaign.

Joseph Martial Poitras.

The Italian Campaign

Ortona

At the eastern end of the Italian front, on the Adriatic coast, the 1st Canadian Division engaged in house-to-house combat with Germany's 1st Paratroop Division in Ortona. The duel began on December 21, 1943 and was still raging four days later. Historian Mark Zuehlke has described the efforts made to bring Christmas spirit to our soldiers despite the shells, machine guns, death, and war just blocks away. Among these efforts was a complete Christmas dinner with Christmas pudding and mince pie — all served on white tablecloths. Companies ate the meals in rotation while listening to carols sung by an impromptu choir accompanied by a piper and organist.[147] Archie Nicholas was there:

> *I went to the Van Doos* [22nd Regiment], *I think there was nine of us. I spoke the Duck Lake French. Once they got to know my name and I could speak French I was very welcome. All nine of us stayed with the Van Doos for three weeks. We went in action with them. They were a rough bunch but they were a good bunch to be with. But you knew that the Van Doos were ahead of you. If they wouldn't get through there, nobody would get through there.*

I went in as a cook's helper all the time we were in Ortona 'till we moved out, then we hit the Hitler line. We hit at four o'clock in the morning. Near Casino, it was before we hit Casino. On the front that we attacked … my company commander was Armstrong and my platoon commander was J. Harper Prouse and I don't know if I was his batman or his runner. I think I was his runner so I was very close to the command post. Before the battle, just around twelve o'clock at night we heard one shot over here and one over there and it happened you know. Harper said "this is it Army" you know, because his name was Armstrong we called him "Army." He said "let's go!" and twelve hundred guns opened up. 1200 guns loaded up and we put in the attack on that creeping barrage. We crossed the river on foot. That was again one of our old colonels, we use to call Bald Face Stone, Jim Stone, he got these little bail bridges across the river and we use to cross that without getting wet. We didn't have too much trouble there 'till we hit the mountains and when we hit the mountain climbing up there, they were waiting for us on top of the mountain. The enemy seemed to have, I wouldn't say they were marked out exactly, but they seemed to know exactly the distance from where they were to us. I wasn't too bad in there we lost some afterwards. I went back that day of the next day of the battle of Casino. The only thing that was standing up was the one doorframe. Then they pulled us out, we were on our way to Rome.

In August that same year I was wounded for the first time. The B company was in the reserve and C company went in. They went in quite a ways and they got cut up. We were in B company and some of them were taken prisoner. So then they order B company in there. They'd gone in a day before, late in the afternoon towards the evening they ordered B company to the same place and we went a little too far. We had to retreat so we had to take back some wounded and we had some guys that hadn't been in action too long. They didn't have enough training or maybe they didn't have the violent experience. When you are taking somebody out you fire on the spot there where the Jerries are, while these come back and you come back so far yourself you turn around and fire. When I passed this certain group on the way back they stopped hard and the Jerries opened and got me.

So I got back to where we were and we couldn't find the officer. There was some prisoners in the bottom of some cellar and another guy and myself were ordered to go in there. So we shot the door open with the Tommy gun and when we bust through the door we could hear "Don't shoot Canada! Don't shoot Canada!" They were British hostages that had been taken prisoner. They were being kept in there. I was wounded and you know those German officers they had these nice P38 Lugers. And when I went to pick up one I wanted one too that's where I found out that it was just a little bit worse than I thought. I went to pick it up and ooh it hurt, so I was ordered out, and we took them out.

German officers weren't the worst ones. Some of these Paratroopers, I've seen one of them get wounded and you know to sort of help them out and they'd spit at you. Well they don't last long spitting on the Canadian soldiers. Not in battle. You had to touch them a little bit with your firearm to let them know that you were boss and you meant business.

That first time I marched back we were short of men. I had to go back to the line and Sergeant Major Almer asked me if I was able to help march back these prisoners. I marched them back to the line and that's how I got to the hospital. I was in the hospital for 30 days. It was just a flesh wound, I had one bullet in me. When I woke up in the hospital they had this bullet all bent up in a saucer. I kept it for as long I could, 'till I was wounded the second time. It was in the northern part our last battle in Italy.

This was our last battle: we were going over to join the Canadians in Holland. Then were going into this attack and I was on the extreme left. We were looking this way, you know, that was our objective. Probably if we would have held that objective that would have been our last battle in Italy. Suddenly, all these guys popped out of a hole and opened a machine gun on us and killed the guys in front of me, one behind me, and knocked me down. They were probably about 50 yards away. They nailed the whole section but they didn't even kill us all. There were some of them that got them but it was too late. I crawled in a tank truck and I couldn't walk. I was hit in the hip and they shot my hip out.

The last thing I remember there was Major Armstrong. Well they were shelling and fighting, they were shelling pretty bad and he hooked a pole in my harness and dragged me in a building. He was the company commander. Then I lost consciousness for a while there. I crawled: I remember when the boys called "Come on! Come on! You can make it!" I think that was Barwold, a guy by the name of Barwold from Tofield, Alberta. The next thing I remember is going through fire, you know these jeeps with the A frame? I was tied up on top there and they were shelling and all I could see was fire. Then I lost consciousness again. I woke up in the hospital. This was on the 13th of December, 1944. I woke up the evening before New Years, that's when I came back. I didn't know where I was. Everything was dark for quite awhile. I was wondering where the hell I was. Everything was dark but I could hear a noise. My leg was sore. I kept scratching at it and I was tied up. I was wondering what the hell? I didn't know where I was. I knew I wasn't taken prisoner 'cause when they first tried to give me first aid, they put that little thing that smells bad on your face and I grabbed that and I threw it away. They operated on me that night. They were Canadians. One of those nurses spoke French. I didn't have adequate clothes on or a damn thing and they said they were in the hospital just out of Naples. I stayed in there 'till April and they were going to fly me out. I wasn't in very good shape. I had infection, I couldn't eat. I had a cast up to here and it stunk. I don't know what it was actually, but for me to eat they use to wet some towels and stuff. They'd give me a drink of brandy and a couple of bottles of stout a day. They got me ready the night before. They said you'd be flying out in the morning. We're going to fly you out to England but in the meantime now next morning just before we left, somebody approached me and asked if I would mind giving my place to somebody else. Well I wasn't very fussy about flying anyways. I've never been in the air before, so I had no experience with flying.

I didn't walk for a long time after that. About two and a half years. Operation after operation and nothing would work.[148]

Top: A jeep ambulance of the Royal Canadian Army Medical Corps bringing in two wounded Canadian soldiers on the Moro River front south of San Leonardo di Orona, Italy, 10 December 1943.
Bottom: Archie Nicholas.

Joseph Louis Rivard, of Harp Tree/Willow Bunch, also took part in the Battle of Ortona. A community history book from Willow Bunch mentioned Rivard's involvement in this battle:

> *Pte. J. L. Rivard of Harptree, Sask., was one of the Canadian soldiers attached to an anti-tank detachment that supported the storming of Cass* [sic — Casa] *Berardi, the action which won for Major Paul Tiquet the Victoria Cross. Cass* [sic] *Berardi itself, a 200 year old fortified house, was used by Rivard and his chums at one time as a billet.*[149]

Louis Roy was wounded by an artillery shell and spent a month in hospital. Harvey Edward Pratt was in Italy with the SLI, a machine gunner,

Royal Canadian Artillery. He was wounded in Italy, and came home with malaria and a defective heart. Corporal R. Isbister (Shell Lake) was wounded near Ortona. He commented to a reporter when he returned home, that the resistance in the sector was "tough." "We were mortared, machine-gunned and shelled … They threw everything at us but the kitchen sink."[150]

Joseph Louis Rivard.

Morris Joseph Poitras served with the 1st Field Company, RCE. He was responsible for detecting mines and building bridges for the frontline troops. In the assault on Ortona, he was accidentally buried under a bombed-out building and was reported as Missing in Action. Some time later, he was found and identified in a Naples hospital. Returning to service, Poitras was wounded again at Monte Cassino.[151]

Private Joseph Antoine (Paynton), of the Hastings and Prince Edward Regiment, returned home because he was shell-shocked.[152] He reported that he and another member of the regiment were sniping from a big brick building when it was shelled. They were forced to stay hidden in the rubble for a night before their regiment moved forward to their position.[153]

Louis Roy.

Private Jerry Umpherville (Glen Mary) was killed at Coriano Ridge, the last important ridge in the Allies' advance in central Italy below the Gothic Line. The Germans were dug in and resisted all attacks to their positions between September 4 and 12, 1944. The Allies were successful on September 12 in dislodging the German parachute and panzer troops.

Charles Umpherville, Italy.

This was some of the heaviest fighting in the Italian Campaign.

We lost many Métis men during the Italian Campaign, including Pte. Robert Maxwell Umpherville (Glen Mary), Fus. Alexander Settee (Cumberland House), and Tpr. William Douglas Sinclair of the 1st Armoured Canadian Regiment (Punnichy). Private Eugene Morin (Green Lake) with the Westminster (Motor) Regiment died on November 18, 1944. Private Stanley Joseph Landry (Meadow Lake) died on December 15, 1944. Both are buried at the Ravenna War Cemetery. Paul Edward De La Ronde died May 18, 1944, and is buried in the Cassino War Cemetery. Fusilier Thomas Bear (Meadow Lake) died January 13, 1945, and is buried in Ravenna War Cemetery. Gunner John Peltier (Lebret), with the Royal Canadian Artillery, 17th Field Regiment, died when "an enemy shell scored a direct hit on his slit trench."[154]

Signore Tomasso, an Italian barber, cuts the hair of Private R. J. Tims of the Anti-Aircraft Support Company, Saskatoon Light Infantry (M.G.), watched by Private Tommy Bear, Ortona, Italy, 10 January 1944.

There were some happy stories from the Italian Campaign. The following is the story of Métis soldier, Corporal W. M. "Bill" Camponi,

Thomas Bear Gravesite.

> *Seeing his grandparents three hours after he landed in Italy, was the experience of Corporal W. M. Camponi, 23, of Saskatoon …*
>
> *The minute he arrived at Reggio, a town on the toe of Italy's boot, Camponi made enquiries and was soon directed to his grandparents by Italian police. His grandfather ran the bakery in town.*
>
> *He found his grandfather and grandmother in good health and learned that they had lost everything of value, confiscated from them by the Germans before they pulled out.*[155]

It is ironic that Bill Camponi's Italian grandparents should have lost everything to an invading army, because his maternal grandparents had lost everything they had at Batoche when his grandfather had fought beside Riel.

First Special Service Force: Hill 720

> *Unlike Hong Kong, the bloody Italian Christmas of 1943 at least led to victory, but it is still remarkable how readily commanders threw their soldiers at the enemy on Dec. 25 — not once, but twice. On the western side of the Italian front, southeast of Rome, the Allies sought control of a spot called Monte Sammucro, where the Germans held a height known as Hill 720. The task was handed to a unique, Canadian-American formation, the First Special Service Force. This joint unit seized the hill, at the cost of 65 dead or wounded.*[156]

The First Special Service Force was deployed during the Italian Campaign in support of an operation in the European Theatre of War. This elite commando regiment, nicknamed "The Devil's Brigade," was formed in 1942. Between 1942 and 1944, about 2,500 soldiers were chosen to serve in this joint Canadian-American military unit. We were there. Sergeant Claude Adams from MacDowall was in the force:

The unit deployed to the Aleutian Islands in 1943 and then moved to Italy, fighting at the amphibious landings at Anzio, in the liberation of Rome and into southern France.

It suffered one of the highest casualty rates of any Allied unit in the war and was disbanded in 1945.

But it was also one of the most effective combat units ever fielded. The force earned its nickname during the vicious fighting in Italy, when the troops recovered a diary from the body of a German officer in which he wrote: "The black devils are all around us every time we come into line and we never hear them." [157]

The First Special Service Force became legendary when they attacked the German-held mountain in central Italy called Monte la Diffensa, a key stronghold blocking the Allied advance to Rome.

Top to Bottom: Forcemen of the First Special Service Force boarding a Douglas C-47 aircraft during parachute training at Fort William Harrison, Helena, Montana, United States, August, 1942. Canadian Soldiers aboard a troopship arriving at Greenock, Scotland, 31 August 1942. Unidentified Forceman of the First Special Service Force during a winter training exercise, Blossburg, Montana, United States, January 1943. Bottom Right: Major-General E.G. Weeks, Major-General in charge of Administration, talking with personnel of No.1 Canadian Special Service Battalion, which is being disbanded, Aldershot, England, 9 January 1945. Claude Adams is in the bottom right-hand corner of the photograph.

The commandos of the special services force snuck up on the German defenders by scrambling up a sheer rock face considered unclimbable at night. The Canadians and Americans completely surprised the Germans and took the mountain in two hours . . .

Brigade members blackened their faces with burnt wine corks and launched night patrols into enemy territory that unnerved the Germans and earned them a reputation for ferocity in combat.[158]

Top: Personnel of the First Special Force being briefed before setting out on a patrol, Anzio beach-head, Italy, 20 April 1944. Lt. H. Rayner of Toronto in the foreground. Bottom: Members of the First Special Service Force preparing a meal, Anzio beach-head, Italy, late April 1944.

The Normandy (D-Day) Landings

D-Day, Juno Beach, June 6, 1944. These words would leave a tragic mark on Saskatchewan's Métis people. More Métis died on this day than during the entire 1885 Resistance.

The Plan
The Canadian 3rd Division planned a two-brigade frontal attack on Juno Beach. The 7th Canadian Infantry Brigade would land on Mike Sector and the 8th on Nana. Within the Mike and Nana Sectors were the villages of Courseulles-sur-Mer and Bernières-sur-Mer, and the western edges of St. Aubin-sur-Mer. Though generally well suited for a landing, the beaches had a sea approach that was complicated by rocky offshore ledges. Fortunately, there were few hindrances to block the exit of the infantry or vehicles from the beaches.[159]

The Canadians' D-Day plan called for the infantry and armour to seize an area extending almost ten miles inland. Initial objectives, including seaside towns, were encompassed within a line designated as "Yew" and a second phase line called "Elm." The final objective of the first day included the high ground west of Caen and was codenamed "Oak." By the time Oak was reached, the divisional reserve, the 9th Canadian Infantry Brigade, and the tanks of the Sherbrooke Fusiliers were ashore, and were in position to reinforce the rest of the division during the anticipated German counterattack.[160]

Paratroopers of the 1st Canadian Parachute Battalion in a transit camp staging area prior to D-Day, England, ca. 1-5 June 1944.

The Reality
David Dumont recalled:

> *We didn't know until it was, of course a few days before … I remember one fellow broke his thumb boxing you know he couldn't even go to hospital without guards and all that until we boarded the boat and went to France. I got sick there again, seasick. Holy smokes everybody had been issued what the army called "puke," "vomit bag" or something, you know my God you had a little bag you had to puke in there and throw it overboard. Oh, it was rough in the channel.*
>
> *We landed, oh I'd say roughly about 8:00 o'clock in the morning. The Americans were first because of a certain way the tide came in, you know, sea tide. Oh, the water was so deep. When I hit the water it was too deep for you see, and I had to struggle … and I wasn't far though that I started walking and my God we had these damn buddies, why they ever made us wear them I don't know. My pants were all filled with water and all that. You know you couldn't run with them. Even I had to pull the pants out of my buddies you know, to let the water out. Oh, I thought that was funny, and yet you didn't have time to laugh about it. There was a lot of machine gun fire, you know. We were just lucky I never lost a man out of our platoon, you know. I was with my sergeant. I think we even had an officer. We lost so many officers. George Gardiner was our sergeant. I don't think we lost a man, but two, three days after we lost quite a few, you know; counter attack after we were inland. Went right through, and I think we went three, four miles the first day, maybe more. We went right in. We could have went further, but our back wasn't covered, what they call in the army our rear wasn't covered so we got pulled back once.*[161]

Charles "Charlie" Fosseneuve from Cumberland House was there too:

I was with the armoured corps. I was a gun layer. You do the same thing as a rifleman. You would point at him and fire and somebody else fired the trigger for you. As soon as there is elevation, error up and down, traversal gun, the guy, the sergeant behind you, tells you, gives you the order, what the degree is, so the gun is put so many degrees in so many minutes and at so much elevation. You do it all yourself, that gun layer, and as soon as you're finished you say you are ready and the guy sergeant says "fire!" and the other guy pulls the trigger for you. You don't open up your instruments there unless you're commanded. All the time, that's what we'll do. As soon as your gun is ready you say "ready," you aim and fire. Very seldom we'd point Charlie like that. We done it a few times but in open field like that. It was mostly hand targets like that.

Top: Infantrymen in a Landing Craft Assault (LCA) going ashore from H. M. C. S. Prince Henry off the Normandy beachhead, France, 6 June 1944. Bottom: Reinforcements going ashore from a LCA from H.M. C. S. Henry off the Normandy bridgehead, June 1944.

When we went in, hey, we fired 200 rounds per gun right on top of our infantry like when they're landing. We fired right over top of their heads like that, so the guys, the Germans, go down in their trenches. We landed in about six feet of water, ourselves with the tanks and everything. The tanks got great big exhaust pipes way up in the air so that the water didn't get to the motor. Well, even the jeeps and everything. It's all water proof vehicles.

We landed at Courseulles. I never got scared actually. Not really. The only thing, this plane came around there and guys were bombing at us, you know, when they landed and but after that, you see, we took the 7th Army, the German Army and we got in some surprises. They didn't expect us. After we slaughtered them we just kept on going.[162]

D-Day took an awful toll on the Canadian military. We felt the loss in our communities. On June 6, 1944, we lost more of our young men than on

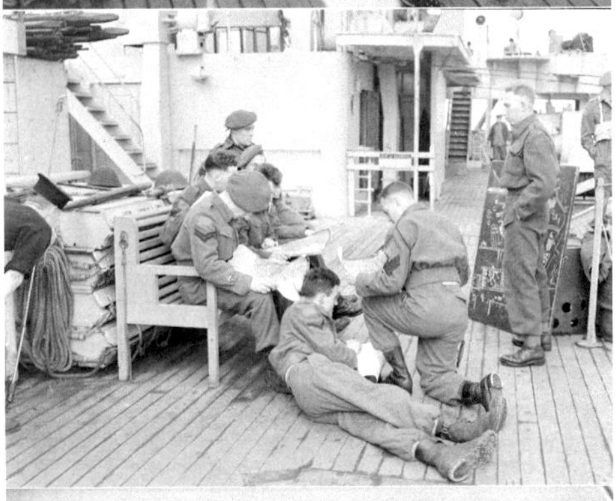

Top to Bottom: Infantrymen of the Regina Rifle Regiment en route to France studying a map of Courseulles-sur-Mer, France, ca. 8-10 June 1944. Personnel of the Regina Rifles Regiment aboard a landing craft en route to NAN Green Beach, Courseulles-su-Mer, France, 6 June 1944. Unidentified Canadian soldiers landing on Juno Beach, Courseulles-sur-Mer, France, 6 June 1944.

any other day in the war. We know we lost Rfn. Jean-Baptiste Delorme (Prince Albert); Rfn. Mathew Joseph Desjarlais (Lebret); Rfn. Bill Andrew Daniels (Balcarres); Rfn. Joseph Flammand (Meadow Lake); Rfn. Archie Isbister (Mont Nebo); Rfn. Russel Rudolph Isbister (Mont Nebo); Rfn. Anton Pelletier (Lestock); Pte. Joseph George Poitras (Fort Qu'Appelle)[163]; and Rfn. Joseph Pelletier Jr. (Lebret). How many more is unknown.

We had many wounded on Normandy's beaches, including "Private Joseph A. Collins of Meadow Lake [who] experienced only a brief period of action. With the assault forces of D-Day, he was injured in the left thigh by a German land mine."[164]

Vital Morin remembered the sights and sounds of the invasion:

Two days after the D-Day landings, [Vital] *Morin and the Regina Rifles (the Johns) waded ashore in Normandy, passing by the bodies of slain comrades and ducking the incoming "moaning Minnies" German rockets that came in "crying like children," Morin recalled.*

At 19, Morin experienced his first taste of continental European culture as he and his regiment advanced on the beautiful port city of Caen, and in a furious battle saw its wonders demolished.[165]

Private Edwin Slater (Frenchman Butte) arrived in France with the 34th Field Company,

Joseph Alfred Collins.

Corps of Royal Canadian Engineers (RCE). They crossed the Channel at night, and by dawn were approaching the French coast. Nets clinging to the ships' sides lifted the trucks out of the ships' holds and the waiting landing craft. Soldiers drove the trucks off the landing craft. The water was so deep that Slater remembered that it was almost over the trucks' hoods and well up on the boxes. They just stepped on the gas and drove![166]

The SSR landed at Courseulles on July 7-8, 1944, and began to fight their way inland. Cumberland House Métis, Private George Lloyd Budd, lost his life upon landing. Within the next two months, when the Canadian Army, including the Regina Rifles and the SSR, spearheaded the push into the French countryside, we lost many Métis soldiers, including Rfn. Patrick Louie Anderson (Regina); Fus. Thomas Bear (Meadow Lake); Pte. Alexis Raphael Beaulieu (Fort Qu'Appelle); Rfn. Anthony William Blondeau (Estevan); Rfn. George Charles Boyer (Yorkton); Rfn. Vern Colin Isbister (Mont Nebo); Pte. Albert Kelly (Fort Qu'Appelle); Pte. Albert Joseph LaRose (Battleford); Rfn. Napoleon Morin (Prince Albert); Pte. Maurice E. Nokusis; Pte. David Whitford; Pte. Raymond Parisien (Fort Qu'Appelle); L/Clp. John Pelletier (Lintlaw); Cpl. James Alvin Sayese (Prince Albert); L/Sgt. Elie Victor Sinclair (Regina); and Tpr. Leslie J. Tate (MacDowall). How many more perished remains unknown.

For some of our men, death came at the hands of the 12th SS Panzer Division. This force, commanded by Kurt Meyer, executed Canadian POWs in a series of

Top: Unidentified infantryman of "D" Company, Regina Rifle Regiment on guard duty in forward post, Normandy, France, 10 June 1944.
Bottom: M.E. (Maurice Edward) Nokusis, Bény-Sur-Mer Canadian War Cemetery, France.

atrocities conducted during the Allies' push into Normandy. Among those murdered were the following Saskatchewan Métis: Rfn. W. Napoleon Morin (Cumberland House); Rfn. Norman Joseph Morin, son of John James Morin (Green Lake); Fus. George Fontaine (Clayton); John Donald Dumont, a relative of Gabriel Dumont; and Spr. John Ionel. The murder of POWs was in defiance of the Geneva Conventions, which regulated the treatment of POWs. Joseph McGillivary, from Cumberland House, told how he captured SS Obersturmbannführer Kurt Meyer, the man responsible for the murder of more than 150 Canadian service members[167]:

> *Before we got to Germany, I was the one that captured that General. I got him in a house. When I got him, and he didn't want to come with me. He didn't like that I had captured him. I told him, "You don't come, I'll shoot you." I already slammed a shell home, and I would have shot him right there in the living room. An officer told me not to do that, and I caved in. A major that had just come from Canada. "You don't do that," he told me, "You'll be up for murder." I told him to look what he had done to our people. He had shot lots of them.*[168]

However, the Americans received credit for the capture. After the war, Kurt Meyer was put on trial in Canada and was imprisoned. He would later serve as an advisor to the Canadian Army.[169]

Solomon Goulet remembered how the soldiers "used to just run to stay alive, not sleeping for days at a time. And when sleep finally came, it was so deep that they needed guards to protect them. He too, took his two-hour shift, protecting the men, all through the night."[170]

Some of our men moved inland. William A. Dumont was a scout behind the lines:

> *I got up as far as Falaise and then I was wounded and I lost a leg. I did most of my scouting at night. It was like we use to go to the back of the German lines. I was in the free French underground. Their contact was right with me all the time, his name was John Messier. He was in France and I met him in Normandy. We were together most of the time. The night I was wounded he was the one that carried me back from the frontlines. On the 18th of August of 1944, I was wounded by a machine gun. I was scouting the back at night and they fired on the six line they called them. The Germans put their guns on six lines they got to be firing on six lines you see at night, it's pitch black. I got hit in the leg, blew my leg off. Well, not all, like there was a little piece hanging there.*
>
> *John didn't get hit. I don't know where he was. Finally he came up to me and he says you know we will take you back to the stretcher-bearers where*

we can get something for you. They carried me back, but I don't know who was with him. That was the last I seen of John then they amputated my leg the next day. Of course, I had gangrene in it. I was hit by tracer bullets they call them and of course I went to the hospital in the first time then they transferred me to the 102nd General British Hospital … and that's when they were bombing Falaise. I was in action from June 6 to August the 18th.[171]

Private G. O. Parenteau of the South Saskatchewan Regiment, Rocquancourt, France, 11 August 1944.

Joseph McGillivary was a sniper:

I was never in one country. I was moved wherever they needed me. There were eight of us, eight snipers. Four white men and four Indians. The four white men were all killed and the four Indians came back, though some of us were wounded. I was wounded on August 14, 1944 at a place called Falaise. That's where we caught the Germans six times, we trapped them. Got in a circle and they were trying to fight their way out but we wouldn't let them out. That's where I was wounded. Even our Divisional Commander was wounded. He was in the next bed to me in the hospital. He was Major General Keller. He was wounded.

Joseph McGillivary.

They always thought us a good shot. Most Natives were very good on the rifle, matter of fact, all of them that I know. That's how they used to live in the old days. That's how they picked me.

I was good on the map. I was on the frontline most of the time, I had to learn to soldier. I could even pinpoint where the artillery was coming from and that was a help too. One time a British officer put down his papers and I said, "What is your position on that gunfire we just heard?" I told him mine. He told me that I must have seen his papers. I told him that was my calculations. Then he placed his beside mine, and they were both the same. He thought I was copying from his calculations. I told him that I don't do that, I was trained for that. He thought it was remarkable that a sniper would know this. You had to go by the contours of the land. You had to know all that. Many times I would just check where I was and I would be right on the spot.[172]

Some of our men were taken prisoner and spent the rest of the war in captivity. Vital Morin told of their experience:

We were already on land and proceeding into Caen, which is the first city in France. And it took quite a while here before we were able to capture that city. From there on we went on all the way through to France and to Belgium and then into Holland and then finally down into Germany. And we were stationed at Nijmegen, which is in Holland, for pretty well most of the winter. We were there for about two months or more without even moving. Just patrolling around and just checking. And then a second front opened up around February or around the middle of February and then that's when we started advancing again. And we went and we, my regiment, went in and we captured Kleve, the first German city. And then from there we proceeded to Hochwald Forest where I was captured and I was taken prisoner of war in Germany.[173]

According to Ed White,

His [Vital's] *unit was told to advance across an open field into the forest. When they reached the edge of the forest, the German machine guns opened up, cutting down the men in the field and slashing through Morin's unit. The two comrades with him were shot through the head.*

Morin kept his head down, and rather than a bullet felt the impact of a boot as a German kicked him and ordered him to get up and surrender.

Of 33 men in Morin's unit, only seven survived the ambush to be imprisoned about 140 kilometres east of Berlin in Stalag 11-B.[174]

Our men were also couriers and despatch riders:

Rifleman George Desjarlais' experiences hinge on the loss of three motorbikes. It began at Caen when Desjarlais of Lestock, a despatch rider, was lying in a ditch during heavy shelling. A shell hit and wrecked his motorbike but Desjarlais escaped without a scratch.

While riding over the road under shellfire at Falaise, Desjarlais suddenly found himself on the road with nothing but the handlebars. "I meant to bring them back with me but lost track of them while in hospital in England," he said.

But it wasn't shelling that sent Desjarlais back to Canada. His third bike was wrecked in a collision with a jeep. Desjarlais was leading a convoy during a night attack going into Holland when the jeep came up from "nowhere" in the darkness. The convoy was travelling without lights through rain and mud.[175]

Peter Pelletier was in the march across the French countryside, as well:

They had just took Caen a few days before we got there because it was still smoldering when we got there. That was the hole for the armour to get in. I don't remember about fear … We weren't very often up close. We sat for 2 weeks when we first went in.

We were getting fired on. Mostly 88s [heavy artillery]. *All you heard was crack, bang! We got a few mortars. You didn't know where they were going to go. We were there for 2 weeks until that drive started, on August 7, when they started to head for Falaise gap. That was pretty heavy action . . .*[176]

Charles Fosseneuve discussed the importance of freeing Europe's ports:

Above: Canadian Street Patrol in France.
Top Right: Infantrymen of the Regina Rifle Regiment and a despatch rider firing into a damaged building, Caen, France, 10 July 1944.
Bottom Right: Peter Pelletier.

There were just pockets of resistance here and there, and they took all the coastline, Calais, all the coast ports where our ships could come give us material. That's why we took all these ports, so the ships could land and bring our fresh food, bread and everything like that. Same with Holland. We took all the Leopold Canal. We took all that so the ships could come in and bring our supplies instead of back over the land, because it would be a lot faster if the ships brought our groceries.[177]

David Dumont was there too:

We stayed put for a while, oh for quite awhile … you know we had to defend ourselves and all that until the, I forget, July or August, I think we went in Falaise … You know the Americans come this way and we went that way and we got a few thousand prisoners …

We went pretty well right across France on trucks, tanks and everything that you could get a ride on up too, oh hell I couldn't say went too fast right across France anyways. We didn't have to do much travel we went to Rouen and we fought around there — the beaches of Great Grands Falaise and all that. In Falaise we had to wade in groups. We go across that way you know for about a mile but it wasn't deep but may be 3 or 4 feet I had to go in there we kept on going 'cause they had flooded the whole thing. We had Frenchmen as guides you know, they knew where about the road was and all that. To go into Calais, oh we had a struggle here and there. What is next, Belgium? I had a little Frenchman that

Above: Charles, Gordon, and Frank Fosseneuve, 1942. Below: David Dumont.

stayed with us you know, gave him a rifle and all that but I had to let him go on the account of he wasn't allowed in Belgium.[178]

Some of our men were captured by the enemy. Euclide Boyer was one of these:

I never went into Belgium. Never got out of France. I got wounded and taken prisoner.

Well, they were crossfiring on us. We were in a little town. They crossfired on us and we were pinned right down. They were well camouflaged, we couldn't see them. They were on both sides of this road. There was only about two that came back from our regiment that didn't get killed or taken prisoner. The rest were taken prisoner or killed.

We didn't know if we were even going to live very long after we were taken prisoner, because we were up against the SS troops, some of the toughest men that Hitler had, and it was all made up of young fellows under 20. They knew nothing else but fight. They were good soldiers. They didn't treat us all that bad, but the only thing was that you didn't have much food. The medical supplies were running low. They'd put bandages on your wounds and wrap it up with crepe paper.

When they took us in there, we didn't know how we were going to be treated but all that mattered at that time was to hope to God that they don't torture you too much … After they got us back from the line they put us in an old barn there, and of course we had guards outside there. And we were in pain. We didn't feel much like going anywhere.

We were only there a matter of hours. And then they moved us by truck to Paris. And we got in there and they unloaded us in kind of a big hall there. And there were rows and rows of stretchers full of wounded soldiers and they were not all Canadians, they were English, Americans, and some Germans. We were mixed up. So we got into this big hospital, and I was on a stretcher by this time and I was getting weaker and they had no more room and there was no beds, so they put me off the main hallway into the nurses office and that's where I laid for the night, on a stretcher, on the floor. And then I was dry and I really wanted a drink of water, and the nurses were all grey nuns. And they all spoke French. So I asked one of the nuns when they come by for a drink. I could get along with them real good with French. But you had to watch that too, because most of the Germans could talk French, because they had occupied that part of France for over 4 years. Anyway, the nurse went and got me a cup of wine. You don't drink water in France. She was real nice. And she felt sorry for us. And they were very nice.

In my shoulder I had a lot of pain, and next morning when they found a bed for me finally, and I went to bed and then some young Germans, wounded German soldiers too, and one came up to my bed and started talking.[179]

Belgium

The Leopold Canal

"Operation Switchback," the battle for the Breskens Pocket during the Battle of the Scheldt, was the first crucial step in opening the Belgian port of Antwerp. The battle began on October 6, 1944 with the 7th Canadian Infantry Brigade crossing the Leopold Canal in northern Belgium not far from the Dutch border. The Regina Rifles "drew the heavily defended sector near the Breskens road."[180] It was here that one of our Métis soldiers earned the Distinguished Conduct Medal. Historians who chronicled the military history of the Regina Rifles describe him:

> *Sammy Letendre, a Métis from Northern Saskatchewan, became our only winner of the coveted DCM, Distinguished Conduct Medal. Always a bit of a renegade, he was quite fearless in battle. Eventually, after a series of heroics, throwing enemy grenades back at his foes at the Leopold Canal, he was promoted to Corporal. His Company Commander said that besides being a great combat soldier, Letendre was also a good barber at the young age of 19 or 20. There was never a dull moment with Sammy around. He could easily have been awarded a Victoria Cross.*[181]

We had other Métis soldiers in the liberation of Belgium. These included Pte. James Lavalley (Marieval), Pte. Joseph Abraham Laliberte (Green Lake), Pte. Pierre Carriere, a SSR sniper (Cumberland House), Gnr. John Amyotte (Indian Head), Tpr. Leo Joseph Belanger (Île-à-la-Crosse), Pte. Simeon Bloomfield (Cumberland House), and Peter Pelletier (Qu'Appelle Valley), who served in the artillery.

Belgium also became the resting place of some of our men. Private Victor Vernon Carriere (Cumberland House) is buried at Schoonselhof Cemetery, Antwerp. Private Emile St. Germain (St. Laurent) also lost his life in Belgium.

Sapper, W. H. Lindstom, 2nd Field Company, Royal Canadian Engineers (R.C.E.) sweeping for mines and road blocks near Kappellen, Belgium, 5 October 1944.

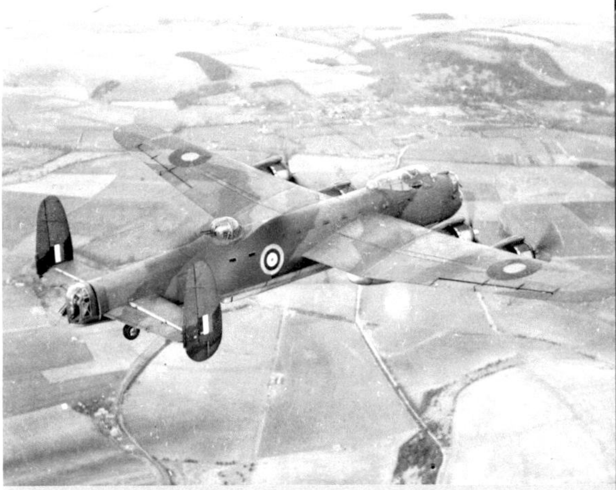

Above: Avro Lancaster in flight.
Right: Leo Belanger.

The Netherlands

After crossing the Rhine, between April 1-12, 1945, the Regina Rifles were involved in seven attacks on the Wehrmacht. Bresaylor's Douglas Dobie — a descendant of Donald Macdonald and Nancy Ferguson, Red River Métis — wrote about the soldiers' feelings as they prepared for the Battle of Wehl, Holland in the February 1991 edition of the *Legion Bugle*:

> *We advanced to within two miles of our objective before unloading from our vehicles and then moved on foot to within a mile of where Jerry (the German force) was thought to be. It was then not quite midnight, so we halted at a Dutch farmhouse for a few hours, awaiting "H" hour. Most of us managed to get a few hours sleep, though some just sat and smoked to pass the time.*
>
> *Around 3:00 a.m. the section's corporals called for O-Group to get the "gen" on the daylight assault so the remainder of us, the riflemen, put on our equipment ready to move.*
>
> *Just before we shoved off at 4:00 o'clock, the whole platoon assembled in the farmyard and the rum issue was handed out. The lieutenant gave us the dope on everything he had learned and the orders received.*
>
> *Looking at those men gathered in that barn at dawn that morning gave a fellow a great feeling of comradeship that exists in a frontline fighting battalion.*
>
> *Each one knew there was a chance he would not come out alive but that worried no one. Good soldiers are all fatalists and so it was with that day.*[182]

When the battle was over, the Germans were defeated. Dobie wrote of the aftermath:

> *All that morning it was raining and very miserable, though while the excitement was on, no one noticed the weather. When things quietened down, the Dutch people came out of their cellars and took us into their houses. They were bewildered, and could hardly believe they were liberated; but could hardly do enough for us. It was noon then and our cooks rolled in with the cookers and were soon dishing out the rations. Our last meal had been the evening before so we were more than ready for them. We still had 50% of our men on guard in case of a counterattack, but an hour later the Queen's Own Regiment of 18th Brigade came through us and went on ahead so we could then relax and rest.*
>
> *To go through the hell of a morning like that, beat the Germans and liberate a city, find you have very light casualties when you get your objective, is the greatest thrill anyone can have. Life is sweet when your platoon sits down after the show and talks it all over, and cleans the weapons. We were sure of a two-day stay at that city, so we were a very happy bunch of guys with no worries.*
>
> *… We did get shelled that night, but that was the usual procedure anyway, so it didn't*

Top to Bottom: German prisoners guarded by infantrymen of the South Saskatchewan Regiment, Hoogerheide, Netherlands, 15 October 1944. A Sherman Vc Firefly tank of The Fort Garry Horse near the Beveland Canal, Netherlands, ca. 29 October 1944. Unloading of sacks of Christmas mail at 2nd Canadian Corps Post Office, Canadian Postal Corps (C. P. C.), Oss, Netherlands, 6 December 1944.

bother us. A canteen ration came up from B. H. Q. along with the past week's mail, and that called for some letters to be written. We each received from the canteen three chocolate bars, cigarettes and two bottles of English beer. It was the first we'd had for a month and tasted mighty good. We went to bed that night for the first real sleep without boots and pants off, which we'd had on for ten days! Life on the front can be mighty pleasant at times!![183]

Conrad Fleury.

The Black Watch Royal Highland Regiment of Canada was one of the regiments in which our men served. The Black Watch landed in Normandy shortly after D-Day, and participated in some thirty engagements throughout France, Belgium, the Netherlands, and Germany. It was at the fight for Holland that one of our men, Pte. Benjamin Lucie (Glen Mary) was killed. Benjamin Lucie was laid to rest in the Bergen-Op-Zoom Canadian War Cemetery, Noord-Brabant.

Sergeant Conrad Réne Fleury (Green Lake) was one of the men who had landed with the Regina Rifles on Juno Beach on D-Day. He survived every battle that his regiment fought until April 22, 1945. He is buried in Holten Canadian War Cemetery, Overijssel, Netherlands. Lance Rifleman William Daniels (Big River), Royal Winnipeg Rifles, Royal Canadian Infantry Corps (RCIC) died the same day as Sergeant Fleury, and is also buried in Holten Canadian War Cemetery, Overijssel. Rifleman John George Belanger (North Battleford), of the Regina Rifles, RCIC lies at the Groesbeek Canadian War Cemetery, Gelderland, Netherlands.

Into Germany

One of the obstacles on leaving Holland and entering Germany was the Rhine River. The first task the engineers were asked to perform was build a "Bailey Bridge." It was a very difficult task. The Rhine is a good-sized river, and all the work needed to be done at night to avoid detection. The job had to be done quickly and efficiently. The landing sights had to be inspected so that everything

Top Row: Regimental Aid Party treating an infantryman of the South Saskatchewan Regiment who was wounded by sniper fire while crossing a canal north of Laren, Netherlands, 7 April 1945. Regimental Aid Party of the South Saskatchewan Regiment resting on the southern bank of canal north of Laren, Netherlands, 7 April 1945. (L-R): Privates Vic Aubichon, Emile Guerin, Lionel Drouin, Eric Hebert. Bottom Row: Rfn. William Andrew Daniels. John Belanger.

could proceed without problems. Checking the landing sights was a dangerous assignment because it meant advancing into enemy territory with only darkness as cover. Edwin Slater and another soldier volunteered to accompany the commanding officer on an inspection tour. During the check, the commanding officer was seriously wounded and the other soldier was killed. Slater had to get the information to the engineers so that they could start their work, and at the same time, he carried the wounded commanding officer back to the Canadian position.

Vital Morin, a prisoner in Germany, told the story of his imprisonment and liberation:

> *And I was stationed at Stalag 11-B, roughly around 90 miles out of Berlin. The exact location I don't know because I didn't know the country at all. After spending close to three months in the prison camp … I almost starved to death … because there was hardly any grub. Just one*

Canadian Soldiers Display a German Flag. Lieut. Ken Bell, photographer, Xanten (Germany), 9 March 1945.

meal a day and it was just soup and a piece of rye bread is all we got in one day. So there was pretty slim pickings for grub for eating there so I lost quite a bit of weight. Roughly about 30 pounds, I guess, in three months.

The prisoner of war experience wasn't too awfully hard. I mean, that the Germans themselves were not too rough, but we did have guards there and we were all fenced in and at prison camp it's a fair size because it had all nationalities there. They had Russians in there and they had French and they had Belgians and Hollanders. And they even had, I think, pretty well all the people that fought against the Germans and roughly around 40 or 50 thousand of prisoners of war in that prison camp. This was a fair size one and as far as treating us rough, it wasn't rough except that we didn't have anything. Nothing to eat. All we had was water to drink and very little blankets. We just had one little blanket and we had to lay on straw there and a little bit of a bunk. A little wooden bunk. And that's about all we had there and we had to keep inside the compound because there was guards all over the place …[184]

After about three months in captivity, the prisoners were liberated:

Vital Morin, 1945.

… and then all of a sudden, I mean, we could hear these guns coming. And first we heard the artillery. The bigger the guns, I mean. They were making a little more noise. We could hear them possibly maybe 10-20 miles away and then finally we started hearing the small rifle shots and we knew that they were getting fairly close. And then all of a sudden, I just hear the roaring of the tanks and everything else that came right in to our prison camp, and this is when we got liberated.

Everybody just about went crazy there. We all ran to all the buildings that were available. And they were looking for grub. That's mostly what we were looking for. And they tried to hold us back so we wouldn't eat ourselves to death there because everybody was so hungry.

And we were liberated just before the war ended and taken on into one of the bombers which was driven back about 60 miles from the prison camp where they had an airport where the bombers landed and flew us back to London. I stayed in the hospital roughly 3 weeks there to recuperate.[185]

The May 7, 1945 edition of the Regina *Leader-Post* listed the names of Saskatchewan men liberated from German camps, and among them was

Pte. Alphonse Carriere, son of Lionel Carriere of Cumberland House.[186] Private William John Sanregret, son of Mrs. Alice Sanregret, was among those liberated on May 16, 1945. Our men, who had been prisoners since the Dieppe raid, were released as the Allies crossed Germany. These included Pte. Paul Delorme, Pte. Peter Gaudry, Cpl. Jeanotte, and Pte. A. E. Kelly.

Norman McAuley was trained as a Borfos gunner. After landing with the Canadian troops shortly after D-Day, he fought through France into Holland and Belgium, and was tasked with the job of cleaning out German machine gun nests at close quarters. As the war was ending, his unit was positioned on the outskirts of Berlin awaiting orders to advance. In the final days of the war, the Russians took the German capital.[187]

VE Day: The End of the War in Europe

Peter Pelletier wrote:

> *For us, the war ended suddenly one evening. We were supporting the 2nd Division as they advanced to Oldenburg. We were still fighting, our guns loaded. Then about six or seven o'clock we got an order to cease firing and that*

Top Row: Pte. John Charette. Rfn. A. Folster, Pte. R. J. Racette, and Pte. G. W. Sherman. Pte. T. E. St. Germaine.
Bottom Row: Sgt. Raymond Joseph La Rocque. Sgt. W. J. Ouelette. Rfn. J. C. Wright, Paddockwood; Pte. E. Pritchard, Baljennie; Pte. C. W. Reid, Regina and Hemingford, Que.; Gnr. A. Prince, Abernethy.

was it. We had to wait three or four days to get everyone unloaded, because you couldn't get the shell back out. While we were waiting, a chum said, "Let's go back and have coffee." So we walked back to the kitchen, set up in a half-track sitting near a barn. Suddenly, we heard the putt-putt-putt sound of German 37-mm shells popping off around us. My friend got a piece of shrapnel in his instep and I got a piece in my arm. Of course, we all started raising hell about the shelling and we were heading for our guns to start again. Instead, we were ordered, "Stay where you are. They're just clearing their guns." But they cleared them right amongst us, right where we were having coffee. The war wasn't officially over yet, not for four more days.[188]

Peter Pelletier.

Vital Morin remembered the day the war was won in Europe:

I was in London, England, when the war ended. I just come out of the hospital. And everybody on the streets. Celebrated all night long there. And I don't think they were policing at all, because everybody was partying all over the place. When the war ended, they can just see them all night long, just hollering and having a hell of a time.[189]

Some of the POWs were invited to Buckingham Palace. Vital Morin was among them:

Morin was among the first Allied soldiers allowed to return home. But before leaving England, he and about 200 other former POW's were invited to Buckingham Palace, where they met and had a picnic lunch with King George VI.[190]

German Occupation

A number of our Métis soldiers did not return to their communities after the fighting was over, but stayed in Germany to supervise the peace. They were part of the Canadian Army Occupation Force.

The War in the Pacific

The end of the war in Europe did not bring peace to the world. Métis soldiers joined the American fight against the Japanese in the Pacific. Airman 1st Class Louis L. Blondeau (Estevan), serving with the 436th RCAF Squadron, was killed on March 14, 1945 in Burma.

Coming Home

Who Came Back

In the Second World War
I was still in school.
All the uncles on my Dad's side
were all in the army.
And it seems all my grandmother's brothers
were all in the army

We lost one of my uncles.
Never came back
on my Dad's side.

And we never had no deaths
on my grandmother's side.
They all come back.
— Rose Fleury[191]

As the ships reached Halifax or Quebec City, the Saskatoon *Star-Phoenix* and the Regina *Leader-Post* published the names of the returnees. From available newspaper articles of the time, it is possible to find names of survivors. Leading Aircraftman D. J. Vandale (Saskatoon), Pte. G. Fayant (Batoche), Pte. T. E. LaPlante (Duck Lake), Sgt. J. E. Umpherville (Glen Mary), Pte. E. G. Pruden (Cochin), and Cpl. R. D. Inkster (Regina) were on the Pasteur. On the Île de France were: Gnr. C. J. Fosseneuve, Gnr. A. Michaud (North Makwa), Pte. I. H. Caron (Batoche), Spr. F. A. Caron (Saskatoon), Rfn. R. R. Pocha (MacDowall), and Spr. W. Umpherville (Prince Albert). Abroad the *HMCS Puncher* were: Signalman D. A. Cromartie (Birch Hills), Rfn. N. V. Cromarty (Prince Albert), Pte. H. P. Sayers (Battleford), and Pte. E. G. Pruden (Cochin). Returning on the Queen Elizabeth were: L/Cpl. C. J. Trotchie (Saskatoon), Fus. N. Settee (Cumberland House), L/Cpl. C. A. Chaboyer (Cumberland House), Tpr. H. R. Fidler (Mont Nebo), Fus. L. Nabess

(Cumberland House), Tpr. J. B. Ouellette (Battleford), Pte. E. Pritchard (Baljennie), and Gnr. A. Prince (Abernethy).

Other men were mentioned in articles announcing welcoming home ceremonies. They included Pte. J. E. Klyne (Regina), Pte. P. Malbeuf (Regina), L/Cpl. L. Klyne (Balcarres), Cpl. L. H. Desjarlais (Fort Qu'Appelle), L/Cpl. M. J. Poitras (Fort Qu'Appelle), Gnr. P. J. Blondeau (Lebret), Pte. A. Morin (Cumberland House), Acting (A)/Company Quarter Master Sgt. (CQMS) V. J. Bellegarde (Balcarres), Rfn. W. Henry (Prince Albert), Pte. G. Desnomie (Lorlie), Tpr. R. R. Young (Meadow Lake), Pte. W. A. Arsenault (Big River), Pte. James Paul (Duck Lake), Pte. W. B. Blondeau (Outram), Rfn. P. McGillis (St. Victor), Gnr. E. J. Flammand (Regina), Tpr. A. C. Blondeau (Estevan), Gnr. J. Fisher (Lebret), L/Bmdr. T. W. Halcro (Prince Albert), Gnr. McKay, 44th Field (Prince Albert), and Pte. Joseph A. Collins (Meadow Lake).

Norm Henderson and Nathan Settee.

Archie Nicolas was one of our men who came home wounded:

> *I come home on the hospital ship, the Lady Nelson. I come to Regina here. I was on the hospital train and I was there a week and the folks got me. It didn't feel very good, I mean you weren't in very good shape. I was sick with infection. There was a doctor in there by the name of Doctor Ryan Colonel. He looked at the papers without looking at me. They had put a splint in my leg and it had a spring. I was in a cast that had a styling pin below my knee here and had a big board up here with a spring to keep the tension. This doctor said, "He's been in this cast this long, well from December to April." He said, "This thing must be healed." He took the cast off, lifted my leg, and punctured the flesh. This reactivated the infection. There was nothing they could do for me. They wrapped me up one night and they put me through a little window in the train and they shipped me to Winnipeg, Deer Lodge Hospital. I was there for over two years.*
>
> *First of all, they had to clear the infection, with penicillin and operations. I was getting pretty well fed up there. Well you know in Winnipeg you're in bed, you can't move, your leg is sore. The infection was so bad they put me in a private room at Deer Lodge Hospital. I was in there a year by myself. Finally, I started*

getting better after half a dozen operations, and in May of '47 I come back. I come back to Duck Lake. I was still on crutches.[192]

Charles Fosseneuve from Cumberland House related his experience:

There must have been almost a million Canadians going then … I think there was 20 thousand (or two thousand) people on that ship when we came across. Took us half an hour to walk around the outside deck. Swimming pool right in front you could swim anytime. It was cold ice water. There were big ships. Queen Mary's bigger than that.

I came home in the fall. Just before freeze up, anyways. I stayed all winter in the Army in Regina. They came up in the spring. I was discharged in '46, March. And then came out trapping for a month, spring trapping. I don't remember, how I felt. I came to Cumberland House, my mother was still living that time. Otherwise, if my mother had died I would never come to Cumberland House 'cause I had nothing to come home for. She was still living when I came back in '46, and she died in '47 of cancer and in the meantime I got married.[193]

Charles Fosseneuve.

William Carriere recalled:

So what I did, I waited for my brothers. Jim was in Italy and I got a letter from him saying that he was in London and he'd be there for about six weeks. On the first of October. I got discharged from the army and I went and met him in Saskatoon — they were all in the Saskatoon Light Infantry. It was rather sad to be there. There was lots of them parents went to that place there in Saskatoon. It was very sad. I was happy to see my brother because it had been five years since I saw him there. But he had a wonderful time there. … Not one car was allowed to run on the street in Saskatoon. Everything was just dead.

And I remember five kegs of that beer, and they had a big orchestra — we had a lot of fun. There was a lot of things that I remember. But it was nice to see your brother that you joined up with at the same time, same place where they have that big celebration for all the boys that came back. That's where they stayed, right in that place where they have that big celebration.

It was three-day celebration. Then we want to get a boat there in Le Pas, to get to Cumberland. Two days by train and two coming up by boat, and from there it was on your own.[194]

Saskatoon Light Infantry parades on 21st Street. Saskatoon Light Infantry parades on 21st Street East from the CN Station to Kiwanis Park for the homecoming ceremony. Crowds and cards line street. October 3, 1945.

Discharge

Most of our Métis soldiers were discharged in Regina. Some were given help to return to civilian life. Prosper Lariviere's case may be typical of this experience. Born in Île-à-la-Crosse, Prosper was educated to Grade 6 in French at the Beauval Indian School. He finished school in 1927, and from 1927-31 he was a labourer on the home farm. He then had his own trap line, fished for an employer, and worked as a teamster on farms. While in the Army, he served a total of 63 months, of which 48 months was overseas in the U.K., France, Belgium, and Holland. For nearly a year, he was the battalion sniper. His war service gratuity and Re-establishment Credit were applied to buying a half share in his uncle's general store. He was discharged from the Army September 19, 1945 after over five years of service.[195]

1939-45 Service Medal (Back and Front), Joseph Alexander Fayant.

For many Métis veterans, their treatment on

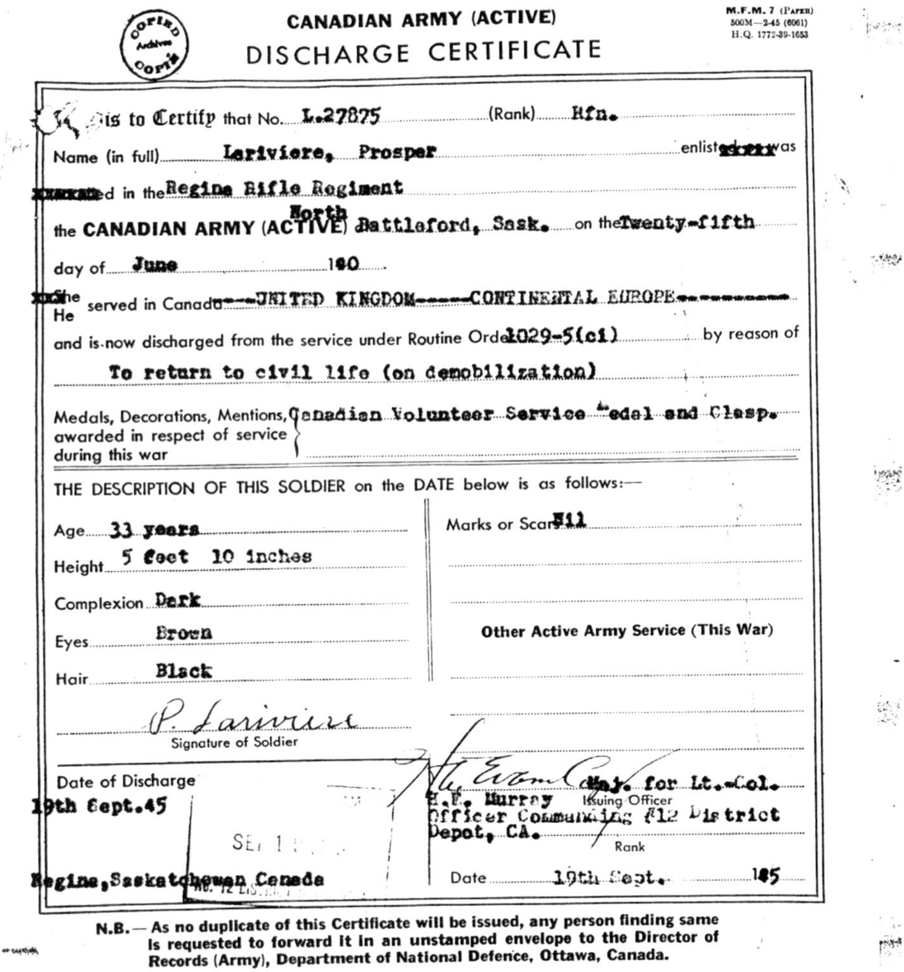

M.F.M. 7 (Paper)
500M—2-45 (6061)
H.Q. 1772-39-1653

CANADIAN ARMY (ACTIVE)

DISCHARGE CERTIFICATE

This is to Certify that No. L.27875 (Rank) Rfn.
Name (in full) Lariviere, Prosper enlisted was
[redacted]ed in the Regina Rifle Regiment
the CANADIAN ARMY (ACTIVE) North Battleford, Sask. on the Twenty-fifth
day of June 1940

He served in Canada---UNITED KINGDOM-----CONTINENTAL EUROPE---------
and is now discharged from the service under Routine Order 1029-5(c1) by reason of
To return to civil life (on demobilization)

Medals, Decorations, Mentions, awarded in respect of service during this war: Canadian Volunteer Service Medal and Clasp.

THE DESCRIPTION OF THIS SOLDIER on the DATE below is as follows:—

Age 33 years
Height 5 feet 10 inches
Complexion Dark
Eyes Brown
Hair Black

Marks or Scars Nil

Other Active Army Service (This War)

P. Lariviere
Signature of Soldier

Date of Discharge
19th Sept.45

Regina, Saskatchewan Canada

Maj. for Lt.-Col.
H.F. Murray Issuing Officer
Officer Commanding #12 District
Depot, CA.
Rank

Date 19th Sept. 1945

N.B.—As no duplicate of this Certificate will be issued, any person finding same is requested to forward it in an unstamped envelope to the Director of Records (Army), Department of National Defence, Ottawa, Canada.

Prosper Lariviere, Discharge Certificate, WWII.

returning home was unexpectedly harsh. In the words of David Dumont, "they kicked me out and they didn't say thank you, shake hands, or anything."[196]

Many of the Métis soldiers came home wounded, like Pte. John LaRose, who came home with a metal plate in his head. Corporal Paul Pelletier (Fort Qu'Appelle) had been wounded twice. For some, they came home to the hospital. Edward King shared his story:

> *We got to Regina at 3:30 a.m., July 20, 1945. There was a band playing. We were taken by ambulance to the military hospital at the exhibition grounds army camp. I was carried on a stretcher on to a bed. It was coming daylight. The ward they put me in was big. There were about twenty beds. Some of the soldiers were wounded badly . . .*[197]

Euclide Boyer brought home a souvenir:

> *I received two gun shot wounds in action and as a matter of fact I came back with a bullet in my shoulder and I carried it around for 17 years and they took it out of me in University Hospital right here in Saskatoon.*[198]

Euclide Boyer.

Archie Nicolas came home wounded, and he didn't want to be discharged:

> *I was getting, you know $7.50, may not mean a lot to people today, but then you get $7.50 a month more while you're still in uniform. When you're out of uniform, I mean they take that $7.50 away from you. You get 15 dollars a month more when you're overseas. When we start out we figured out because we were on duty, we were getting five and a half cents an hour. So they wanted to discharge me and I said, "No I won't sign my discharge." You see the Jackson (war with Japan) is still going. This was in Winnipeg and I said, "No I won't sign." So now, they transferred me back to Saskatoon here to 121, and in the meantime 121 had been transferred somewhere in Quebec so by the time the papers come back and they had to transfer me from one command to another, from my regiment to my depot where I enlisted, and from my depot to the Winnipeg depot, Fort Oxford Barracks, and there one morning they had a major or something come up and he signed my discharge for me. That's the part I didn't like, and I'd been in there a year already in the hospital. They took me off the payroll. I was losing $7.50 a month.*[199]

Many brought back diseases, as their fathers had from the Great War. Corporal William Regan, a machine gunner who had fought through Sicily and Italy with the SLI, had malaria. Many had tuberculosis, which was contagious, and made them a danger to their communities. They came home with metal plates and shrapnel. Some still carried bullets in their bodies. Back injuries were common, as were injuries to the limbs. One man had lost an eye. Others had suffered hearing loss. Combat Stress was recognized in some of our returned soldiers. Those who had been prisoners of war had many debilitating illnesses. Fred Malbeuf, liberated from a Japanese prison of war camp, remembered:

> *When I left Tokyo and the war was over, I came home on a stretcher. We went to San Francisco, from there we took Coast Rind back to Vancouver. I was in a hospital in Vancouver. We had our check up and we took a hospital train to Saskatoon. I got off in Saskatoon and into the sanatorium. I couldn't go very far. I weighed 200 pounds when I went. I had tuberculosis in the spine and T.B. in the chest. 2 operations, the spine and the chest. 5 ribs removed.*
>
> *When I got to Saskatoon Sanatorium, I never thought of anything. I was so weak I didn't know where I was. I was in Saskatoon for two days. Then I got a phone call from Regina from the armory. I had to go report there. I waited there so long that I fell asleep on the bench. Finally someone came and got me. They said, "Mr. Malbeuf, the officer wants to see you upstairs." I didn't know if I could make it upstairs. I told him someone would have to help me. I got help up. After I was finished there, I went to a military hospital for a week, from there to the General Hospital. I was in the General Hospital for about 1 month. Then I got my strength. They were going to send me to the sanatorium but I told them no. I wanted a pass so I could go home. So they gave me a pass for a week. I was able to go home. I was able to walk by then.*[200]

Alfred Malbeuf, Right.

William A. Dumont told of coming home:

> *I was discharged January 1945, the end of January 1945. I wasn't home 'till November. That was a long trip on the Letitia coming home on the hospital ship and just the Russian boat, the small one. I left England on the 29th of November because I know it was the last week in November and I arrived home the day before Christmas. I arrived in Lloydminster on the 23rd or the 22nd of December. That was a nice Christmas. Of course, I could talk Cree too.*[201]

Left: Hospital Ship, *Oranje*, WWII. Right: William Dumont.

War Brides

Several Métis soldiers met and married their wives in England. Their wives — and, in some cases, children — came to Canada after the war. Willard Dumont was with the SSR. He spent the war years in England training troops. His wife, Vera, was a war bride.[202] Jake Chartrand (Bengough) brought home a war bride, as did Laurence and Eddie Pruden (Cochin) who married English girls before returning to Canada.[203] Norman McAuley returned to La Ronge with his English bride, Hettie. Norman was instrumental in starting the Legion in La Ronge and served as its first president. The Ladies' Auxiliary was also founded in 1962. Hettie McAuley was its first president.[204]

After the War

Helping His Brother After the War

But I don't think too many of them
got that much out of it.
In fact, one of my brothers that had went to war —
he came back and he wasn't
one bit better off.
Because when he come back
he still didn't have a home.

And after me staying back
from the war,
I still had to help him out
to get a home.

So I don't think
that anyone gains anything
by going to war.[205]
— Médéric McDougall

The following poem shows the way our communities responded to the return of their men and women from battle.

Settling Down After the War
I don't know what they called that —
Soldiers Settlement Board
or what it was —
I never took too much interest in it,
but I heard some things about that.

I do believe that if somebody
wanted to take advantage of this
and know how to go about it —
and it could be that they got
some help out of it.

But a lot of our people
weren't educated
and by not being educated
you don't know how
to take advantage of these things.

So you usually lose out
and somebody gets the kick.
That's the way I've seen it.

So I know a lot of our people
certainly didn't benefit
by going to war anyway.[206]
— Médéric McDougall

There are many stories of life after the war. The following are just a few.

> I [Euclide Boyer] *came back and I got married a year later. My wife's name is Helen Lucier. We raised twelve kids. Seven boys and five girls. None of them got less than grade 11. They were all bushwackers to begin with, but later on they started their own business, some of them, and go in different things. I brought up my family without any social help, welfare or anything. And I worked and I made it with my own two hands, and sweat.*
>
> *Those days I use to drink a lot and I use to wash out all the sorrows and memories. Every soldier is your buddy in the army. And some are more special than others. And you get that in civilian life too. That's very hard when you see your buddies getting knocked off and dying on both sides of you. It's just very, very hard to take. But I always got thinking that if your time is up, your time is up. If it's not your number, you're going to go through somehow.*[207]

William Sayese described his postwar life to Mike Tymchak:

> MT: *So you came back to Cumberland House and I'm sure there was a happy reunion with your family.*
> WS: *Was there ever! The Army wanted to keep me, you know; they wanted me to stay because they were going to train young soldiers for the peace army. "It's enough," I said, "I've had this uniform for four years and I want to take it off now." So I did. I'm sorry now I didn't stay. I'd be sitting pretty today; I'd have been retired now.*
> *MT: You'd have a pension I suppose?*
> WS: *I would have had a good pension. I would have been retired now.*
> MT: *What did you do when you got back to Cumberland House?*
> WS: *It was good then; it was really good times then. Oh, the fur was a good price.*
> MT: *Did you do some trapping?*
> WS: *I did some trapping and I make a good living then.*
> MT: *Did you ever fish?*
> WS: *Yes, I done that too: trapping and fishing.*[208]

Many who had been prisoners of war suffered long-lasting physical and psychological effects. Fred Malbeuf returned from a Japanese prison camp, and found the transition hard:

> *My brother Ernest got a job on the railroad in Sintaluta as soon as he got home. He got married right away. Got a job on the railroad and started working. I*

did my best. I tried. I used to get a job but I couldn't keep it. I couldn't handle it and I would quit. I'm not kicking today. I'm satisfied with the pension I'm getting right now. I think I deserve it. All of us deserve it.

I'm satisfied. All I went through. I got a good experience out of it. You talk to a lot of people, especially the young people. Talk about war. It goes through one ear and out the other. They don't believe you. I know what happened to us over there. I don't need to read it. There is no use me telling you about the guys who got beat up, or hanged, or starved.

These things happened. I saw it with my own eyes. I know.[209]

Alfred Malbeuf.

In the words of Brereton Greenhous:

> *Nearly every man who came home* [from the Japanese POW camps] *had physical and psychological problems of one kind or another, and many of them would suffer the effects the rest of their lives. There were two more battles left for the survivors to fight, one for understanding and one for compassion and one for compensation, but those bureaucratic struggles are another story.*[210]

Finding work was the most important job for many Métis veterans. They were willing to go where the work was. Many northern veterans found jobs in the resource sector in northern Saskatchewan. Truck drivers were in demand and could easily get work hauling logs. Jim Brady, a veteran himself, was hired by the CCF government to set up cooperatives in Cumberland House. Many veterans worked with him at the lumber project and the fish plant. Many, like Nathan Settee (Cumberland House), worked as fire fighters for the Department of Natural Resources.

Many Métis soldiers found they could not stay home after they had travelled for so many years. Charlie Umpherville (Glen Mary) told a researcher:

Charles Umpherville.

> *Living conditions in Glen Mary were the same* [as when he left]. *Came home — stayed home, helped*

dad on the farm. Things were starting to look up when we came back but things didn't look up for a couple of years after we got back. I worked on the farm. Ended up in Prince George for two years. I went there for logging. Lots of northern Saskatchewan boys went there. After B.C., came home for 2-3 weeks. That's it — can't stay, gotta go. I had the, I don't know, that wandering feeling. I couldn't stay home.[211]

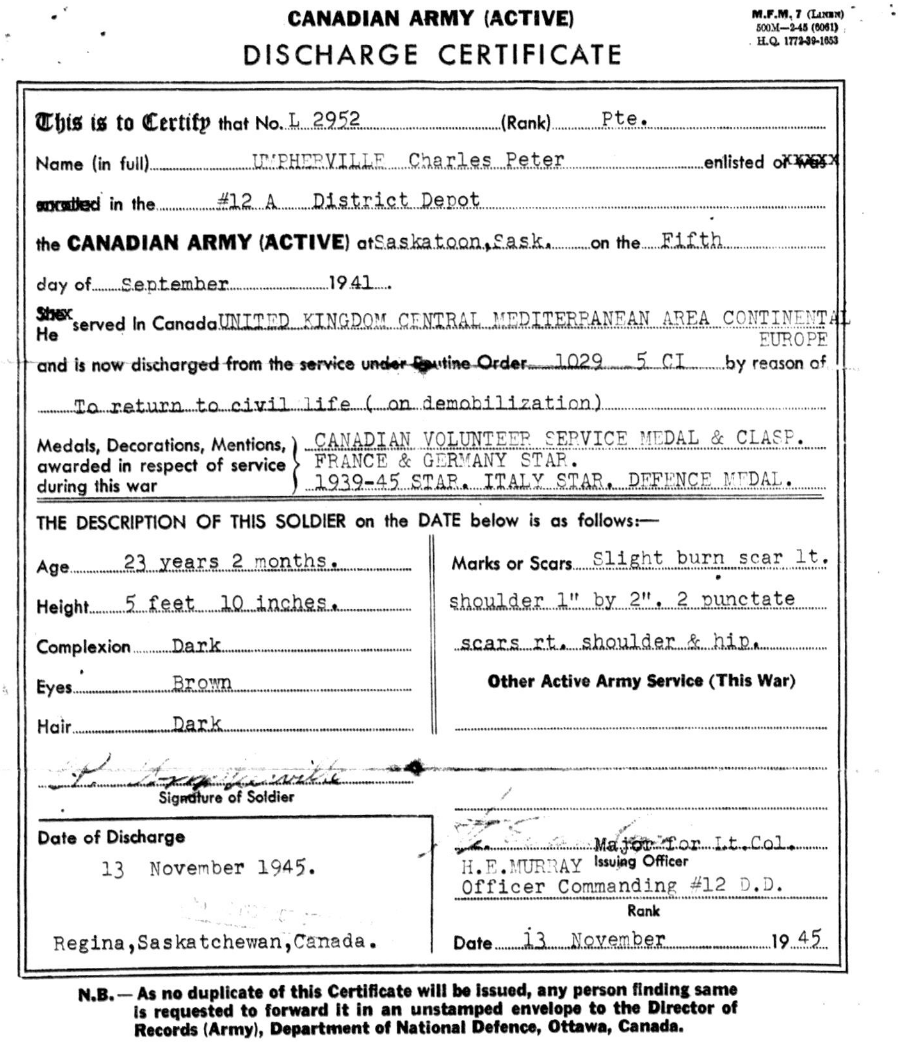

CANADIAN ARMY (ACTIVE)

DISCHARGE CERTIFICATE

M.F.M. 7 (Linen)
500M—2-45 (6061)
H.Q. 1772-39-1653

This is to Certify that No. L 2952 (Rank) Pte.

Name (in full) UMPHERVILLE Charles Peter enlisted ~~or was~~

~~enrolled~~ in the #12 A District Depot

the CANADIAN ARMY (ACTIVE) at Saskatoon, Sask. on the Fifth

day of September 1941.

~~She~~ He served in Canada UNITED KINGDOM CENTRAL MEDITERRANEAN AREA CONTINENTAL EUROPE

and is now discharged from the service under Routine Order 1029 5 CI by reason of

To return to civil life (on demobilization)

Medals, Decorations, Mentions, awarded in respect of service during this war: CANADIAN VOLUNTEER SERVICE MEDAL & CLASP. FRANCE & GERMANY STAR. 1939-45 STAR. ITALY STAR. DEFENCE MEDAL.

THE DESCRIPTION OF THIS SOLDIER on the DATE below is as follows:—

Age 23 years 2 months.

Height 5 feet 10 inches.

Complexion Dark

Eyes Brown

Hair Dark

Marks or Scars Slight burn scar lt. shoulder 1" by 2". 2 punctate scars rt. shoulder & hip.

Other Active Army Service (This War)

Signature of Soldier

Date of Discharge

13 November 1945.

Regina, Saskatchewan, Canada.

Major for Lt. Col.
H.E. MURRAY Issuing Officer
Officer Commanding #12 D.D.
Rank

Date 13 November 1945

N.B.—As no duplicate of this Certificate will be issued, any person finding same is requested to forward it in an unstamped envelope to the Director of Records (Army), Department of National Defence, Ottawa, Canada.

Charles Umpherville, Discharge Certificate, November 13, 1945.

Claude Adams took to the road as well. He was a gifted fiddle player, and for almost two years he toured North America as part of Wilf Carter's band.[212] Gabriel Dorion left his home in Cumberland House to go logging in Ontario. As he said, "You had to go out somewhere else to make a living."[213] There were not enough opportunities in many home communities for the men to get work.

Some of the veterans ended up in the cities. James Lavalley, a Métis soldier from Marieval, started farming on a *Veterans' Land Act* grant, but a fire traumatized his family, and he decided to leave the farm:

> *Just over night we made up our minds that we were going to leave. We had a little car, packed up the kids and we left in the morning. The only thing we had was our kids and twenty bucks. We went to Regina. Found a job right away. We had hard times the first year. We found a place to stay, a little one bedroom house. At that time there was a lot of work. You didn't have to look for work, work looked for you. That time there was so much work in Regina. If someone wanted work, there was no problem to find work.*
>
> *I was dry walling. I was working construction first for six years. Then I worked for the city for six months, I guess. I didn't like it. I was on night shift all the time, midnight shift. They wouldn't change you. So I quit there and I went cement finishing. 'Cause as I say there was a lot of work. I still have hard times, this is as far as I can lift my arm, I got pins in me [from] cement finishing, yeah. I was off work for two and a half years. In and out of the hospital. But after that, I went to school, went back to school. Came out and went to apply for a job at the university. Maintenance mechanic. I worked there until I was sixty-five.*[214]

James Lavalley.

After the war, many Métis veterans moved to cities, where there was work. There was a major shift in the Saskatchewan Métis population from the road allowances and small communities to the urban centres. Métis soldiers had travelled much and had worked side by side with non-Aboriginal people. Moving away from their communities did not scare them any more.

Veterans Looking After their Own

Returned soldiers could see the needs in many of their communities. In Cumberland House, for example, a branch of the Royal Canadian Legion was established in 1946. It was started through a meeting between Mr. Wellan and Joe Johnson. Pierre Dorion was chosen to be president, Edward Sahyes as first vice-president, and Mr. Fraser as secretary.[215]

Left to Right: Alex Morin. Edward Sahyes. Pierre Carriere.

The Legion members had to borrow the community hall to have meetings, but it was too small for social gatherings. Money was raised to build a larger hall. The new hall burned down after only a year of service, but as the community realized the important work of the Legion, they supported the rebuilding of a new Legion building.[216] The Cumberland House branch was supported by other Legion branches, especially The Pas branch.[217] William Carriere recalled:

> *I was President then and made dances every Friday; we made a little money. Picture shows are still held today. Children were charged 10 cents and adults, twenty-five cents. We had to raise the charges because we were going into debt. We weren't charging enough; no profit was made.*[218]

Legions became the social centres of many small communities. Cadets were organized for the young boys. The Ladies' Auxiliary brought the wives of service members together. According to William Carriere, "There is also a Ladies' Auxiliary that's our backbone. They help us quite a bit. Bingos, banquets and wedding dances"[219] were held in the hall. Norman McAuley, a Métis veteran, was the founder and first president[220] of La Ronge's branch of the Legion. At Duck Lake, as well, our men helped build the Legion. J. Fisher and W. A. Dumont were on the executive in the early years.

Re-enlisting

Edward King relates how many Métis re-enlisted back into the military following the Second World War:

> *Ray DeLaronde and Fred Morin came to visit me. We were listening to the radio when we heard they needed men for the Regina Rifles. That was when we decided to enlist. It was the second time for Ray and me. We went to the beer parlour* [in Meadow Lake]. *There we met more men who were interested in enlisting. All we had to do was go to the bus depot and sign our names. Then they would give us a ticket to Regina.*
>
> *Some of the World War II veterans who enlisted then are: Ray DeLaronde, Joseph Merasty, Levis Leggitt, George Ducharme and I. Men enlisting for the first time — Fred Morin, Eugene Morin, Stanley Morin, Don Morin, Ernest Aubichon, Martin Aubichon, Stanley Laliberte, George Rayman, Daniel Ross, Harvey Sanregret, William Fiddler, Clarence Fiddler, Pat Merasty, Alfred McCallum, Gabe Aubichon, Edward Arnault, Clarence Murray, Clarence Laliberte, Eli Caplette, Paul Caplette, Max Gervais and Ronald Collins.*
>
> *... About 40 men went up for an interview. The men that enlisted in the Regina Rifles stayed at Regina. The others enlisted for The Royal Canadian Army Service Corps. They were shipped to Ontario.*
>
> *... The Company had 80% Natives from Duck Lake, Green Lake, Meadow Lake, Battleford and Prince Albert. We had Sergeant Somerville from Cumberland House.*[221]

Opposite Page Top: Volunteers for the Korean War, 27th Brigade, Regina Rifles, Hanover, Germany, 1950. Bottom Left: Sgt. Martin Aubichon (M), ___ Hill (Prince Albert) (M), ___ Prosper (Duck Lake), Boyer (M) (Prince Albert), ___ Lacombe (Regina); Second Left: _____ (Prince Albert), ___ Greyeyes (M) (Duck Lake), _____, Fisher (M)(Lebret), ___ Lariviere (Île-à-la-Cross or Beauval); Third Left: _____ Anderson (Prince Albert area), ____ Desjarlais (M) (Fort Qu'Apelle), _____, ___ Runs (Duck Lake), ___Holbett (Duck Lake), ___(Black) (M) (Beardy's First Nation); Top Right: ___(Morin) (M) (Meadow Lake), ___Laliberte (M) (Green Lake), ____, ____, ___Beauchense, ___Callaghen, ____ (Lois Dolby). Opposite Page Bottom Left to Right: Joseph and Lawrence Fiddler (Ptes.), and Unknown. Joseph George Merasty.

Top: Albert Morin, Back Row, 2nd from Left, Saskatoon Light Infantry. Middle Left to Right: Alexander Poitras. Alex Malbeuf. Charles Aubichon. Bottom Left to Right: Albert Merasty with son Peter. Joseph Flammond. Leonard Morin.

Top: Lawrence Morin, Group of Soldiers. Middle Left to Right: Louis Nolin. Ralph Aubichon and J.-B. (Jean-Baptiste)(Chip) Ouelette. Bottom Left to Right: Alfred Malbeuf, Right. Roy L. McDonald (Norquay).

Top Left to Right: Victor (and Justine) Daniels. Wilfrid Poirier. Alfred Ouellette. Middle Left to Right: Alphonse Collins. Alphonse Merasty and Alex Bear. Armand Morin and Peter Laliberte. Bottom Left to Right: John-Baptiste Maurice. Joseph Martin. Louis Blondeau.

Top Left to Right: Louis Poitras and Unknown Man. Ora Madden. Middle Left to Right: Ralph Aubichon. John Buskey. Bottom: Max Lucier (Centre).

Top Left to Right: Leo Pruden. Louis Laboucane. Peter Laliberte. Middle Left to Right: Raymond Delaronde (Pte.) and Edward King (Pte.), Meadow Lake, SK, 1943. Solomon Krein. Vital Poitras. Bottom Left to Right: Stan Durocher and Charles Umpherville. William Tanner.

Top Left to Right: Jules J. Morin. Lawrence Carey. John Fiddler. Middle Left to Right: John Flamont and mother, Alice. Emile Laboucane. H. J. Myette. Bottom Left: Harold Ross.

Top Left to Right: George Pambrun. Dan Pelletier. Gaspard Morin. Middle Left to Right: Cyprian Corrigal. Ernest Joseph Boyer. Métis Soldiers [ca. 1940-1945]. Bottom Left to Right: Frank Howse (John Nelson?), Métis, while serving in Army, 1943. Vital and Alex (Alexander) Poitras (Ptes.).

Top Left to Right: Edwin, Leon, and Norbert Morin. Leo Bourassa.
Bottom Left to Right: Rose, Edward, Patsy, Elmer, and Pat Parenteau. James Wilard Shorrt.

Korea

On June 25, 1950, the North Koreans invaded South Korea. That afternoon, in New York City, the United Nations Security Council voted to take action against North Korea. As a member of the United Nations, Canada was involved. Canada did not declare war on North Korea, maintaining that the operation was a police action. On June 30, 1950, United Nations command headquarters was established in Tokyo under General Douglas McArthur. On July 12, three Canadian destroyers were sent to the waters around Korea to serve with the United Nations. The RCAF provided resources for transporting supplies by air. By August 7, the Canadian government authorized the recruitment of the Canadian Army Special Force (CASF).

For many Métis, enlisting for the fighting in Korea seemed the best thing to do. Among the Canadian soldiers who fought in Korea were the following Saskatchewan Métis:

Edward Arnault	Charles Arnold	Robert Aubichon
Ernest Aubichon	Gabe Aubichon	Martin Aubichon
Joe A. Bishop	Edward Gilbert Blondeau	Maurice J. Blondeau
Edward A. Boyer	Bernie Brown	Harvey Brown
Angelo (Tony) Camponi	Leonard Camponi	Ron Camponi
Eli Caplette	Paul Caplette	Ann Chartier
Thomas Chartier	Maxime Collins	Ron Collins
Anthony (Tony) Desjarlais	Henry (Ron) Desjarlais	Georges Napoleon Ducharme
Ambroise J. Durocher	Donald Fayant	Joseph Fayant
Peter Joseph Fayant	Leon Ferguson[222]	Ernest Ferguson
Clarence Fiddler	William Fiddler	Armand Fisher
James Fisher	Lawrence Fisher	Arnold Gervais
Max Gervais	Gregg Hamilton	George Henry
Louis Henry	Marcel (Joe) Henry	Cliff Hessdorfer
Raymond Lajour	Clarence Laliberte	Peter Laliberte
Stanley Laliberte	Floyd Larocque	Norbert Lesset
Joseph McGillivray	Leonard Mckenzie	Joseph Merasty
Pat Merasty	Réne Michaud	Herschel Misener
Dineam Montour	Bernard Morin	Don Morin
Eugene Morin	Fred Morin	Stanley Morin

Clarence Paul Murray
Lionel Nabess
Allan Nault
Archie Hubert Nicholas
Robert F. Nicholas
James Ouellette
Marcel Paul
John Pederson
Claude Petit
Murray Petit
Norris Petit
Reo Pilon
George Raymond
Peter Raymond
Hilliard Robillard
Joe Robillard
Daniel Ross
Harold Ross
Robert Ross
Harry Sanregret
Harvey Sanregret
Percy Sangrey
Ken Umpherville
John Wheeler Jr.
John J. Wheeler Sr.

Top Left to Right: Ambroise J. Durocher. Daniel Ross, Stanley Morin, Harry Sanregret, and Unknown Man. Edward G. Blondeau. Middle Left to Right: Eli Caplette (Cpl.). Eugene Morin and Stanley Laliberte. Fred Merasty and Dan Ross. Cliff Hessdorfer, circa 1942. Bottom Left to Right: Joseph Fayant. Harry Sanregret, Stanley Morin, and Arnold Gervais.

Top Left to Right: Leon Ferguson. Maxime Collins and Clarence Laliberte. Raymond Delaronde (Pte.) and William M. Fiddler Jr. (Pte.), 1951. Middle Left to Right: Ronald Collins. Leon Ferguson, Ft. Lewis, Washington, 1951. Bottom: William Jr. and Clarence Fiddler (with parents and siblings).

Left: Claude Petit (Left), with Bren Gun, Mountain Training on the way to Korea, Jasper, Alberta.
Right: Claude Petit, Saskatchewan Order of Merit recipient.

Two men from Cumberland House served in Korea after the armistice was signed on July 29, 1953. They were Joseph Cadotte and Sangadore Joseph Morin.

For Claude Petit, enlisting was a family thing. "All my cousins and relations were going in the Army. My uncle was in the regiment I served."[223] His older brother Norris joined the Army as well. Both brothers were underage. His uncle, Murray, served in Korea with his two nephews. It was a family affair for the Camponis as well. Four Camponi brothers were in the Army after the Second World War: Ron, Len, Bill, and Tony. Three of the brothers met in Korea.

Cpl. Len Camponi, a veteran of 14 months' service in the Far East war theatre as a member of "C" Squadron, Lord Strathcona's Horse, found to his surprise that his newly arrived replacement as crew commander of the tank "Calvados" was none other than his brother, Cpl. Ron Camponi, of "B" Squadron, who to Len's further amazement and delight was accompanied by younger brother Tony.

On November 25, 1950, the 2nd Battalion of the Princess Patricia's Light Infantry (PPCLI) set sail for Korea. They arrived in Pusan (now Busan) in December. In mid-February, 1951, they joined the battle with the 27th British Commonwealth Infantry Brigade advancing toward the 38th Parallel, the divide between North and South Korea.[224]

Vincent R. Courtenay chronicled soldiers' experiences in the first days of the Korean War in his book, *Patricias in the Korean War*:

> *It was three days ago that we came here. It was fifty-some horrible hours ago, two hundred thousand seconds ago. You have lived a new kind of life in every one of them. You have been in agony through most of them. Death has come your way without letting up. You have not slept. You have not eaten. You have tried to do both. The worry of death has already made you old. Yet many, like yourself, are just eighteen.*[225]

The Korean War was officially a police action, but as far as Ron Camponi was concerned, "it was no such thing as police action, it was a bloody war …" It reminded him of his father's description of the conditions Canadian soldiers had faced in the First World War:

> *And actually the type of war we had, when we got there, everyone was dug in as it was like trenches. They had their guns zeroed in on our trenches, it was mostly hills, you were on a hill you know. And that was harder on the nerves, than if you could jump in your tank and move and get the hell out of there if you're being shelled, but we couldn't because we were dug in like pillboxes … And the infantry would go out on patrols and we would cover them. We would register targets during the day and then they would tell us what targets because we could fire at night, with the instruments, we just lay them on that target and if they'd call for fire, we'd just lay ahead of them or whatever they wanted.*[226]

The war in Korea challenged the UN commanders to rethink their tactics. It soon became clear that the battles would be won by small sections of men led by corporals or privates. This meant that individual soldiers became much more important to the success of the conflict than had ever been imagined:

Top to Bottom: Frontlines, Korean War, 1952. Handing out rations in the front lines, Korea, 1952. Soldiers of the Princess Patricia's Canadian Light Infantry, Korea, March 17, 1953.

Top Left to Right: Ron Camponi. Maxime Collins and Unknown Soldier. Middle Left to Right: Private John J. Wheeler, 1st Battalion P. P. C. L. I and his son John with sniper rifle at Korean front, 20 February 1952. Unknown and Eugene Morin. Unknown Métis Soldier. Bottom Left to Right: Unknown Métis Soldier and Another Soldier. Unknown Métis Soldiers.

Those private soldiers who sometimes were looked down upon or even bullied by senior noncommissioned officers were the ones on who every mission rested. The value of the individual soldier was espoused before, but not truly believed. Now without every man doing his all, it was clear that no planning officer or command officer, no matter how well trained and quick of mind, could exercise much power in the field, without their will and determination. The power was with the Privates![227]

Harold Ross remembered that the conditions in Korea were worse than in Europe during the Second World War. "We were in the front for one solid year and never in a building during that time."[228] Norris Petit described what it was like to live at the front line in Korea:

Harold Ross.

We were moved to A Echelon, living in pup tents, and we received our first bombing. That really scared us. The bombs weren't landing too far away, and some of the guys started jumping up. The guy I was with was really hyper, and he ran right out of the tent in the middle of the night. It was scary, and if you're not scared, then you're not human.[229]

Left to Right: Norris and Claude Petit (Top Left) on Leave. Norris Petit.

One of the scariest things were airdropped enemy pamphlets that told the soldiers to go back home. Obviously, the North Koreans and Chinese knew exactly who and where their enemies were. Norris Petit commented, "They knew we were there, we couldn't believe it."[230]

Maurice Blondeau was trained to load the 25-pounders that were aimed at the enemy positions at night: "And you don't know where they are. See, they were coming out the side of the mountain. They'd shove their nozzles out and back again. You never knew where they were."[231]

Ron Camponi described the role of tanks in Korea:

Royal Canadian Army Service Corps trucks taking supplies along a mountain road north of Pusan, January 1951.

> *We were entrenched at the 38th Parallel and they were entrenched across the valley. There was a lot of shelling and a lot of patrols. But we didn't actually go on patrols. The infantry went on patrols of course, we were sort of dug in our tanks. We were there as support. I think the shelling was really hard on the nerves because you can't move, you can't go anywhere. We can't move our tanks. We were sort of in one position all the time. That's the kind of action, depends on what you call action. We didn't go up with our tanks because first of all it was terrible country for tanks, because it was all rice paddies and mountains. So if you ever got off the rice paddies, you almost disappeared in swamps. It wasn't that you couldn't go across country, there was no country to go. So it really wasn't a good place for tanks to fight, more infantry support is all we did.*[232]

Because of the terrain and the enemies' tactic of using hills to conceal their activities, the CASF employed fighting patrols as a way of locating enemy positions. Fighting patrols varied from other patrols in that the men in the patrol had to go into enemy territory until they made contact with the enemy, and instigated a fight with them. Claude Petit said:

> *There were plenty of fighting patrols for advance contact. You contact the enemy and then you have a briefing afterwards to figure out what their position is and what they are doing. The patrol has to go until they contact the enemy. You've got two kinds of men, usually about 20: get-away men, radio men, an officer, a sergeant, two corporals, two lance corporals. You've got a lot of knowledge. You*

go until you contact the enemy, you shoot it up a little bit, then you come back. You try to bring your casualties back, because you are going to get casualties, you can expect that.[233]

Fighting patrols were dangerous: casualties were expected. Reo Pilon (Duck Lake) was badly wounded while on a fighting patrol.

Joseph McGillivary (Cumberland House) received (along with other members of the PPCLI) the US Presidential Citation for his fighting in the Battle of Kap'yong (Hill 677), which started April 23, 1951. McGillivary had been trained as a sniper in the Second World War. He was number one on the Vickers machine gun crew for the two days that the battle raged at Kap'yong. The five other members of the crew were lost, and he had to get help from a line company.[234]

Albert (Hap) Boyer brought some of his Métis culture with him to Korea. This fiddle player joined the Army in 1951:

> *Wherever he was stationed, he entertained people with his fiddling. In Korea he started a band and one of his officers decided his band needed a name. He had a stand made out of painted wooden beer boxes and painted the name "Hap Boyer's Homesteaders" on it. The name stuck.*[235]

Top to Bottom: Particias on Patrol, February 1951. PPCLI Personnel on Patrol. Joseph McGillivary. Albert "Hap" Boyer (with fiddle), Brian Cyr (maroon jacket), Claude Adams (Legion blazer).

Leon Ferguson said that the last thing the men did when leaving Korea was visit the cemetery in Busan to pay their respects to the soldiers who had died.[236]

Leon Ferguson.

We lost men in Korea too. Lance Corporal Rene Michaud, serving with the PPCLI, died June 24, 1953, and is buried at the United Nations Cemetery at Busan. Pte. Georges Napoleon Ducharme (South Makwa), PPCLI, died on January 12, 1952 in Korea. He is buried in the Yokohama War Cemetery, Japan. Private Robert Ross (Green Lake), serving with the 48th Highlanders of Canada, died in training.

Alexandrine Nicolas, mother of two soldiers in Korea, described her son, Robert's, return to Duck Lake after his discharge.

> *Anyway, he came back in 1953. His shoulder blade was all mashed. His arm was open and his side was all opened. The station agent used to come at the door here and bring me telegrams and that was — it happened some time in May, I guess, early May in 1953. So, all at once he says to me, he came smiling in July. The last days of July. "Well," he says, "this isn't a sad one." He was smiling, you know, and the station agent brought the telegram. And he says, "Your son is coming back on the 30th. They want you to go and meet him at the airport in Saskatoon." So, I had these welfare children and I hired my sister-in-law to stay with my three welfare children. And my daughter and I took the train and went to Saskatoon to meet Robert.*[237]

David C. Bercuson, a military historian, wrote this about the famous PPCL:

> *… war is still war and the primary job of all soldiers — killing others and offering themselves up to be killed — has not changed since the dawn of time. The same attributes of courage, steadfastness, loyalty, dedication to a higher cause, and a love for comrades in arms that exceeds love of self, motivated and sustained the Patricias in those first days in the Ypres Salient, at Bellewaerde Ridge, at the Hitler Line, at Kap'yong, and at the Medak Pocket.*[238]

Top Left to Right: Claude Petit with other Korean War Veterans, Korean War Anniversary Thank You Banquet, 2010. Clarence Fiddler. Left: Maurice Blondeau, Unknown, and Claude and Norris Petit.

Korean veterans had to wait for decades to receive thanks for their service. According to Claude Petit, former President of the National Aboriginal Veterans' Association,

> *It took us 40 years to get recognized and to get our medals … For many of those forty years of silence the Korean War wasn't even called a war but rather a United Nations police action. Looking at the number of people who died as UN forces battled the North Korean and Chinese armies up and down the peninsula make it clear Korea was no police action.*[239]

Left to Right: Korea Volunteer Force Medal (Back and Front), Joseph Alexander Fayant. Korean War Service Medal (Back and Front), Joseph Alexander Fayant.

Top Left to Right: United Nations Korean War Medal (Back and Front), Joseph Alexander Fayant. Bobby (Robert) Morin with Grandmother Maria (Gaspard) Morin, 1960s. Second Row Left to Right: Edward King, 1950s, Regina Rifles. Claude Petit (Left), Canadian Army, PPCLI, Germany, 1964. Wilber Fisher. Third Row Left to Right: Janet Blaze. Claude Goulet and Roy Fosseneuve. Norris Petit and Son. Bottom: Leon Ferguson, Prince Albert, 1971.

Continuing Service in the Military

Albert "Hap" Boyer spent 21 years in the Army, performing in Japan, Germany, as well as Cyprus. While he was in Europe with the Army, he had a fifteen-minute show on Radio Canadian Army Europe. Most of the Métis veterans became even more nationalistic as they fought for Canada and for Métis rights upon their return home. In 1995, Willard Dumont built and donated a Red River cart to Fort Walsh National Historic Site to remind visitors of the Métis peoples' contribution to the colourful and exciting history of the Cypress Hills.

The Continuing Fight of the Métis Veterans

> *You remember the last European war, thousands of our loved ones died in the field of battle — sacrificed their life for the people, and for Canada, and for the rights of the Indians and Half-breeds — that we haven't got. No we haven't got. The only consolation we have is to know that our dear loved ones died a soldier's death and were buried on the field of battle. What did we get out of that? Nothing! What have they done? Now you take how the white man — how they celebrate that day! They were drinking, dancing, and yelling. What have we got to shout about — us poor half-breeds? We stood at the side of our white friends, shedding tears of sorrow to know that our dear loved ones died in vain because we haven't got the freedom we fought for.*[240]

As the Second World War was concluding in Europe, the *Veterans Rehabilitation Act* (the *Veterans Charter*), was enacted to assist returning veterans. This Charter included provisions so that veterans could receive land through the *Veterans Land Act* (1942). Education and training were also available, and there was a re-establishment credit. To administer the benefits, a new department was set up, the Department of Veterans Affairs (DVA, now VAC). A discharged soldier stopped receiving services from the military and came under the direction of the federal bureaucracy:

> *The Canadian government provided special benefits to veterans who had seen active duty. These include land and cash grants, to start farms, disability pensions if wounded, health benefits and other entitlements. Veterans were to be given priority or preference in the federal service.*[241]

The *Veterans Land Act* was intended to assist returning veterans to become established landowners. This legislation was based on the assumption that getting into agriculture would be a good way to rehabilitate soldiers. Acquiring land would have been a significant change for our people. At the time, many Métis lived as squatters in road allowance communities because we had lost land through the Métis Scrip system, and had not been able to get title for many of our lands. However, most Métis soldiers did not benefit from the *Veterans Land Act*. A survey undertaken by the National Métis Veterans Association showed that only about one per cent of Métis veterans received land under the Act.[242]

Duck Lake Métis Veterans, Late 1950s.

The Act's provisions applied differently to veterans applying to settle on Crown Land. Through the processes undertaken in the 1930s and '40s to resettle our people from road allowances, many Métis veterans returned to communities on Crown Land. Other Métis communities were not surveyed, and the Act pertained to surveyed land only. Therefore, for many Métis veterans, the Act did not cover any land around their home communities. The province owned the land around the Métis Colonies, which were established after the Second World War. Therefore, the land on the farming colonies, such as those in Lebret, Willow Bunch, and Green Lake, was not open for individual ownership. Other provisions applied to the purchase of trapping, fur farming, or household equipment. These could have assisted Métis veterans in our communities. However, the provisions were restricted to First Nations veterans. Métis veterans need not apply.

Cliff Hessdorfer.

The education and training option did not benefit Métis veterans, either. The vast majority of Métis servicemen and women could not take advantage of this benefit. Many Métis soldiers were unschooled, or minimally schooled. At the time of the First World War, neither the federal nor the provincial government took responsibility for Métis schooling. It was not until 1944 that the provincial government in Saskatchewan dedicated resources to ensuring that all Métis children (even those whose parents did not own land and thus paid no property taxes) had access to schooling. The offer of a university education or trades training was meaningless for most Métis soldiers who did not have the basic prerequisites for advanced education.[243]

Some Métis soldiers used the Re-establishment Credit. In most cases, those who were able to get assistance were living in urban centres. The process for obtaining the Re-establishment Credit required a proposal from the Métis soldier, which outlined what was required. A DVA official then determined the amount needed. The DVA issued a goods voucher for the prescribed purpose, and the Department made a direct payment to the supplier. Such a complicated system required that a returned soldier had easy access to a DVA office. Many Métis veterans lived a long way from the nearest DVA office. As a result, the vast majority of Métis veterans did not receive this benefit. As Donna Pinay wrote:

Top: Charles Umpherville.
Bottom: Claude Adams and Max Lucier.

> *Many of our veterans were forced to return to the poverty and unemployment rampant in our communities. While in the war, they had a sense of accomplishment and self-worth — they knew they were capable of doing anything as well as anyone else. For many, it was difficult to adjust to civilian life, particularly for those who returned to unemployment. For others, it meant leaving their communities to secure employment elsewhere.*
>
> *For some, it was hard to secure employment particularly on reserves, and in rural and northern areas. It must have been difficult to adjust from being an active participant in a major war effort, to being unemployed.*[244]

Many Métis soldiers came home from war — whether the First World War, the Second World War, or the Korean War — with physical injuries. In many cases, the families provided the healing. Often, returned soldiers had to fight to get the services they required to live a comfortable and dignified life. Agnes Carriere's account of her husband, Pierre Carriere's, post-war experience provides an example of what Métis soldiers and their families had to bear. Her son, John, translated her memories from Cree into English, and told his father's story:

> *My father was wounded severely on his face, head and neck. I do not know how much this wound affected his daily life. He was independent and self employed. The head wound affected him severely when chopping wood and chiselling ice with the ice chisel. He talked about his ears ringing all the time and I remember up to 1962 that he had been bleeding just about every night. In the early 60's, my father was seeing a dentist. While the doctor was working pulling out a tooth, he found a piece of his* [Pierre's] *broken jaw.*
>
> *Most of the complaints that my father talked about the hospital was the poor treatment, and he would not stay long. His right eye was affected. He was just about blind and could not close his eyelid. His right side of his face was paralyzed and his face was twisted because of the war wound.*
>
> *When we were growing up there was a sick saying from some Cumberland House people that we were the twisted face children. That affected my parents. If the Army had looked after him by doing plastic surgery, as it was stated in his records, he would not have gone through the humiliation.*
>
> *When my father was released from the hospital after the war in the winter of 1945, my mother said it was -40 degrees. He had to ride in a horse and buggy from The Pas, Manitoba. The only clothes he had were on his back. He had no money. He had no letters to tell him how he was to follow up with his treatment, and no notice of what arrangements the Canadian government or Canadian Army had for my father to be looked after.*
>
> *There was no hospital in Cumberland House and after the war the veterans and some other people built a hospital.*
>
> *My mother talks about the time when my father came home after the war. He walked into the house. They did not recognize his face. It was black and blue and puffed up. My sister Anne was five years old and she ran away from him. There was no warning as to how he looked or how badly he was wounded.*
>
> *After the war, my father tried other jobs that were available in our small town, but he always ended up being independent and self-employed. Around the time he was 53 years old I believe his health deteriorated further due to the wounds he received in World War II. My mother recalls that they did receive a*

pension of $67.00 from 1946 to around 1970.

I believe an old Veterans doctor that used to come to Cumberland House in the late 1960s told my father, with the wounds he received in the war he should have been receiving more than $67.00. He told my father that others, meaning white veterans, were receiving more money and that the D.V.A. was looking after the veterans' wives and the rest of the families.

My parents, Pierre and Agnes Carriere had raised eight children — Anne, Verna, Donna, Franklin, John, Ken, Clifford, and Les. With what we know now is that if my parents were looked after by the Canadian Army and the Canadian Government right away, as the war records and hospital release records show, my father would not have had to work so damn hard to raise his family. I believe he would have lived longer.[245]

Métis veterans struggled to get the medical help they needed. Wilfred Henry described his battle to get help:

On my service book it says, "wounded" so why don't they have a record? My wife was working for John Diefenbaker at one time, and he helped to get a little bit. John went back and said that it wasn't enough, so I got a little bit more. He went back again and finally, I was getting close to $2,000 a month. Now they expect us to make do with $1,000.

Wilfred John Henry.

The pain is continuous. I still get medicine from the doctor to rub on my head. I've said many times that I thank God I married a good wife. She looks after me. Sometimes I tell her where it hurts and she rubs it to help take the pain away. I take pills for the pain and sleeping pills to put me out. Sometimes I still scream at nights, especially if I've been talking about the war. It all comes back. During the Gulf War, my wife had quite a time with me. It was like I was right there.

I couldn't go to work because I couldn't bend over without blacking out. The disability pension wasn't enough but we had to make do. It was more than what we are getting now. The minute I hit 65, they cut me right off. Other veterans have told me they have been able to get what they need and I should go after the Department of Veterans Affairs, but it's hard because I'm not able to make my case well. My memory has been affected. The pain in my head often makes me forget what I'm going to say.

Veterans need help. If they were in special homes or hospitals, it would cost the government a lot more. They want veterans to be independent and stay in their own homes. The people in government didn't experience what we did. They're from a generation that doesn't understand the pain soldiers went through.[246]

Old comrades decided that they needed to assist each other in receiving the help that they and their families were entitled to receive. The Saskatchewan Métis Veterans Association was formed in 1985. The first executive consisted of Euclide Boyer, president for seven years, Edward King, vice-president for seven years, and Tony Camponi, secretary. The next executive elected in Saskatoon in 1992, included Vital Morin, president, Leon Belanger, vice-president, Tony Camponi, treasurer (for thirteen years), and Charlie Fosseneuve, secretary. The following year, in 1993, Vital Morin was elected for six years, Leon Belanger and Charlie Fosseneuve retained their positions, and Edward King took over as treasurer. The organization continues to this day to fight for Métis veterans.

Top: Edward King. Bottom: Vital Morin.

As time passed, the community became more aware of the contributions and sacrifices made by their men and women in wartime. In November 1988, Donna Pinay wrote an article in *New Breed Magazine* — then the magazine of Saskatchewan's Métis and Non-Status Indians — entitled "In Recognition of Our Veterans," which provided an analysis of the service to Aboriginal veterans to Canada and their treatment by their country:

Few veterans speak freely of their actual war experiences — it is too painful a memory. They will speak of their enlistment, of the comradeship among all, and perhaps of the more humorous or lighter sides of their service, but not of the war and destruction of human life they witnessed on a firsthand basis. They saw the horrors of war and lost friends and comrades. Others bore the emotional and physical scars of war.[247]

The article goes on:

There was no place for racism in the war — lives and freedom were at stake. Camaraderie developed which crossed racial and ethnic lines. Veterans speak of the great sense of comradeship and friendship, of the good times and of the cooperation among one another. Differences were put aside as there was no alternative. Everyone had to depend on one another and they lived, and sometimes died together. There was a great sense of friendship, of caring and co-operation.[248]

This spirit of community and service enabled many returning Métis soldiers to use their skills, organizational abilities, and knowledge to address problems in their own communities. "They were no longer prepared to accept the conditions facing our people and began to work towards organizing our people to better their situation,"[249] wrote Pinay. She described Métis soldiers as "pioneers in race relations or cross-cultural awareness."[250] They taught their non-Aboriginal comrades that they were equal partners in the war effort. "They were respected for their skills and abilities and they also learned that racism is put aside in crisis."[251]

Top: Cliff Hessdorfer, Frank Tomkins, Leon Ferguson, and Charles Umpherville. Bottom: Métis Veterans, Prince Albert Métis Fall Festival, 1998. Left to right in the back row are: Claude Goulet, Nathan Setee, Charles Fosseneuve, Peter Tompkins, Cliff Hessdorfer, Marcel Giraud, Charles Umperville, Frank Tompkins, Harold Lagimodiere, Roy Fosseneuve, and Ronald Collins. Left to right in the front row are: Norman Henderson, Max Lucier, Stanley Durocher, Alex Dreaver, Solomon Goulet, Roderick Bear, and Edward King.

> *They worked for our people, confident and assured that they could attain improved social and economic conditions. Despite oppressive government policies, many of our veterans were no longer prepared to accept this oppression or second-class treatment.*[252]

In the early 1990s, fifty years after the Second World War, the Senate of Canada's Standing Committee on Aboriginal Affairs began an investigation into the postwar lives of Aboriginal soldiers. The committee planned to hold hearings in Ottawa with veterans and bureaucrats responsible for veterans in order to accept briefs from veterans and veteran associations, and to travel the country to hear from Aboriginal veterans directly. In preparation for the hearings, the Gabriel Dumont Institute spearheaded an effort to locate and document the experiences of as many Métis veterans as possible. Unfortunately, by the time the investigation got underway, most First World War veterans had died and their stories were not recorded, but many Second World War and Korean veterans came forward to share their experiences. Some did not wish to be interviewed.

The researchers heard many heartbreaking stories, revealing a great deal of neglect and suffering for those who had fought for their country. Many veterans and their families had to struggle to meet their most basic needs.

On June 6, 1994, at the Senate Standing Committee on Aboriginal Affairs, Vital Morin recounted the experience of Saskatchewan's Métis soldiers as they returned home:

Top to Bottom: Edith Hilda Merrifield. Joseph George Merasty. Lawrence Sayese. Len Desjarlais.

Men told stories of coming back to Canada. They spoke of finding their families gone, their land being awarded to someone else. Some of their wives had remarried because they were told their men were dead. We heard that many of our ex-soldiers were placed in mental hospitals because they had no home. Many of our men were denied military funerals. In short, many of our veterans went from being respected soldiers to being treated like bums and vagrants. We feel strongly that Métis veterans were treated as second-class veterans and second-class Canadian citizens.[253]

Métis Veterans were hopeful after meeting with the senators in 1994. When the Métis veterans told their stories during the hearings, the chairperson spoke of the committee's commitment to addressing the issues raised by Métis veterans. Typical of this sensitivity was the chairperson's closing remarks on November 15, 1994:

The manner in which this committee has been approaching this subject is that it was not only the individual veteran who was affected by going to war, but the whole family was part of the process. It affected the veteran, his spouse and their children. We hope that time will not be against us because we want to honour the families … We must never forget: One man or woman does not go alone into war; it affects a family, generation after generation. We will approach it that way and we hope some justice will be done.[254]

On November 16, 1994, in his closing statement to the Senate Committee on Aboriginal Peoples regarding the treatment of Aboriginal veterans, Métis veteran Vital Morin said, "I would like to thank you, Madam Chairman, for the good words. I think you are quite sincere

Top to Bottom: Leo Belanger. Max Lucier. Norm Henderson. Ora Madden.

in trying your best to see if something can be done for us. I hope that you people can succeed and do something before we leave this world …"[255]

Chairperson Raynell Andreychuk addressed Mr. Morin and others in the Métis delegation:

> *As I indicated before we commenced, we were here to talk about veterans, their families and their dependants whether they have passed away or whether they are still with us. We will try not to make that distinction.*
>
> *… We will also concentrate on the fact that the policies after the war were Government of Canada policies and that there is inherently a difference of benefits between Aboriginals and others. We will have to determine whether that was fair, appropriate or discriminatory right from the start — a government that sent its young people to war treated them differently when they came home. We will have to look at why 50 years have gone by and why we are still grappling with it.*
>
> *All I can say is that the members of this committee have taken this exercise seriously. We feel very strongly that we want to get a report that is concrete, one that can be acted upon and one that will not allow too much more time to pass before this issue is brought to the attention of government.*[256]

Sadly, Vital Morin passed away in November, 2000.

In the mid-1990s, when the Royal Commission on Aboriginal Peoples travelled the country and received representations from older and infirm Métis veterans, the veterans were encouraged to think they would soon receive the recognition and the benefits promised by the government they had fought to protect. Once again, they were disappointed. A 2001 report to the Canadian government from the National Métis Veterans Association stated:

> *Métis veterans have told the story of their betrayal. They have told it at the Senate Standing Committee Hearings on the Aboriginal Soldier After the War. They have told it to the Commissioners of the Royal Commission on Aboriginal Peoples. For proud, strong men and women, for the "Otipemisiwak," the free people, as the Cree called the Métis, it is humiliating enough to tell the stories of betrayal once but when their struggles are disregarded and efforts are made to discredit their words, the insult is compounded.*[257]

A lawsuit on behalf of Métis veterans was filed in 2004[258], but to date, justice has not been served. Métis veterans still await compensation. Many of the men who were fighting for justice will never see it. They have died during this battle with their own government.

Taking Care of Our Veterans

Many soldiers came home with unseen injuries of the spirit and the mind. One of the veterans interviewed by the Gabriel Dumont Institute in 1993 spoke of a soldier he knew who had been at D-Day in 1944. He described the soldier's tragic postwar life: "He committed suicide last March 28. He was always sick. He had to come to Saskatoon 2-3 times a week. Psychiatrist, specialist. He was in very bad shape, so he decided enough of that."[259]

Wilfred Henry spoke of the psychological after effects that he had from being buried alive twice while in the service, and the DVA's response to his condition:

> *I had nightmares of that experience many times. I would wake up screaming and I'd wake up my children. They didn't know what I was crying about. I gave my wife lots of trouble trying to look after me. I had so much pain in my head all the time, I couldn't stand it. There were times, before I was married, I just about took a gun and went into the bush and shot myself. That's how I felt.*
>
> *When I got married I could be quite a violent boy, when I had pain. But when I reported it, they told me they had no record of it, that it's never been reported that I was buried alive. My commanding officer knew it and the rest of the fellows knew it. The officer said, "Henry, you're alive, thank God that's the main thing." I told*

Back Row: Frank Tomkins, Leon Ferguson, Claude Petit, Cliff Hessdorfer
Front Row: Vital Morin, Joseph Fayant, Leo Belanger, Charles Umpherville, and Edward King.

him I had pains in my head, and he was going to send me back and get someone else to take my place, but I didn't want to leave. Some of my friends might get killed and I wouldn't know about it. I wanted to tough it out.[260]

Top: Métis Veterans Colour Guard, Prince Albert Métis Rendezvous, 1995.
Bottom: Métis Veterans Colour Guard, Prince Albert Métis Fall Festival, 1997.

Such suffering from combatants and former combatants was known as "shell shock" or "battle fatigue" during the First World War. Whatever it is called, it is the result of a soldier witnessing or experiencing a terrible event or tragedy which so haunts his or her memories that the individual's personal health and personality are affected. A background paper prepared for the Canadian Parliamentary Information and Research Service, *Post-traumatic Stress Disorder and Mental Health of Military Personnel and Veterans,* states:

> *The potential psychological after-effects of involvement in military operations are usually described by the medical term "post-traumatic stress disorder" (PTSD), or the military and police term, "operational stress injury." These after-effects are more difficult to anticipate than physical injuries because they are less visible, reluctantly reported by those who suffer from them, and because the symptoms may only appear years after the traumatic event. Our understanding of the condition is therefore imperfect, and there are no certainties, except for the distress of those affected.*[261]

The document affirms that the "diagnosis of PTSD is becoming well established in the psychiatric community."[262] The diagnosis is based on three symptoms: intrusive recollections (e.g., distressing dreams, flashbacks, or hallucination), avoidance and emotional numbness (e.g., avoidance of circumstances that remind the individual of the traumatic event, or feeling detached from others), and increased arousal (e.g., difficulty sleeping, hyper-vigilance, and irritability).[263] If these symptoms persist more than three months, they are considered "chronic." Further complicating the issue is that symptoms may not appear for months or even years. The condition, known as "lifetime prevalence," may produce symptoms at any point in a person's life.[264]

Recently, a Métis Korean War veteran attended a PTSD lecture. He had been suffering ever since his return from Korea over 60 years ago. When the lecturer explained PTSD's symptoms, the veteran was suddenly provided with an explanation for his continuing problems. He is finally receiving counselling and finding relief after all these years. He wants veterans and their families to visit their local DVA office to receive information on PTSD and to seek any available help.

Claude Petit (Left) and Unknown Veteran.

Legacy

The late Mary Rose Boyer wrote a tribute to the five men in her Métis family who went to war. She closed the article by describing the legacy that these men have left her:

> *A man who could not read showed me you could still contribute and raise a family and be worthy in the eyes of the community, another showed me that despite three years in an enemy prison camp, you could still forgive and get on with your life, another showed me that hands trained to kill in war time can be gentle enough*

Frank Tomkins, Armand Fisher, Harold Ross, Peter Pelletier, Edith Merrifield, Charlie Fosseneuve, and Maurice Blondeau.

to warm a child's face and that bravery could be fun. Another showed me that in war, young men and women and their contributions are lost forever and it is our duty to see that wars do not happen. They showed me that substances could be abused to cover the pain of dead buddies and that the terrors of fierce battles could be erased with determination and focus. I learned I could live a good life and meet any challenge because they had good lives after facing far more serious challenges of death, terror and the destruction in foreign lands without family and at an age when most people are just completing high school and starting a family.

All of these men, because of their contributions and examples, made me proud to be a member of their family and proud to be a Métis girl from the Souris River Valley. That was quite possibly the best legacy.[265]

Ensuring that We and Future Generations Never Forget

I have written this book to remember and acknowledge those Métis from Saskatchewan who went to war in three twentieth century wars: the First and Second World Wars, and the Korean War. This book tells the stories of ordinary men and women who were put in extraordinary situations in which they performed incredible deeds. These heroes fought for us all. They understood the fragility of peace and the need at times to fight to protect it. It is still worth fighting for their values.

These are lessons that we all need to remember. It is our responsibility to ensure that we do not forget our veterans and their contributions. It is our responsibility to ensure that our history includes their stories. Future generations must continue to tell their stories as well.

Canada 125 Service Medal (Back and Front), Joseph Alexander Fayant.

Afterword: First and Second World War Memorial Tours, 2010-2011

First World War Memorial Tour, France and Belgium, 2011

In preparing for the First World War Memorial Tour, it was important for me to determine the battles and operations that involved Saskatchewan's Métis soldiers. By examining their dates of enlistment and their battalions, I was able to establish where selected Métis soldiers may have served.

GDI initially compiled the list of Saskatchewan Métis soldiers as part of a presentation for a Senate Hearing on the treatment of Aboriginal soldiers after the wars. From this list, GDI researchers interviewed those soldiers who consented, and some of the interviews were used for the book, *Remembrances: Interviews with Métis Veterans*. By this time, in the early 1990s, very few First World War veterans were able to participate. The emphasis was on the needs of Second World War and Korean War veterans.

In 2001, the National Métis Veterans Association furthered this initial research for six months. Since that time, the search for the names of Métis First World War soldiers has continued by a few committed community members.

Information on First World War soldiers is available at Library and Archives Canada (*http://www.bac-lac.gc.ca*). On this website, it is possible to download a Métis enlistee's attestation paper.

Not all Métis soldiers returned. Many are buried in cemeteries in Europe or are commemorated on monuments for the missing. The Internet has made it relatively easy to find the burial place or place of commemoration of fallen Métis soldiers. The Commonwealth War Graves Commission (*http://www.cwgc.org*) provides the burial plot or place of remembrance for every Commonwealth soldier killed in the First, Second, and Korean Wars. Those who have given their lives in service to Canada are remembered by the Canadian people in the *Books of Remembrance*, which are located in the Peace Tower of the Parliament Buildings in Ottawa. Copies of the pages of individual soldiers are available online through Veterans Affairs Canada (*http://www.veterans.gc.ca*). The Canadian Virtual War Memorial (*http://www.virtualmemorial.gc.ca*) contains the names of Canadian service members who died in the wars. This website provides the opportunity for family and friends to add pictures or information to an individual's memorial.

Knowing this information beforehand proved useful for the trip to France and Belgium. It was foggy when we left Toronto. A drizzly day turned into a misty evening. Reading Tim Cook's *Sharp End*, the weather seemed uncannily fitting for the beginning of a tour of First World War memorial sites.

As I travelled 678 mph at a height of 35,000 feet, I found it hard to imagine what the young Métis boys must have experienced travelling on the water at 10 knots for days on the same journey almost 100 years ago. They would have been thinking of what lay ahead of them, with excitement obscuring the fear of the unknown and the enemy. While in Canada, they were introduced in a preliminary way to drilling and following military discipline and protocols. They were a little better prepared than they had been when they joined up, but just a little. They had their kits — their uniforms and the notorious Ross rifles which became the snipers' favourite for their accuracy but the curse of infantrymen for their unreliability.

The First World War was to be the "war to end all wars." It combined the most modern of weaponry and scientific knowledge with the ancient technique of sending men against the enemy in face-to-face combat. The troop ships carried not only decks of soldiers with the latest gear and guns of the most modern technology, but also in the ships' holds were horses — which were still valuable to move the "Great Guns."

In London, we visited the Imperial War Museum. It is a chilling reminder of how many wars Britain has fought. Although the Canadians were with the British on many campaigns, Canadian content is meagre, and it is impossible to find reference to the contribution of Canadian Aboriginal soldiers.

We went to see the Canadian Memorial in the gardens of Buckingham Palace. It is an intriguing creation of moving water and sculpted maple leaves. The time of day and the season affect the patterns that you see. According to the guide, in fall when the leaves are falling off the maple trees in the park, it is hard to tell which leaves are real and which are sculpted. The mood created is one of beauty and serenity. If a war memorial can bring a feeling of peace, it is this one.

We left London to catch the ferry at Dover, on England's southern coast. When we arrived, the white cliffs of Dover (immortalized by Vera Lynn's wartime song) were obscured by mist and clouds. It was not a good day to get a picture.

The distance from Dover, England to Calais, France is insignificant in Canadian terms. Our ferry eased into the Channel through a narrow break in the sea wall. Gulls darted back and forth. With the fog, the sky and sea melded, light grey muted the darker tones of the sea. Occasional white caps added a touch of brightness to the blue-grey water. I can only imagine the effect this weather would have had on an inexperienced soldier being transported to the battlefields of Europe. With the sea and sky as one, and no visible clues as to where you were, it would have seemed like you were passing from the known world to an unknown reality waiting ominously on the other side of the fog.

Sanctuary Woods—Hill 62. Ieper, Belgium, in the background.

We landed in France and went through customs in Calais, then boarded a bus and passed through the French countryside to Belgium, where we were to stay for three nights, the centre of the protracted Battles of Ypres and Passchendaele (the third battle of Ypres), both part of our Canadian history.

The contemporary city of Ieper (Ypres in French), in the centre of Flemish Belgium, has the elegant spires and delicate appearance of a medieval cityscape. The city faces inward to the Gort Market — the original centre of the medieval textile trade. Here the commercial transactions of the day were made: wool was bought, cloth was sold, workers were hired and bankers haggled with businessmen over prices.

Today, outdoor cafes ring the square. Tourists dodge buses and cars to take that perfect picture of the city's architecture. If they did not know any better, they would think that these beautiful buildings were constructed hundreds of years ago in the 13th and 14th centuries. In thinking this they would be wrong.

When Métis soldiers saw this beautiful city in the First World War, it was a pile of rubble. Between 1914 and 1918, the city was shelled and bombarded. The people of Ieper watched their churches, homes, and everything they identified with in their historic city reduced to debris. The stately buildings you see today were all rebuilt after the war using the plans prepared by the original builders to replicate every detail. The people of Ieper were determined not to let the war take their beautiful city from them. The city itself, that its people rebuilt, stone by stone, is a monument to the power of the human spirit.

The fighting was centred in this area in 1914. The German invasion of Belgium was the action that brought Britain and its colonies and dominions into the war against Germany. Great Britain was committed to going to war in support of Belgium under the terms of an 1839 treaty. This treaty

Close Up, Poppy, Northern France.

signed by two European heads of state plunged our country into a war on European soil. It sent Saskatchewan Métis soldiers to fight in the Belgian countryside. It was the reason why Canadian soldiers lie in countless cemeteries in this countryside. It is why Canadian John McCrae's haunting poem, which has come to symbolize the sacrifice of all wars, is called "In Flanders Fields." This is Flanders. This part of Europe has a strong connection to Canada.

The Soldiers Missing and Without a Grave

The First World War was tragic in that many of the soldiers who lost their lives were never found. In the relentless bombardment of the battlefields, soldiers' bodies, which had been buried by their friends where they had fallen, were destroyed and their remains never identified. These soldiers remain unknown, but not forgotten.

The Menin Gate, in Ieper, Belgium is one of the memorials to the missing. The British government decided that the Menin Gate would be an appropriate place for remembrance because between 1914 and 1918, hundreds of thousands of Allied soldiers passed this way when going to the battlefields. One hundred and sixty panels were erected to remember the names of over 55,000 missing young men who left home to fight for freedom. Among the names on the Memorial is Napoleon Nault, a Métis soldier from Cochin, Saskatchewan.

In Ieper, they remember the First World War. The Menin Gate memorializes the names of soldiers with no known grave. Many bodies could not be identified. For many, their bodies were

Menin Gate, Western Entrance.

destroyed in the incessant shelling, in the violence of the fighting in the Ypres Salient. Each night at 8 p.m., the "Last Post" ceremony is held at the Menin Gate. Those who attend influence the ceremony. One night it may be Australians who are remembering their fallen. The next, it might be Scots with their bagpipes and laments. People come from all over the world to be part of this ceremony. In silence, everyone respectfully watches and listens as the missing soldiers are remembered. Members of the audience express their personal connection to the soldiers and this place by placing wreaths.

Menin Gate Memorial.

The Menin Gate did not have enough space to display the names of all the missing. The Thiepval Memorial, a huge brick and stone edifice with massive square pillars and graceful arches, was commissioned to commemorate 72,000 officers and men who were killed during the Battle of the Somme and who have no known graves.

Tyne Cot Memorial to the Missing, Passchendaele.

The Thiepval Memorial, the Tyne Cot Cemetery, and the Vimy Memorial all stand as reminders of the sacrifices of these men who never received a proper burial and have no individual gravesite.

The Vimy Memorial

Vimy — the word has become synonymous with Canada's contribution to the First World War. Nearly every person in Canada has heard of it.

The spires of the Vimy Memorial rise above the countryside and they can be seen for many minutes before you enter the memorial park. It took eleven years to craft this 40-storey monument. Twenty sculpted figures evoke the mood of melancholy and sacrifice that overcomes you in this gigantic

Top: Vimy Ridge Memorial, Viewed from the Northeast. Middle Left to Right: Vimy Ridge Memorial, Viewed from the Southeast. Vimy Ridge Memorial, Mother Canada Statue. Bottom Left to Right: Vimy Ridge Memorial, Breaking the Swords Statue. Vimy Ridge Memorial, Mourning Parents, the Female. Vimy Ridge Memorial, Mourning Parents, the Male.

tombstone to 11,000 young Canadian soldiers who were "missing and presumed dead," and did not receive their own burial place and gravestone.

The words at the base of the monument say, in English and French:

> *To the Valour of their countrymen in the Great War and in memory of their sixty thousand dead this monument is raised to the people of Canada.*

Among the names etched on the monument are the names of Saskatchewan Métis soldiers who never came home, including Edward J. Baptiste, Battleford; Joseph Bourassa, Prince Albert; Wilfred Whitford, Birch Hills; Oswald Victor Keddie, Cumberland House; Herbert Bruce Kennedy, Duck Lake; George T. Bird, Duck Lake; Frank Nicol Dreaver, Saskatoon; and Joseph Boileau, Lebret.

Vimy Ridge Memorial, Fallen Soldiers Names.

Cemeteries

There are so many cemeteries with so many graves. It is possible to see only a few graves of Saskatchewan's Métis soldiers. Some bodies were found, but they were never identified. They were buried with a headstone that read only, "A Soldier of the Great War." All are remembered. The local people keep the cemeteries immaculate.

We know that there is at least one Métis soldier from the First World War buried in each of the following cemeteries: Raillencourt Communal Cemetery Extension, Nord Department, France; Drury Crucifix Cemetery, Pas-de-Calais, France; Villers Station Cemetery, Pas-de-Calais, France; Givenchy-en-Gohelle Canadian Cemetery, Pas-de-Calais, France; Larch Wood (Railway Cutting) Cemetery, Ieper, Belgium; Warvillers Churchyard Extension, Somme, France; Aix-Noulette Communal Cemetery Extension, Pas-de-Calais, France; Wancourt British Cemetery, Pas-de-Calais, France; Sains-les-Marquion British Cemetery, Pas-de-Calais, France; Ecoivres Military Cemetery, Pas-de-Calais, France; Hersin Communal Cemetery Extension, Pas-de-Calais, France; Barlin Communal Cemetery Extension, Pas-de-Calais, France; Aldershot Military Cemetery, Hampshire, UK;

Hourges Orchard Cemetery, Domart-Sur-La-Luce, Somme, France; Haynecourt British Cemetery, Nord Department, France; Passchendaele New British Cemetery, Belgium; Niagara Cemetery, IWUY, Nord Department, France; Etaples Military Cemetery, Pas-de-Calais, France; Nine Elms Military Cemetery, Pas-de-Calais, France; Grayshott (St. Joseph) Roman Catholic Churchyard, Hampshire, UK; and Aubigny Communal Cemetery Extension, Pas-de-Calais, France.

Deville Wood Memorial, Cross of Sacrifice, Somme.

It would be possible to visit all of these cemeteries and remember each Métis soldier who is in foreign fields. Someday, a tour might be arranged for that purpose. A tour of First World War Memorial sites is a sobering but uplifting experience. It forces us to grapple with questions of identity, loyalty, duty, honour, and values which we need to examine in light of each of our lives. A generation of young men faced these questions and offered their lives for what they believed in.

Left: Adanac Cemetery, Somme. Right: Vimy Ridge, Givenchy Road Canadian Cemetery.

Second World War Memorial Tour, France, 2010

July 11, 2010 dawned grey with the threat of rain. The weather reflected our sombre mood as we travelled to the Normandy beaches and to the cemeteries that contain thousands of young men who gave their lives to liberate Europe. Our ship, the Avalon Creativity, docked at Rouen and we left for the beaches in buses. It was a three-hour trip through the Norman countryside. Normandy is very rural — known for its dairy cattle, horses, and apples. The cattle provide the unpasteurized milk to make cheeses such as Camembert, Pont-l'évêque, and Neufchâtel. In former times, workhorses such as Percherons came from Normandy and many of these helped to turn Prairie landscapes into wheat fields. Today, Norman stud farms produce some of the world's greatest racehorses. Locally grown apples form the base for tortes, desserts, cider, and Calvados Brandy — also used extensively in Norman cooking.

Our guide through the Normandy countryside, Brigitte Muller-Konrad, explained that the first settlers to travel to New France in the 17th and 18th centuries were from Normandy. Tradesmen and families, chosen specifically for their skills necessary to build the colony of New France, seized the opportunity of obtaining and settling a new land. Some of the first families to emigrate from Normandy to New France were the Pelletiers, Boyers, Bouchers, Rivards, Goulets, Landrys, and Lamberts.

These family names were the same as many of the Métis soldiers who served in France. On June 6, 1944, when Métis soldiers set foot on the Normandy beaches, they were actually stepping onto their ancestral land. Although the Métis soldiers may not have realized this, the Normans recognized them as relatives by the way they spoke. Our guide Brigitte told us that the local Norman citizens were surprised when so many Canadian soldiers spoke French in their Norman dialect.

The night before the trip to the Normandy Beaches, the Tour Manager, Gusta Krusemeijer, provided the British, Canadian, and American participants with an informative background on the D-Day landings. She explained that of all the forces that landed on June 6, 1944, only the Canadian troops reached their objective. The Regina Rifles, the Royal Canadian Engineers, and the Royal Winnipeg Rifles were among the Canadian troops to land that day.

Gusta showed dramatically how the war affected people growing up in Europe. Gusta is Dutch. She is too young to have been alive during the war, but the power of the Second World War is so profound that she finds it hard to make her presentation without being overcome by her emotions. For her, it is still painful to talk about the war. I had the opportunity to tell her that

Métis veterans have told me that for them returning to Holland has been a special privilege. It is in Holland that many Métis veterans are made to feel that what they did as soldiers made a difference. Dutch people, young or old, understood and appreciated the veterans' sacrifices. The Dutch people made them feel that they were right in what they did. In the Netherlands, Métis soldiers have seen for themselves that they made a difference in people's lives, and their experiences have been validated.

In her presentation, Gusta said that she continues to tell the story of the war because she wants people to remember that we should not take our freedom for granted. It is not free. It was won at a high price. It is important to remember that the Métis communities of Saskatchewan paid a high price for our freedom.

Our bus had both Canadian and British visitors. Our first stop was Arromanches-les-Bains, where the Royal Navy created a port (Mulberry Harbour) so that they could unload supplies to support the Allied operation in Europe. When the Royal Navy sailed to France, the ships carried with them hollow cement forms to fill and sink, forming docking areas for supply ships to maintain the large advancing force. Accompanying the British ships were derelict freighters that were sunk to protect the manmade harbour. Today, some remnants of the British formations can still be seen in the waters off the village, while onshore, stores sell souvenirs and historical postcards.

In the D-Day invasion plan, airborne divisions were to cover the activities of the ground forces. During the night, before the landings were scheduled, paratroopers and gliders filled with soldiers were deposited behind the German lines. The job of the Allied soldiers behind enemy lines was to capture or destroy key installations such as bridges to ensure that the German Army would not be able to amass its forces and quell the invasion. The zone between the Rivers Orne and Dives was to be secured by the British 6th Airborne Division. As part of this pre-invasion force, the men of the 1st Canadian Battalion were entrusted with destroying bridges at Varaville and Robehomme.

These small groups of military personnel had to capture strategic sites. It was a dangerous but necessary operation. Many lost their lives either by being shot out of the sky as they dropped or in the battles to achieve their targets. Ranville British War Cemetery is the resting place of the paratroopers, glider pilots, and troopers who landed behind the lines the night before the D-Day landings.

As I walked through the rows of graves of British paratroopers, my eyes were attracted to a gravestone with a maple leaf. I was drawn to the grave in a strange, urgent way. When I saw the name — Lt. Lloyd Herman Adams — I knew that he was a Saskatchewan Métis soldier. I have since found out that Lt. Adams was born at Lindsay Scottish Métis settlement near Prince Albert. He was the son of Horace Adams and Aglentine Hodgson, daughter of Albert Hodgson and Elizabeth Jane Inkster of Clouston. Lieutenant Adams joined the PPCLI in 1937 at Winnipeg. He transferred to the Winnipeg Rifles in 1942 and took officer training. In the fall of 1943, he went to England as a training officer transferring to the 1st Canadian Paratroop Battalion. He was one of the first Canadians to give their lives in the liberation of Europe. I placed the first Métis sash on his grave and wondered at the force that had brought me to it amidst so many other graves.

L. H. (Lloyd) Adams, Bény-Sur-Mer Canadian War Cemetery, France.

"Operation Overlord" as it was called in official documents, took place on June 6, 1944. The operation involved the 7th Canadian Infantry Brigade under Brigadier Harry W. Foster, comprised of the Royal Winnipeg Rifles, the Regina Rifle Regiment and the 1st Battalion, the Canadian Scottish Regiment; the 8th Canadian Infantry Brigade under Brigadier Kenneth Blackader, including the Queen's Own Rifles of Canada, Le Régiment de la Chaudière, and the North Shore (New Brunswick) Regiment; and the 9th Canadian Infantry Brigade, composed of the Highland Light Infantry of Canada, the Stormont Dundas and Glengarry Highlanders, and the North Nova Scotia Highlanders. The 2nd Canadian Armoured Brigade was attached to the operation. This included the 6th Armoured Regiment, or 1st Hussars, the 10th Armoured Regiment, or Fort Garry Horse, and the 27th Armoured Regiment, or the Sherbrooke Fusiliers.

The A company of the Regina Rifles landed in their sector, known now as Juno Beach, at 8:05 a.m. The soldiers were to attack a powerful complex of concrete shelters that the Germans had built to defend the coastline around the village of Courseulles-sur-Mer. Fourteen Sherman tanks had landed and were engaged in the battle. None were destroyed by the German anti-tank guns. With the rising tide, Companies C and D, arriving a little later, lost some of their barges, which were exploded by mines no longer visible on the beach. However, by 10:00 a.m., the Regina Rifles had secured Courseulles.

They were ready for their advance inland. This was slowed down when German fire began again from a network of underground fortifications. After a further fight with the remaining defenders, Courseulles was in Allied hands.

For the men in the landing parties, the order had come down that they were not to stop for colleagues hit by German fire or those swept under the waves. Each soldier was to keep going; to keep his mind on the objective of reaching land. For many, rushing past dying friends and comrades in arms was the hardest part of the operation. Leaving their buddies to die was something they could never forget.

Courseulles, a small fishing village on the Norman coast, became an invaluable link in the supply chain. From June 8, 1944, some 2,000 tonnes of supplies were shipped to Courseulles daily. This was the contribution of the Canadians.

The Government of Canada has opened the Juno Beach Centre near the beach. It has a rather sombre design, which fits the landscape. An inukshuk stands outside the building, facing toward Canada. For visitors, the tour is organized in such a way that you can recapture some of the feelings the soldiers must have experienced as they approached land. You begin the tour standing in a small space

Top to Bottom: Juno Beach Centre. Juno Beach Centre Statue. Juno Beach, Ranville Cemetery. Juno Beach, Ranville Cemetery.

with the other tourists entering the exhibition. The space is cramped, the lighting dim, and around the room are scenes familiar to anyone who has examined pictures of the landing craft and the landing itself. You soon realize that you are standing in the landing craft, and the images of the landing are illuminated on the walls around you. You hear the sounds of shelling, gunfire, and men shouting. Lights flash. The swell of the sea is all around you. After what seems like a very long time, the landing craft doors are opened, and you are free to leave, as the men would have out of the end of the vehicle. You are left with an inkling of what our soldiers must have felt with the knowledge that outside the confines of that small, cramped craft, someone was waiting to kill you.

Juno Beach, where the Canadian Army came ashore, is today a place where families lie in the sun, picnic, play games, and spend lazy summer days. Seeing this reality made me readjust the images in my mind and the feelings that I brought with me to this spot on the coast of France. I had to remind myself that when our men came, the French people had been prisoners of the Nazi regime for four years. The beaches where our men fought and died had once been where the French had picnicked and sunbathed. For them, reclaiming this beach as a place of celebration must have been necessary for their healing. I had to chase the images of this place as a place of death and horror from my mind and acknowledge the fact that the French people had reclaimed it.

This does not mean that the sacrifices of our young men are forgotten. To this day, these young men who perished to liberate people they had never met are remembered. They have a burial site. They have a stone to tell the world of their sacrifice. Each stone is the same, adorned with a maple leaf, under which the name, regiment, and age of the soldier are etched. The stones are simple and elegant.

The French government gave the Canadian government the opportunity to pick land for Canadian cemeteries. The Bény-sur-Mer Canadian War Cemetery is in the village of Bény-sur-Mer, a few kilometres inland from the beach where the Canadians landed on June 6, 1944. The cemetery is beside the village church and the community's cemetery in its courtyard. It is as if the Canadian cemetery and graves of the Canadian soldiers are an extension of the community. The location is significant for its lack of pretension and the way that it blends into the French village and countryside.

The war cemeteries in this part of France are considered part of the country of the men who lie in them. Each country is responsible for the design and upkeep of the cemetery where their countrymen are buried. To the European guides, the cemeteries reveal each country's character:

the American cemeteries are simple and elegant with crosses in large grassy fields, while the British and Canadian graveyards are separated into sections by stone walls and arches, trees, and shrubs, and the gravestones are surrounded by flowerbeds.

On the day of the landing and the next days of fighting, a number of Saskatchewan Métis soldiers were killed. These men are buried in Bény-sur-Mer. What strikes one about the land around Bény-sur-Mer is its flatness. It is on a coastal plain. The land would have been familiar and homelike for the Métis men from the Canadian Prairies.

Top to Bottom: Rows of graves, Bény-Sur-Mer Canadian War Cemetery, France. Bény-Sur-Mer Canadian War Cemetery, France.

Before leaving for France, knowing that I would be visiting the Bény-sur-Mer Canadian War Cemetery, I checked the Commonwealth War Graves Commission website to determine if any Saskatchewan Métis soldiers are buried there. I searched their list of those buried in the cemetery and found approximately twenty who could be Saskatchewan Métis. I was able to verify that twelve were Métis from my previous research. I then made a list of the ones that I knew with the location of the grave. I downloaded a copy of the map of the cemetery from the website and marked the graves of the Saskatchewan Métis soldiers on it.

In visiting Gabriel Dumont Institute before the trip, Publishing Director Karon Shmon gave me small Métis sashes to put on the graves of Métis soldiers. I was honoured to take this symbol of the Métis people to place on the graves of Saskatchewan Métis soldiers so far from home. I placed sashes on several soldiers' graves. Matthew Joseph Desjarlais was one of the Métis from the Qu'Appelle Valley reported by the Saskatchewan Métis Society to the Regina *Leader-Post* in 1942, as serving in Canada's armed forces. Rifleman Desjarlais (Lebret), son of Alex and Flora Desjarlais, was one of

Top Left to Right: Pte. Matthew Desjarlais. M. J. (Matthew Joseph) Desjarlais, Bény-Sur-Mer Canadian War Cemetery, France. B. A. (Bill Andrew) Daniels, Bény-Sur-Mer Canadian War Cemetery, France. Right: R. R. (Russell Rudolph) Isbister, Bény-Sur-Mer Canadian War Cemetery, France. Bottom: J. (Joseph) Flammand, Bény-Sur-Mer Canadian War Cemetery, France. J. B (John Baptiste) Delorme, Bény-Sur-Mer Canadian War Cemetery, France.

the sixty-five Saskatchewanians killed on D-Day, is buried at Bény-sur-Mer. In the grave beside Matthew Desjarlais is Rfn. Bill Andrew Daniels from Balcarres, also killed on D-Day. His parents, Angus and Helen Daniels, moved to the area from Montana.

Rifleman Russell Rudolph Isbister of the Royal Winnipeg Rifles was a member of the Isbister family (Mont Nebo) who lost three men in the first days of the Allied landing in France. Russell died on June 6, 1944, as did his brother Archie. They were the sons of William Joseph Dreaver and Ada Isbister. Their cousin, Vern Colin (Tony) was killed in a German counter-offensive on June 8, 1944.

Rifleman Joseph Flammand (Joe), son of Samuel and Celeste Flammand of Meadow Lake, was a Métis whose ancestors had originally settled in Fort Qu'Appelle. However, they were forced to flee to Montana, eventually homesteading in the Meadow Lake area. Joseph was killed fighting for Canada on D-Day.

Rifleman John Baptiste Delorme died on

D-Day. He came from Prince Albert and was killed with the other 359 Canadians who gave their lives that day.

Lance Sergeant Elie Victor Sinclair was among the seventy-one Métis soldiers reported by the Saskatchewan Métis Society from the Qu'appelle Valley. He was the son of Louis and Mary Sinclair, both born in Lebret. He was married to the former Marcelline St. Denis who lived in Regina at the time of his death.

Rifleman Anthony William Blondeau, 33, son of Samuel and Sarah Blondeau (Estevan), died near Caen on June 10, 1944. His brother, James Blondeau, also served in the Canadian military.

Private Soloman Kline, a member of the Canadian Scottish Regiment, had been a farmer from the St. Joseph de Dauphinais district southwest of Ituna. He was the son of Modeste Kline. When he died overseas, 34-year-old Solomon left behind his wife Elizabeth (Richard) and their four children.

Rifleman George Charles Boyer was fatally wounded by a shell splinter that pierced his side during the battle for Carpiquet. He died on July 4, 1944. George was raised on a farm at Ste. Marthe, and was listed as coming from Welby on his death notice.

Top: E. V. (Elie Victor) Sinclair, Bény-Sur-Mer Canadian War Cemetery, France.
Middle: A. W. (Anthony William) Blondeau, Bény-Sur-Mer Canadian War Cemetery, France.
Bottom Left to Right: James Blondeau. S. (Solomon) Kline, Bény-Sur-Mer Canadian War Cemetery, France. G. C. (George Charles) Boyer, Bény-Sur-Mer Canadian War Cemetery, France.

Fighting inland, Canadian troops were pitted against some of the fiercest of Hitler's forces, the 12th SS Panzer Hitlerjugend Division. At the time, this Division was made up of Hitler Youth raised and trained to support Hitler and their fatherland with absolute fanaticism. They would stop at nothing to win the day. In 1944, they did not want to be encumbered by prisoners. Prisoners would slow down their progress and would be particularly inconvenient when they were in retreat. Research has shown that prisoners were summarily executed by these boy soldiers. These executions were in direct contravention of the Geneva Convention.

Among those buried at Bény-sur-Mer is Rfn. Norman Joseph Morin of Green Lake, son of John James Morin, who was shot execution-style by the infamous 12th SS Panzer Division at the battle for Bretteville l'Orgueilleuse and Norrey-en-Bassin.

Patrick Louie Anderson died June 18, 1944. He was the 25-year-old son of Joseph and Anna Belle Anderson of Regina.

When the Royal Canadian Armoured Corps came ashore, they were the targets of the anti-tank guns of the defenders. Trooper John Donald Dumont (Lorlie), with the 6th Armed Regiment, 1st Hussars, gave his life on June 11, 1944 in one of those tanks.

Buried with the Saskatchewan Métis soldiers, alongside others from Meadow Lake, is Daniel (Mike) Fulton, whose story is told with great affection in Edward King's memoir. Fulton was with the 18th field Company of the Royal Canadian Engineers. He died July 8, 1944.

Top to Bottom: N. J. (Norman Joseph) Morin, Bény-Sur-Mer Canadian War Cemetery, France. P. L. (Patrick Louie) Anderson, Bény-Sur-Mer Canadian War Cemetery, France. J. D. (John Donald) Dumont, Bény-Sur-Mer Canadian War Cemetery, France. D. (Daniel) Fulton, Bény-Sur-Mer Canadian War Cemetery, France.

There is no doubt that other Saskatchewan Métis soldiers are at rest in the cemeteries that I visited. However, these were the ones that I was able to pay tribute to on this tour. Brigitte held the bus so that I would have time to locate the graves, secure the sashes and take pictures. As I re-entered the bus, I pinned one of the sash pins on her. She was extremely pleased, and said that she was happy to have been a part of something so important. Returning to the ship, I presented Gusta with a sash, and she too expressed her appreciation for being involved in remembering the Métis soldiers.

There was something deeply spiritual about being able to bring sashes to the fallen Métis soldiers. Other passengers on the tour wanted to be part of this experience. As I got back on the bus and after returning to the ship, people would seek me out to find out if I had been able to find the graves. People were eager to know more about the soldiers and more about the Métis. I hope I told the story well.

Bibliography

Books, CDs, and DVDs

Barkwell, Lawrence. *Metis Soldiers in the War of the 1812*. Saskatoon: Gabriel Dumont Institute, 2012. The Virtual Museum of Métis History and Culture. *http://www.metismuseum.ca/resource.php/13476*.

Barris, Ted. *Juno: Canadians at D-Day, June 6, 1944*. Toronto: Thomas Allen Publishers, 2004.

Barry, Bill with Doug Chisholm and Beth Parsons. *Age Shall Not Weary Them: Saskatchewan Remembers its War Dead*. Regina: People Places Publishing, 2005.

Bercuson, David J. *Blood on the Hills: The Canadian Army in the Korean War*. Toronto: University of Toronto Press, 1999.

______. *Maple Leaf Against Axis: Canada's Second World War*. Toronto: Stoddart Books, 1994.

______. *The Patricias: The Proud History of a Fighting Regiment*. Toronto: Stoddart Books, 2001.

Bernier, Serge. "Participation des Canadiens Français aux combats: evaluation et tentative de quantification," *Association Québécois d'histoire politque*, Vol. 3, No. 3/4 (1994): 15-24.

Bresaylor Heritage Museum Association Inc. *Bresaylor Between the Battle and the North Saskatchewan Rivers, 1882-1992*. Battleford: Marian Press Ltd., 1992.

Brode, Patrick. *Casual Slaughters and Accidental Judgments: Canadian War Crimes Prosecutions, 1944-1948*. Toronto: The University of Toronto Press, 1997.

Brown, Angus and Richard Gimblett. *In the Footsteps of the Canadian Corps: Canada's First World War 1914-1918*. Ottawa: Magic Light Publishing, 2006.

Brown, Gordon and Terry Copp, *Look to Your Front … Regina Rifles: A Regiment at War: 1944-45*. Waterloo: Laurier Centre for Military Strategic and Disarmament Studies, 2001.

Boyer, Hap (Albert). *Fiddling Métis Style*. Liner Notes. CD. Saskatoon: Turtle Island Music, 2006.

Boyer, Mary Rose. *A Metis Family Legacy: Five Men Who Went to War*. Handout: 2005.

Burns, Patricia. *They Were So Young: Montrealers Remember World War II*. Montreal: Véhicule Press, 2002.

Cave, Nigel. *Vimy Ridge*. Barnsley, South Yorkshire: Pen & Sword, 2009.

Chappell, Mike. *The Canadian Army at War. Men-At-Arms Series*. London: Osprey Books, 1996.

Christie, Norm. *The Canadians at Mount Sorrel, June 2nd-June 14th, 1916. For King & Empire: Volume VIII*. Ottawa: CEF Books, 2000.

______. *The Canadians at Vimy, April 1917, Arleux, April 28, 1917, Fresnoy, May 3, 1917. For King & Empire: Volume III*. Winnipeg: Bunker to Bunker Books, 1996.

______. *The Canadians at Ypres, 22nd-26th April, 1915. For King & Empire: Volume I*. (Revised Edition). Ottawa: CEF Books, 2005.

Cook, Tim. *At the Sharp End: Canadians Fighting the Great War, 1914 to 1916*. Vol. I. Toronto: Penguin Group, 2007.

______. *Shock Troops: Canadians fighting the Great War 1917-1918*. Toronto: Penguin Publishers, 2008.

Copp, Terry. (Ed.) *A Nation at War, 1939-1945. Essays from Legion Magazine*. Waterloo: The Laurier Centre for Military Strategic and Disarmament Studies, 2004.

______. *Cinderella Army: The Canadians in Northwest Europe, 1944-1945*. Toronto: University of Toronto Press, 2006.

______. *Fields of Fire: The Canadians in Normandy*. Toronto: University of Toronto Press, 2003.

Courtney, Vincent R. *Patricias in the Korean War.* Windsor: North American Heritage Publishing Co., 1999.

Cyr, A. Brian. *Métis Veterans of Manitoba: From Buffalo to Battlefields.* Winnipeg: Manitoba Metis Federation, 2009.

Dempsey, L. James. *Warriors of the King: Prairie Indians in World War I.* Regina: Canadian Plains Research Center, 1999.

Duck Lake History Committee. *Their Dreams—Our Memories: A History of Duck Lake and District.* Vol. I. Duck Lake, SK: 1988.

Fort Pitt Historical Society. *Fort Pitt History Unfolding.* Frenchman Butte: Fort Pitt History Society, 1985.

Gabriel Dumont Institute. *Remembrances: Interviews with Métis Veterans.* Saskatoon: Gabriel Dumont Institute, 1997.

Gaffen, Fred. *Forgotten Soldiers.* Penticton: Theytus Books, 1985.

Gilbert, Martin. *The Battle of the Somme: The Heroism and Horror of War.* Toronto: McClelland and Stewart

Granfield, Linda and Janet Wilson (Illustrator). *In Flanders Fields: The Story of the Poem by John MacCrae.* Toronto: Lester Publishing, 1993.

Granatstein, J. L. *Canada's Army: Waging War and Keeping the Peace.* Toronto: University of Toronto Press, 2002.

Granatstein, J. L. and J. M. Hitsman. *Broken Promises: A History of Conscription in Canada.* Toronto: University of Oxford Press, 1977.

Granatstein, J. L. and Desmond Morton. *Bloody Victory: Canadians and the D-Day Campaign, 1944.* Toronto: Lester Publishing Limited, 1994.

Greenhous, Brereton. *C Force to Hong Kong: A Canadian Catastrophe, 1941-1945.* Toronto: Dundurn Press, 1997.

Gresco, Audrey and Paul (Eds.) *The Book of War Letters: 100 Years of Private Canadian Correspondence.* Toronto: McClelland & Stewart, 2003.

Harrison, Julia. *Metis: People Between Two Worlds.* Vancouver: The Glenbow-Alberta Institute in Association with Douglas & McIntrye, 1985.

Hucker, Jacqueline and Julian Smith. *Vimy: Canada's Memorial to a Generation.* Ottawa: Sanderling Press, 2012.

Innes, Robert Alexander. *The Social-Political Influence of the Second World War Saskatchewan Aboriginal Veterans, 1945-1960.* MA Thesis. Saskatoon: University of Saskatchewan, 2000.

Keegan, John. *The First World War.* New York: Alfred A. Knopf Inc., 1998.

Keery, Paul. *Canada at War: A Graphic History of World War Two.* Michael Wyatt, Illustrator. Toronto: Douglas & McIntyre, 2012.

Keshen, Jeffrey A. *Saints, Sinners and Soldiers: Canada's Second World War.* Vancouver: The University of British Columbia Press, 2004.

______. *Propaganda and Censorship during Canada's Great War.* Edmonton: University of Alberta Press, 1996.

King, Edward. *The Life and Times of Edward King.* Meadow Lake: Self-Published, 2000.

Lambrecht, Eddy. *Gas Clouds Over Flanders: The Second Battle of Ypres.* York, England: G. H. Smith & Son, 2005.

Lamontagne, Manon et al (Eds.) *The Voice of the People: Reminiscences of Prince Albert's Early Citizens 1866-1895.* Prince Albert: Prince Albert Historical Society, 1985.

Lamouche, Carrielynn. "The Face of Service: Alberta Métis in the Second World War," In Ken Tingley (Ed.) *For King and Country: Alberta in the Second World War.* Edmonton: The Provincial Museum of Alberta, 1995: 33-38.

Leach, Norman. *Passchendaele: An Illustrated History. Canada's Triumph and Tragedy on the Fields of Flanders.* Regina: Coteau Books, 2008.

Mackenzie, David (Ed.) *Canada and the First World War. Essays in Honour of Robert Craig Brown.* Toronto: University of Toronto Press, 2005.

Margolian, Howard. *Conduct Unbecoming: The Story of the Murder of Canadian Prisoners of War in Normandy.* Toronto: University of Toronto Press, 1997.

Marteinson, John. *We Stand on Guard: An Illustrated History of the Canadian Army.* Toronto: Ovale Publications, 1992.

Marteinson, John and Michael McNorgan. *The Royal Canadian Armoured Corps: An Illustrated History.* Ottawa: Canadian War Museum, 2000.

McKean, Captain George B. VC, MC, MM. *Scouting Thrills: The Memoir of a Scout Officer in the Great War, 1914-18.* New York: The Macmillan Company, 1919.

Mein, Stewart, A. G. *Up the Johns! The Story of the Royal Regina Rifles.* North Battleford: Senate of the Royal Regina Rifles, 1992.

Meota History Book Committee. *Footsteps in Time: Meota, Prince, Wing, Russell, Fitzgerald, Vyner, St. Michael, Jackfish Creek, Ness, Lavigne, Cochin, Murray Lake, Scentgrass, Glenrose, Moosomin, Saulteaux, and Metinota.* Meota: Meota History Book Committee, 1980.

Métis National Council. *No Longer Forgotten: Métis Nation Veterans.* DVD. Ottawa: Bossy Jossy Productions, 2010.

Neary, Peter and J. L. Granatstein (Eds.) *The Veterans Charter and Post-World War II Canada.* Montreal and Kingston: McGill-Queen's University Press, 1998.

Nicholson, G. W. L. *Canadian Expeditionary Force 1914-1919: Official History of the Canadian Army in the First World War.* Ottawa: Queen's Printer, 1964.

Poulin, Grace. *Invisible Women: WWII Aboriginal Servicewomen in Canada's Second World War. Aboriginal Peoples and the Canadian Military: Historical Perspectives.* Kingston, 2007.

Rocanville History Committee. *Where the Prairie Lily Blows, A History of Rocanville and District.* Vol. 2. Rocanville: Rocanville History Committee, 1997.

Ross, Robert Todd. *The Supercommandos. First Special Service Force, 1942-1944: An Illustrated History*. Atglen, PA: Schiffer Military History, 2000.

Royal Canadian Legion, Saskatchewan Command. *2012 Military Service Recognition Book*. Regina: The Royal Canada Legion, Saskatchewan Command, 2012.

Saskatchewan Indian Veterans Association. *We Were There*. Saskatchewan: Federation of Saskatchewan Indian Nations, 1989.

Schreiber, Shane B. *Shock Army of the British Empire: The Canadian Corps in the Last 100 days of the Great War*. St. Catharines: Vanwell Publishing, 2005.

Shaw, Susan Evans. *Canadians at War: A Guide to the Battlefields of World War I*. Fredericton: Goose Lane Editions, 2011.

Sheffield, R. Scott. *The Red Man's on the Warpath: The Image of the "Indian" and the Second World War*. Vancouver: University of British Columbia Press, 2004.

Shore, Fred and Lawrence Barkwell (Eds.) *Past Reflects to the Present: The Métis Elders' Conference*. Winnipeg: Manitoba Métis Federation, 1997.

Stacey, C. P. *Six Years of War: The Army in Canada, Britain and the Pacific*. Ottawa: 1966.

Stevenson, Micheal, D., "The Mobolisation of Native Canadians during the Second World War," *Journal of the Canadian Historical Association*, Vol. 7, 1996: 205-226.

Summerby, Janice. *Native Soldiers, Foreign Battlefields*. Ottawa: Veterans Affairs Canada, 1993.

Todd, Loretta. *Forgotten Warriors: The Story of Canada's Aboriginal Veterans*. Videocassette. Montreal: National Film Board of Canada, 1996.

Tout, Ken. *The Bloody Battle for Tilly: Normandy 1944*. Phoenix Mill, UK: Sutton Publishing, 2000.

Vance, Jonathan F. *Death So Noble: Memory, Meaning and the First World War*. Vancouver: University of British Columbia Press, 1997.

Venne, Muriel Stanley (Ed.) *Our Women in Uniform*. Edmonton: Institute for the Advancement of Aboriginal Women, 2003.

Wheeler, Victor W. *The 50th Battalion in No Man's Land*. Ottawa: CEF Books, 2000.

Weins, Alfred. *Our Roots, La Ronge*. La Ronge: La Ronge Heritage Committee: 1981.

Willow Bunch Historical Society. *Poplar Poles and Wagon Trails: A Mosaic of Willow Bunch R. M. #42*. Willow Bunch, SK: Willow Bunch Historical Society, 1998.

Winegard, Timothy C. *For King and Kanata: Canadian Indians and the First World War*. Winnipeg: University of Manitoba Press, 2012.

Zuehlke, Mark. *Breakout from Juno: First Canadian Army and the Normandy Campaign, July 4-August 21, 1944*. Vancouver: Douglas & McIntyre, 2011.

______. *Holding Juno: Canada's Heroic Defence of the D-Day Beaches: June 7-12, 1944*. Vancouver: Douglas & McIntyre, 2005.

______. *Juno Beach: Canada's D-Day Victory: June 6, 1944*. Vancouver: Douglas & McIntyre, 2004.

______. *On To Victory: The Canadian Liberation of the Netherlands, March 23-May 5, 1945*. Vancouver: Douglas & McIntyre, 2010.

______. *Operation Husky: The Canadian Invasion of Sicily, July 10-August 7, 1943*. Vancouver: Douglas & McIntyre, 2008.

______. *Ortona*. Toronto: Douglas & McIntyre, 1999.

______. *Terrible Victory: First Canadian Army and the Scheldt Estuary Campaign, September 13-November 6, 1944*. Vancouver: Douglas & McIntyre, 2007.

______. *The Gothic Line: Canada's Month of Hell in World War II Italy*. Vancouver: Douglas & McIntyre, 2003.

______. *The Liri Valley: Canada's World War II Breakthrough to Rome*. Vancouver: Douglas & McIntyre, 2003.

Government and Archival Documents

Brady, J.P. *Jottings from a Record of Service in the North West Europe Campaign, July 9th 1944-May 8th 1945*. The Virtual Museum of Métis History and Culture. *http://www.metismuseum.ca.*

Carriere, John V. *Statement for Pierre Carriere, Regimental number L74343 from Agnes Carriere, wife of Pierre Carriere to National Métis Veterans Association.* November 15, 2001.

Directorate of History and Heritage, National Defence Headquarters. Files 92/226, 145.2W3065 (D1) and 593.065 (D4).

Gardiner, James G. Minister of the Department of National War Services to Z. M. Hamilton, Secretary, Saskatchewan Historical Society. Ottawa, May, 6, 1941. Saskatchewan Archives Board (SAB).

Government of Saskatchewan. *Towards a New Past, Volume II: Found Poems of the Métis*. Regina: Department of Culture and Youth, 1975.

Hamilton Z. M. to Flying Officer Stewart, Air Force Recruiting Headquarters. Regina, July 10, 1940. SAB: R1260 V.16.

McKay, Virginia, and Jean Carriere et al. History and Culture Report — Cumberland House. R. M. Bone fonds, University of Saskatchewan Archives. MG 240 Box 2 I. Northern Sask. Housing Needs Survey. A. General files. Cumberland House. Historical material — 1930-1958, 1969-1974 — folder 2. Database ID: 16176.

Métis National Council. *Towards a Métis Database, Elders' Workshop Report.* Ottawa: Métis National Council, 1990.

Metis Support for Gardiner (1934). SAB: R33.2, III, 37: 1-5-3.

Morin, Vital. *Testimony to the Standing Senate Committee on Aboriginal Peoples. Minutes of the Proceedings of the Standing Senate Committee on Aboriginal Peoples.* June 16, 1994.

Moses, John with Donald Graves and Warren Sinclair. *A Sketch Account of Aboriginal Peoples in the Canadian Military*. Ottawa: Department of National Defence, 2004.

National Métis Veterans Association. *Final Report National Métis Veterans Association*, December 2001.

Nilot, Nicole. Olivier Meriel, Photographer. *Juno Beach: 6 Juin 1944-June 6th 1944.* Juno *Exposition du Centre Juno Beach.* Cabourg, France: Éditions Cahiers du Temps, 2004.

Paré, Jean-Rodrique. *Post-Traumatic Stress Disorder and the Mental Health of Miltary Personnel and Veterans.* Publication No. 2011-97-E. Ottawa: Library of Parliament, 2011. Parliament of Canada. *http://www.parl.gc.ca/Content/LOP/ResearchPublications/2011-97-e.pdf.*

Senate of Canada. *(The) Aboriginal Soldier After the Wars.* Ottawa: Standing Senate Committee on Aboriginal Peoples, 1995.

______. *Minutes of the Proceedings of the Standing Senate Committee on Aboriginal Peoples.* November 15, 16, 1994.

Veteran's Affairs, Canada. *Native Soldiers: Foreign Battlefields.* Ottawa: Government of Canada, 1993.

Magazines and Journals

Adams, Claude, "Ode to the Métis Veterans," *New Breed Magazine*, March-April, 2001: 10.

Bechthold, Michael, "Canada and the Victoria" (Article and insert), Part One. *Legion Magazine*, November-December 2011: 34-35.

Bouvier, Yve, "The War Years: Vital Morin," *New Breed Magazine*, November 1983: 22.

Byers, Daniel, "Mobilising Canada: The National Resources Mobilization Act, the Department of National Defence and Compulsory Military Service in Canada, 1940-1945," *Journal of the Canadian Historical Association*, Vol. 7, 1996: 175-205.

Byrd, Dick, "The Native Soldier," *New Breed Magazine*, Fall 1994: 11.

______, "World War I Indian Soldiers," *New Breed Magazine*, May 1995: 10-11.

Boyer, Mary Rose, "A Métis Family Legacy: Five Men Who Went to War," *New Breed Magazine*, Summer-Fall, 2007: 18-27.

Campbell, Jeff, "Aboriginal Vets Gather in Saskatoon," *New Breed Magazine*, August-September 1993: 5.

Conrad, Lieutenant-Colonel John D., "*Canadian Corps Logistics During the Last Hundred Days, August-November 1918*," *Canadian Army Journal*, Vol. 8.2 (Summer 2005), 86-98.

Cuthand, John, "The War Years: Norman McAuley," *New Breed Magazine*, November 1983: 23.

Devine, Don, "Native Veterans Benefits Still Sought," *New Breed Magazine*, November 1986: 19.

Docken, Dwayne, "No Rememberance [*sic*] for Metis Soldiers," *New Breed Magazine*, Summer 1994: 4-5.

Flamont, Bruce, "Métis Veterans Gala. Excerpt from a Speech by Bruce Flamont, September 30, 2002," *New Breed Magazine*, November-December, 2002: 8-9.

Ferguson, Sue, "A War Scout's Honor: A hero's forgotten story sheds new light on Canada's role in ending the First World War," *Maclean's*, September 8, 2003. *http://www.macleans.ca.*

Granatstein, J. L., "Hong Kong: The Inside Story of Canada's Role in a Doomed Garrison," *Legion Magazine*, November-December 2011: 22-29.

Gravel, Michel with Darren Préfontaine, "François-Xavier Cardinal: Unknown Métis War Hero,"*New Breed Magazine*, March-April 2005: 20-21.

Greenfield, Nathan M., "War Crimes (Hell in Hong Kong),"*Canada's History*, December 2011-January 2012: 36-45.

Hodgson-Smith, Kathy, "Juno Beach (Charlie Fosseneuve)," *New Breed Magazine*, May-June 2003: 26-33.

______, "Métis Veterans Hold Second Annual General Assembly," *New Breed Magazine*, January-February 2003: 23-25.

______, "Métis Veterans Honoured," *New Breed Magazine*, November-December, 2002: 10-11.

______, "Solomon Goulet: Métis Veteran," *New Breed Magazine*, November-December, 2002: 13-15.

______, "The National Métis Veterans Meet in Saskatoon," *New Breed Magazine*, January-April 2002: 4-7.

______, "Traversing Holland and Belgium (Charlie Fosseneuve),"*New Breed Magazine*, May-June 2003: 34-39.

______, "Veterans Association: Métis Veterans Form National Organization to Continue to Lobby for Outstanding Compensation," *New Breed Magazine*, March-April 2001: 7-10.

______, "Who Are These Men (Charlie Fosseneuve and Francis Godon)," *New Breed Magazine*, May-June 2003: 40-41.

iCardz and the Royal Canadian Legion. *Lest We Forget: D-Day Education Cards. Canada at War*. Collectors' cards and CD-Rom. Charlottetown: 2007.

Innes, Robert Alexander. "'I'm on Home Ground Now. I'm Safe': Saskatchewan Aboriginal Veterans in the Immediate Postwar Years, 1945-1946," *American Indian Quarterly*, Summer-Fall 2004, Vol. 28, Nos. 3 &4: 685-718.

King, Edward, "Remembering My Experiences in World War II," *New Breed Magazine*, November 1990: 1-2.

Kovatch, Douglas, "Lack of Justice for Metis Vets," *New Breed Magazine*, Christmas 1999: 16-17.

Laliberte, Larry, "The War Years: Joe Amyotte," *New Breed Magazine*, November 1983: 23.

Lee, Philip, "Love's Story (War Brides: A Canadian Love Story)," *Canada's History*, December 2011-January 2012: 20-27.

Métis National Council, "Métis Veterans Honoured with Golden Jubilee Medals," *New Breed Magazine*, November-December, 2002: 3-7.

Moine, Louise, "Bells Don't Ring Anymore," *New Breed Magazine*, Fall 1994: 12-13.

New Breed Magazine, "Aboriginal Soldiers after the wars," July 1995: 18-19.

______, "Ben Henry: A Warrior's Story," November 1998: 8-10.

______, "Our Man in Korea," November-December, 1993: 16.

______, "The Aboriginal Soldier After the Wars: Standing Senate Committee on Aboriginal Peoples," May 1995: 18.

Pinay, Donna, "Daniel Pelletier — A Veteran of the Two World Wars," *New Breed Magazine*, June 1978: 2-4.

______, "In Recognition of our Veterans," *New Breed Magazine*, November 1988: 2-4.

Poitras, Leona, "Morris Joseph Poitras: Metis War Veteran," *New Breed Magazine*, November 1988: 15.

Préfontaine, Darren R., "Honouring Métis Veterans," *New Breed Magazine*, Fall 2005: 1-2.

______, "Métis Veterans: Remembrances," *The New Nation: La novel naayson*, Winter 2011: 2-3.

______, "Remembering Madame Josephte Tourond and the 1885 Resistance," *The New Nation: La novel naayson*, Summer 2010: 16-17.

Roy, Alma, "Louis Roy: Métis Veteran," *New Breed Magazine*, November-December, 2002: 12.

Sheffield, R. Scott. "Of Pure European Descent and the White Race:" Recruitment Policy and Aboriginal Canadians, 1939-1945, *Canadian Military History*, Vol. 5. [Spring 1996], No. 1: 8-15.

Simpkins, Maureen, "The Sniper in the Shadows," *The Beaver*, August-September 1998: 17-21.

Vizina, Yvonne, "Veterans Honoured!," *New Breed Magazine*, December 1998-January 1999: 14.

Walton, Jack, "Edward King: Veteran, Métis Senator & Rancher," *New Breed Magazine*, January-February 2001: 2-3.

Newspapers

Dobrucki, B. Letter to the editor, "Devil's Brigade Was Aptly Named," *National Post*, December 22, 2006, A19.

(The) *Fort Qu'Appelle Times*, "Lest We Forget: Remembrance Day. Generations of Service," November 9, 2004: B3.

_____, "Military Medal Awarded," November 9, 2004: B6.

(The) *Globe and Mail*, "Canada's Windtalkers," June 13, 2002.

Hill's Happenings, "People and the Cypress Hills," Ed. 5: 6-7.

Kalinowski, Tim, "Profile of a Legendary Early Pioneer [Bill Gunn]," *The Gull Lake Advance*, August 7, 2012: 9.

Parker, James, "Gov't disputes Metis Claim. Metis Soldiers received same benefits as others, Veterans Affairs says," Saskatoon *StarPhoenix*, February 11, 2003.

______, "Metis vets call Ottawa's treatment racist," Saskatoon *StarPhoenix*, February 10, 2003.

Powers, Ned, "Battlefield inspires a lifetime of service [Claude Petit], Saskatoon *StarPhoenix*, October 29, 2002: D1, D4.

______, "Veteran of two Wars [Leon Ferguson], Saskatoon *StarPhoenix*, September 7, 2000: C1, C4.

(The) *National Post*, "Devils get their due as US honours Canadian Soldiers," August 16, 2006.

______, "Metis vets take plight to UN," February 11, 2003.

Regina *Leader-Post*, "Metis Answer Call of Country to War," March 9, 1941.

______, "L. Sgt. Malcolm Budd" (Obituary), September 4, 1944.

______, "Metis Compile Soldier List," September 18, 1942.

______, "Metis Veterans Deserve Better," February 11, 2003.

______, "Quit Free Northland for Army," June 18, 1941.

______, "Pte. Edward Poitras" (Obituary), September 15, 1942.

______, "Pte. John Charette" (Wounded in Action Notice), October 4, 1944.

______, "Pte. Matthew Joseph Desjarlais" (Obituary), August 24, 1944.

______, "Pte. T. E. St. Germaine" (Obituary), January 6, 1942.

______, "Regina Men Now Liberated," May 7, 1945.

______, "Rfn. George Frank Allen Racette" (Wounded in Action Notice), July 26, 1944.

______, "Rfn. William Andrew Daniels" (Obituary), August 7, 1944.

______, "Rfn. Wilfrid Fayant" (Wounded in Action Notice), August 18, 1944.

______, "Saskatchewan Men Heroes in Air Blitz," July 26, 1941.

______, "Saskatchewan Soldier [August Sangret] Charged with Murder," December 7, 1942.

______, "Saskatchewan Soldiers Use Pitchforks … Help Farmers in England Harvest Crops," July 11, 1941.

______, "Sgt. Elie Victor Sinclair" (Obituary), July 4, 1944.

______, "Sgt. Raymond Joseph La Rocque" (Obituary), September 19, 1944.

______, "Wounded come home from the Italian front," April 17, 1944.

______, "24 Metis Enlist in Armed Forces," March 9, 1942.

______, "32 Now Listed Killed," August 26, 1942.

______, November 13, 1941, July 23, 1942, September 18, 1943, January 15, 1945, and July 24, 1945.

Saskatoon *Phoenix/Star-Phoenix/StarPhoenix*, "Died for His Country: Sgt. W. J. Ouelette" (Obituary), January 28, 1945.

______, "Saskatchewan Soldiers are Back from Overseas," April 16, 1945.

______, "Veterans Return," April 24, 1945.

______, "Why Are So Many Metis Enlisting?" September 16, 1916.

White, Ed, "The War for Recognition," *Western People,* November 5, 1998: 8-9.

(The) *Windsor Daily Star,* August 20, 1942.

Oral Histories

Cathy Littlejohn Oral History Collection:
Adams, Claude, in conversation, May, 2001-December, 2001 and June 25, 2001.
Aubichon, Martin and Lloyd Bishop, in conversation, November, 10, 2001.

Gabriel Dumont Institute Oral History Collection — The Virtual Museum of Métis History and Culture. *http://metismuseum.ca.*

Veterans' Interviews:
Askwith, Dorothy; Blondeau, Maurice; Bear, Roderick; Boyer, Euclide; Camponi, Ron; Carriere, William; Chayboyer, Steve; Dumont, David; Dumont, William A.; Fayant, Joe; Ferguson, Leon; Fosseuneuve, Charles; Henry, Wilfred; Hessdorfer, Cliff; King, Edward; Lavalley, Stella and Jim;

Madden, Ora; Malbeuf, Fred; McGillivary, Joe; Merrifield, Edith; Morin, Vital; Nicolas, Archie; Noname, Alfred; Pelletier, Dan, Darcy and Ivan; Pelletier, Paul; Pelletier, Peter; Petit, Claude; Petit, Norris; Pruden, Leo; Ross, Harold; Sanderson, Owen; Sayese, Lawrence; Trotchie, Clarence Joseph; and Umpherville, Charlie.

Oral History Collection:
Bishop, Alex; Nicholas, Alexandrine

Library and Archives Canada — Oral histories of the First World War: Veterans, 1914-1918.
http://www.collectionscanada.gc.ca/first-world-war/interviews/025015-1130-e.html.
Stevens, Lester, 8th Battalion.

Memory Project — Oral histories of Second World War and Korean War Veterans.
http://www.thememoryproject.com.

Delorme, Paul Henry; Petit, Claude; Samuel (née Petit), Alice Marie; Scofield, Ralph Earl; and Venne, Marie Beatrice

Tymchak, Mike.
Unpublished Oral Histories (Research for *Our Heritage: The People of Northern Saskatchewan.* Regina: Department of Northern Saskatchewan, 1975): Bishop, Alex and Sayese, William.

Online Resources and Websites

Aboriginal Veterans Honour List. *http://www.vcn.bc.ca/~jeffrey1/tribute.htm.*

Canadian Aboriginal Veterans and Serving Members Association. *http://canadianaboriginalveterans.ca/national-alliance.*

Canada at War. *http://www.canadaatwar.ca.*

Canadian Expeditionary Force Study Group. *http://www.cefresearch.com/phpBB2.*

Canadian Military Heritage Project. *http://www.rootsweb.ancestry.com.*

Canadian Great War Project. *http://www.canadiangreatwarproject.com.*

Canadiansoldiers.com. *http://www.canadiansoldiers.com.*

(The) Canadian Virtual War Memorial. *http://www.virtualmemorial.gc.ca.*

Canadian War Museum. *http://www.warmuseum.ca.*

CBC Digital Archives. *http://www.cbc.ca/archives.*

Commonwealth War Graves Commission. *http://www.cwgc.org.*

(The) Department of National Defence and the Canadian Forces. *http://www.forces.gc.ca.*

Google News. *http://news.google.com.*

Heroes Remember. Veterans Affairs Canada. *http://www.veterans.gc.ca/eng/collections/hrp/adv_search.*

Hong Kong Veterans Commemorative Association. *http://www.hkvca.ca/index.htm.*

"In memory of Fusilier Thomas Bear who died on January 13, 1945." Veterans Affairs Canada. *http://www.veterans.gc.ca/eng/collections/virtualmem/Detail/2222655.*

Legion Magazine. *http://www.legionmagazine.com.*

Library and Archives Canada. *http://www.collectionscanada.gc.ca.*

Métis Nation Veterans. *http://www.metisveterans.ca.*

Métis Veterans Memorial Monument Project (Gabriel Dumont Institute). *http://www.gdins.org/veteransmonument.*

Mitchell, Howard Cliffton. *The Wartime Exploits of Major H.C. Mitchell, MBE.* Reproduced by L. Col. Gerry Carline, CD, RCA, September 2008. University of Saskatchewan Archives. *http://www.usask.ca/archives/sli/SLI_MajorMitchellsBook.pdf.*

National Aboriginal Veterans Association. *http://www.navavets.ca.*

RCAF Airwomen. *http://www.rcafairwomen.ca.*

Reginarifles.ca. *http://www.reginarifles.ca/index.htm.*

(The) Regimental Rogue. *http://regimentalrogue.com.*

Saskatchewan Virtual War Memorial. *http://www.svwm.ca/home.htm.*

Veteran's Affairs Canada. *http://www.vac-acc.gc.ca.*

(The) Virtual Museum of Métis History and Culture. *http://www.metismuseum.ca.*

War & Peace. National Film Board of Canada. *http://www.nfb.ca/playlist/war-peace.*

(The) War Graves Photographic Project. *http://twgpp.org/index.php.*

Appendix 1: Researching Saskatchewan Métis Veterans

1. For soldiers who served during the First World War, Library Archives Canada (LAC) has digitized the attestation papers online at *http://www.collectionscanada.gc.ca/databases/cef/001042-130-e.html.* An individual signed these papers when he or she joined the military. Using an individual's name or regimental number — the identification number that the enlistee received when he or she enlisted, which remained with them for the entirety of their military service — allows researchers access to the attestation papers for First World War service members and military nurses. Information contained in these documents includes the individual's full name, which may be spelled in a variety of ways. Date and place of birth are recorded, as are the next of kin's name and address. In most, but not all, instances, the relationship to the stated next of kin is included, which provides some genealogical information. The recruits, conscripted soldiers or nurses' trades and callings and marital status are included on the attestation papers. The papers also list any former military service and the soldier's willingness to serve overseas. Often, the document lists the soldier's initial regiment. Sometimes, the soldier's discharge date from the Army is listed, as are the reasons for leaving such as being medically unfit. From the attestation paper, it is possible to learn whether the Métis soldier was a volunteer or a conscript. Further, one can determine whether he was literate as the declaration made on the attestation was signed at the time of enlisting. If the individual was illiterate, the document was signed with an "X," and there was indication on the document that the recruit had been read the form's contents. The date and place of enlistment were also listed.

   One validation of the recruit's Aboriginal ancestry is on the back page of the attestation form. The recruit's physical description is provided. Code for Aboriginal heritage was complexion, dark; eyes, brown; hair, black. His height, chest size while expanded, and girth are noted, as was his religion (a choice from those listed). Distinctive marks and marks indicating congenital "peculiarities" or previous diseases are recorded. The medical officer attested to his fitness for service and the officer of the commanding unit signed his approval of the soldier.

   This process is sometimes complicated by the varied spellings of Métis surnames. Try various spellings of a family name before giving up your search. These varied spellings were sometimes the result of recruiters not being familiar with the names and some recruits being illiterate.

Regimental numbers relate to the location where the soldiers were recruited. Knowing the regimental number of one soldier can lead you to others from the same area. Recruitment for the First World War took place in communities. Therefore, regimental numbers from an area were sequential. Regimental numbers can be cross-referenced, on the LAC website, with the known numbers to search for others from a specific community.

Most attestation papers indicate the recruit's battalion. With this knowledge, the researcher can find the recruit's campaigns. By using the regimental histories for reference, the broad story of the recruit's war experience can be documented. The military member's record can be obtained from LAC for more personal information.

2. The files of the Commonwealth War Graves Commission website (*http://www.cwgc.org*) can be searched to see if the recruit was killed in action. If a record of his death is found, then the date of death, cemetery, and place of burial can be discovered.

3. Finding that the individual died in battle takes the researcher to VAC's Canadian Virtual War Memorial (*http://www.veterans.gc.ca/eng/collections/virtualmem*), where there may be personal information and memorabilia provided by the family. Researchers can then discover a page for fallen service members in the *Book of Remembrance* where the individual's name appears through the Canadian Virtual War Memorial. When searching for fallen servicemen and women, the researcher is redirected to the VAC website (*http://www.veterans.gc.ca/eng/collections/virtualmem*). Information about fallen service personnel can be found at this link.

4. Service records for military members who served in the World Wars and in the Korean War can be obtained through LAC. Please note, however, that only First World War records have been digitized and put online. Because of privacy laws, the records of service people who served in the Second World War and in the Korean War are restricted, and can only be accessed by family members. In this instance, the service record may be requested from VAC.

5. If the Métis soldier's home community is known, it is possible for the researcher to look in local history books to see if there is a picture or perhaps a story about or by the soldier. Often, local histories have stories about service people and their families written by family members. A search of these resources, in local history reading rooms, reveals details about family and community members who went to war.

6. Newspaper searches are another source of information on killed, injured, and returning soldiers. If your community has a local newspaper that was published during the wars, they are a goldmine of stories about local heroes. Some even have indexes. The Saskatchewan Archives Board has back copies of most Saskatchewan newspapers in both its Regina and Saskatoon offices. Many newspaper articles have also been digitized in the archives section of Google News (*http://news.google.com*).

7. Returning soldiers came home to Canada on ships. Local newspapers in Eastern Canada reported all the returning ships, listed the returning soldiers and where they come from in the country. Searching these newspaper ship lists provides another source of Métis soldiers who survived the wars.

8. Much can be learned about the service members' lives by talking to family members or by speaking to the soldiers who served with them.

9. Surviving Métis soldiers can be asked for information.

10. Researching general war histories is necessary to understand the engagements that a particular soldier participated in, as well as the geography, the campaign objectives, the enemy's location, the extent of the fighting, the importance of the battle, and any evidence of individual Métis' soldiers activities.

11. Local Legion branches in Saskatchewan are a good place to locate information or memorabilia available with respect to local Métis soldiers.

12. Regimental museums and archival resources can also be searched for references to individual soldiers.

13. Finding pictures of Métis soldiers is an important aspect of telling the story. This can be done by looking at the digitized photographs available on the LAC website. These photographs can be searched by name, regiment, or location. Other photos are availablc from the Saskatchewan Archives Board and the Glenbow Archives. Family photographs may be available too. Newspaper accounts contain some photographs which can be tracked down. Legion and regimental collections are good sources for photographs.

14. After gathering as much information and resource materials as possible, a story will emerge, which will flesh out a narrative for a particular Métis individual's war service. This involves researching the official story of the units which the soldier served in.

15. The search may lead to various accounts left by Métis soldiers. Local history books are one source of information, as are oral history projects such as the Gabriel Dumont Institute's collection of Métis veterans' interviews on The Virtual Museum of Métis History and Culture. (*http://www.metismuseum.ca/browse/index.php?id=277*).

16. Writing the story is the final step. This involves taking the broad general story of the regiments and combining it with the story told by the Métis soldiers, their families, and whatever research you can find.

17. Finally, chose a format that will best tell the story.

Appendix 2: Abbreviations and Acronyms used in this Book

Able Seaman (AB)
Acting (A)
Alberta (AB)
Battery (Bty.)
Battalion (Bn.)
Belgium (BE)
Black Watch Royal Highland Regiment of Canada (BWRHRC)
Bombardier (Bmdr.)
Canada (CA)
Canadian (CDN)
Canadian Army Medical Corps (RCAMC)
Canadian Army Occupation Force (CAOF)
Canadian Army Special Force (CASF)
Canadian Armoured Division (CAD)
Canadian Engineers Corps (RCE)
Canadian Expeditionary Force (CEF)
Canadian Field Artillery (CFA)
Canadian Forestry Corps (CFC)
Canadian Forces Decoration (CD)
Canadian Garrison Regiment (CGR)
Canadian Infantry Division (CID)
Canadian Intelligence Corps (CIC)
Canadian Mounted Rifles (CMR)
Canadian Railway Troops (CRT)
Canadian Scottish Regiment (CSR)
Canadian Women's Army Corps (CWAC)
Canadian Volunteer Service Medal (CVSM)
Canadiens-Français du Nord-Ouest (CFNW)
Company (Coy.)
Company Quarter Master Sergeant (CQMS)
Conscripted (con.)
Corporal (Cpl.)
Corps of Royal Canadian Engineers (RCE)
Department of Veterans Affairs (DVA)
Depot (Dep.)
Discharged (dis.)
Distinguished Conduct Medal (DCM)
Division (Div.)

Enlisted (en.)
Europe (EUR)
Flying Officer (F/O)
Fort Harry Horse (FGH)
France (FR)
French-CDN Brigade (FCB)
Fusilier (Fus.)
Germany (DE)
Gunner (Gnr.)
His/Her Majesty's Canadian Ship (HMCS)
Hong Kong (HK)
Killed in Action (KIA)
Korean War (KW)
Independent (Ind.)
Italy (IT)
Lance (L) as in L/Cpl.
Leading Aircraftman (LAC)
Le Royal vingt-deuxième 22e Régiment (22e Reg.)/ 22e Bataillon d'infanterie (canadien français) (22e Bn.)
Library and Archives Canada (LAC)
Lieutenant (Lt.)
Lord Strathcona's Horse (LSH)
Loyal Edmonton Regiment (LER)
Machine Gun (MG)
Manitoba Regiment (MR)
Master (M) as in M/Sgt.
Member of the Order of Canada (CM)
Military Medal (MM)
Missing in Action (MIA)
Netherlands (NL)
(Northwest) (NW)
Ontario (ON)
Pilot Officer (PO)
Post-Traumatic Stress Disorder (PTSD)
Prince Albert Volunteers (PVA)
Princess Louise Fusiliers (PLF)
Princess Patricia's Canadian Light Infantry (PPCLI)
Private (Pte.)
Queen's Own Cameron Highlanders of Canada (QOCHC)
Radio Canadian Army Europe (CAE)

Re-enlisted (reen.)
Regiment (Reg.)
Regina Rifle Regiment (RRR)
Reserve (Res.)
Rifleman (Rfn.)
Royal Canadian Air Force (RCAF)
Royal Canadian Air Force Women's Division (RCAF WD)
Royal Canadian Amoured Corps (RCAC)
Royal Canadian Army Services Corps (RCASC)
Royal Canadian Dragoons (RCD)
Royal Canadian Electrical and Mechanical Engineers (RCE)
Royal Canadian Engineers (RCE)
Royal Canadian Infantry Corps (RCIC)
Royal Canadian Navy (RCN)
Royal Canadian Navy Veterans' Reserve (RCN VR)
Royal Canadian Ordnance Corps (RCOC)
Royal Canadian Regiment (RCR)
Royal North-West Mounted Police (RNWMP)
Royal Regiment of Canada (RRC)
Royal Regiment of Canadian Artillery (RCA)
Royal Winnipeg Rifles (RWR)
Sapper (Spr.)
Saskatoon Light Infantry (SLI)
Saskatchewan (SK)
Saskatchewan Light Horse (SLH)
Saskatchewan Métis Society (SMS)
Saskatchewan Order of Merit (SOM)
Saskatchewan Regiment (SR)
Schutzstaffel (SS)
Sergeant (Sgt.)
Sicily (SIC)
Sniper (Snr.)
South Alberta Regiment (SAR)
South Saskatchewan Regiment (SSR)
Squadron (Sqdn.)
Trooper (Tpr.)
United Kingdom (UK)
Veterans Affairs Canada (VAC)
Veterans Guard of Canada (VGC)
Westminster Regiment (WMR)

Winnipeg Grenadiers (WG)
Women's Royal Canadian Naval Service (WREN) (WRCNS)
Wounded in Action (WIA)
Years (yrs)

Appendix 3: Saskatchewan's Métis Soldiers of the First World War, the Second World War, and the Korean War

The following list of Métis soldiers is an ongoing and incomplete list. Doubtless, many other Métis veterans are not included below. I have compiled this list to encourage veterans and families to provide additional information to assist the Gabriel Dumont Institute in developing as complete a list of veterans as possible. If any veterans are not included in this list, please pass their names on to the Institute. If there are any inaccuracies or incomplete information relating to the veterans, please send the corrected information to the Institute.

1. Adams, Cecil George, Pte., MacDowall, **WWII**, RCAMC
2. Adams, Clarence, Pte., Sintaluta/Carry the Kettle, **WWII**, Canadian Infantry Corps, (**KIA**)
3. Adams, Claude, Sgt., MacDowall, **WWII**, CIC/Special Forces
4. Adams, Glen, Battleford, **WWII**
5. Adams, Homer, Lac Pelletier, **WWII**
6. Adams, Leonard, Lac Pelletier, **WWII**
7. Adams, Lewis Henry, Sgt./Major, Maymont, **WWII**, trained men for combat
8. Adams, Lloyd, Lt., Vawn, **WWII**, 1st CDN Parachute Bn. Paratrooper, among the first Allied troops to land on D-Day, (**KIA**, D-Day, Jun. 6, 1944)
9. Adams, Sidney Harold, Spr., Prince Albert, **WWI**, en., Mar. 20, 1916, Winnipeg, 2nd Field Troop., RCE, *504471*
10. Adams, Thomas Leslie, Ridge District, **WWII**, Army
11. Adolphe, Ernest, Touchwood, **WWII**
12. Agnew, Willard Victor, Sgt., DCM, Prince Albert, **WWI**, en., Feb. 4, 1916, Winnipeg, 44th Bn., *308700*
13. Amyotte, Albert, Lebret, **WWII**
14. Amyotte, Frank, Pte., Lebret, **WWII**, SSR, IT/FR/DE, *L-13203*
15. Amyotte, Joe, Balcarres, **WWII**
16. Amyotte (McNeil), John
17. Amyotte John, Gnr., Lebret, **WWII**, 60th/76th Field Bty./support infantry/9th Bty./17th Field Reg., UK/FR/IT (18 mos.)/BE/NL/DE, *L-35045*
18. Amyotte, Paul, L/Cpl., Lebret, **WWII**, SSR, (**WIA**, Dieppe, Aug. 19, 1942), *L-13180*
19. Anderson, Andrew William, MM, **WWI**, 107th (Winnipeg) Bn., *718531*
20. Anderson, Burns, Touchwood, **WWII**
21. Anderson, Colin Oliver, Prince Albert, **WWI**, con., Prince Albert, Oct. 20, 1917, 1st Depot (Dep.) Bn./SR, *256384*
22. Anderson, Earl, Balcarres, **WWII**
23. Anderson, Fred, Touchwood, **WWII**
24. Anderson, George, Touchwood, **WWII**
25. Anderson, Norman, Regina, **WWII**, SSR, *L-13609*
26. Anderson, Oliver, Regina, **WWII**, SSR, (**WIA**, Aug. 19, 1942), *L-13268*
27. Anderson, Patrick Louie, Rfn., **WWII**, RRR, *L-27749*
28. Anderson, William, Regina, **WWII**
29. Andrews, Lyle, Prince Albert, **WWII**
30. Arcand, Alexander, Chellwood/Green Lake, **WWI**, con., Prince Albert, Oct. 24, 1917, 1st Dep./SR, *256362*

31. Arcand, Colin, Pte., Aldina, **WWII**, SLI/RCASC, (**KIA**, Feb. 12, 1947), *L-39140*
32. Arcand, Ernest Joseph, Duck Lake, **WWI**, en., Prince Albert, Jun. 17, 1915/53rd Bn. Reg./52nd Reg. PVA, *441503*
33. Arcand, James, Duck Lake, **WWI**
34. Arcand, Joseph, Duck Lake, grandson of Patrice Fleury, **WWII**
35. Arcand, William John, Duck Lake, **WWI**, en., Camp Hughes, Sept. 25, 1915, 53rd Bn., *441473*
36. Arnault, Alfred, Meota, **WWI**, en., Battleford, Jul. 15, 1915, 65th (SK) Bn., *472114*
37. Arnault, Allan, **WWII**
38. Arnault, Charles, Waterhen/Green Lake, **WWII**, RCASC, CA/UK/IT/SC
39. Arnault, Clarence (Peter), Meadow Lake, **WWI**, en., North Battleford, (**WIA**, gassed and died on the return to Meadow Lake, 1918), *887003*
40. Arnault, Edward, Green Lake, **WWII**, **KW**
41. Arnault, Joseph, North Battleford, **WWI**, en., North Battleford, Feb. 1, 1916, 188th Bn., *887006*
42. Arnault, Norbert, Meadow Lake/Junior, **WWI**, en., North Battleford, Feb. 29, 1916, 188th Bn./233rd Bn. CFNW/178th, *887166*
43. Arneaux, Charlie, Prince Albert, Special Forces, **WWII**
44. Arnold, Charles, Meadow Lake, **KW**
45. Arnold, Fred, Meadow Lake
46. Arnold, Richard, Meadow Lake
47. Aubichon, Charles, Pte., Green Lake, **WWII**, RCASC, *L-8639*
48. Aubichon, Ernest, Green Lake, 1st CID/RRR, **KW**, *SL-4373*
49. Aubichon, Gabriel, Green Lake, **WWII**, **KW**
50. Aubichon, Joe R., Green Lake, **WWII**
51. Aubichon, Martin, Green Lake, **WWII**, RRR, German Occupation, **KW**, *SL-4373*
52. Auchibon, Ralph, Green Lake, Pte., **WWII**, SSR, (**WIA**, Foret de la Londe, Jan. 22, 1944; Groot Meer, Oct. 13, 1944; Schipbeek/Holten Apr. 8, 1945), *L-39152*
53. Aubichon, Robert, Green Lake, **WWII**
54. Aubichon, Victor, **WWII**, SSR
55. Badger, Harry, Pte., Puckahn, **WWI**, en., Prince Albert, Jul. 17, 1916, 243rd Bn., dis., medically unfit, Dec. 6, 1918, *1051104*
56. Badger, George Charles, Pte., Kamsack, WG, (**KIA**, Nov. 5, 1943), *L-13725*
57. Badgley, Dave, Kinistino, **WWII**, (**KIA**)
58. Baldhead, James L., Duck Lake, **WWII**, SSR, (**KIA**, Jul. 20, 1944), *L-74350*
59. Ballantyne, Clifford, Glen Mary, **WWII**
60. Ballantyne, H.R. **WWII**, *L-103263*
61. Ballantyne, John, Battleford, **WWII**
62. Ballantyne, Raymond, Glen Mary, **WWII**
63. Ballantyne, Ronald, Glen Mary, **WWII**
64. Ballantyne, William Douglas, Battleford, **WWI**, en., Prince Albert, Apr. 16, 1917, 243rd Bn., dis., medically unfit, Feb. 26, 1918, *1051655*
65. Ballendine, Alex, Kilwinning Siding, **WWI**, en., North Battleford, April 17, 1916, former RNWMP guide and interpreter, 232nd Bn., *1018223*, *7018223*
66. Ballendine, Donald, Battleford, **WWI**, en., Battleford, Mar. 6, 1916, 232nd Bn., *887848*
67. Ballendine, Henry, Battleford, **WWI**, en., Battleford, Dec. 6, 1915, 232nd Bn., *887803*
68. Ballendine, James, Battleford, son of Fred, **WWI**, en., Valcartier, Sept. 24, 1914, 3 yrs in 232nd Bn., formerly 22nd Bn., SLH, dis., medically unfit, Sept. 16, 1916, *15489*
69. Ballendine, James, Battleford, son of Adam, **WWI**, en., Dec. 6, 1915, 232nd Bn., SLH, Battleford, *887807*
70. Ballendine, John, Meadow Lake, **WWI**

71. Ballendine, William, Battleford, **WWI**, en., Dec. 6, 1915, Battleford, 232nd Bn./SLH, dis., medically unfit, May 25, 1917, *887802*
72. Baptiste, Edward Jean, Pte., Battleford, **WWI**, 46th Bn. (South SK)/SR/4th CDN Div., (**KIA**, Aug. 9, 1918), Vimy Memorial, *887804*
73. Baptiste, Edgar H., Battleford, **WWII**, WG, (**KIA**, Dec. 19, 1941), *L-2957*
74. Baptiste, George, Battleford, **WWI**
75. Beady, Robert
76. Bear, Agathe
77. Bear, Alex, Meadow Lake, **WWII**
78. Bear, Andrew, Buchanan, **WWI**, en., Prince Albert, Dec. 2, 1915, 107th Bn., *886086*
79. Bear, Douglas Bertie, Glen Mary, **WWI**, con., Winnipeg, Jun. 7, 1918, 1st Dep. Bn./MR, *4070720*
80. Bear, G. A., **WWII**, *L-602076*
81. Bear, Gilbert James, Pte., Fort à la Corne, **WWI**, en., Feb. 22, 1916, 107th Pioneer Bn., *886412*
82. Bear, Gilbert, Puckahn, **WWI**, en., Prince Albert, Mar. 15, 1917, 249th (SK) Bn., *1069560*
83. Bear, Joe, Round Lake Mission/Whitewood, **WWI**, en., Moosomin, Mar. 21, 1917, 249th (SK) Bn., *1069595*
84. Bear, Robert, Round Lake Mission/Whitewood, **WWI**, en., Feb. 17, 1917, 249th (SK) Bn., *1069464*
85. Bear, R. T., Pte., **WWII**
86. Bear, Roderick, Glen Mary, **WWII**, RRR
87. Bear, Sidney
88. Bear, Stanley, Horseshoe Bend, **WWII**, SLI
89. Bear, Thomas, Fus., Meadow Lake, **WWII**, PLF/11th Independent (Ind.)/(MG Coy.)/RCIC, (**KIA**, Jan. 13, 1945), *L-2944*
90. Bear, Walter, Prince Albert, **WWII**
91. Beatty, Tom, **WWII**
92. Beatty, Walter, **WWI**
93. Beaudry, Joe O., Rfn., Meadow Lake, **WWII**, RRR, *L-27867*
94. Beaulieu, Alexis Raphael, Pte., son of Octavie and Magloire, Ft. Qu'Appelle, **WWII**, FMR/RCIC, (**KIA**, Jul. 26, 1944), *L-13207*
95. Beddome, Henry Alexander, Red Deer Hill, **WWI**, con., Prince Albert, Oct. 13, 1917, *269050*
96. Beed, Cecil Edgar, L/Cpl., Mont Nebo, **WWII**, SSR, (**KIA**, Jul. 20, 1944), *L-86913*
97. Beeds, Alfred Edward, Pte., Shell Lake, **WWII**, QOCHC, (**KIA**, Jul. 21, 1944), *L-86891*
98. Belanger, George S., **WWII**, SSR, (**WIA**, Verrières Ridge, Jul. 19-25, 1944)
99. Belanger, John George, Rfn., North Battleford, **WWII**, RRR, (**KIA**, Feb. 12, 1945), *L-27814*
100. Belanger, Joseph, Battleford, **WWI**, en., Battleford, Jan. 19, 1915, 16th/22nd/232nd Bn./SLH/FGH, UK/FR/BE, *887805*
101. Belanger, Leo Joseph, Tpr., Île-à-la-Crosse, **WWII**, RCAC, *L-3911*
102. Belcourt, Edward, Gnr., Saskatoon, **WWII**, dis., March 1, 1944, unable to meet required military standards, *L-19793*
103. Belcourt, George, Strasbourg, **WWII**
104. Bell, Roy Munroe, Welwyn, **WWI**, en., Winnipeg, Mar. 28, 1917, Ind. Forestry Coy., *2183375*
105. Bellegarde, Kathleen
106. Bellegarde, Maurice, Rfn., Abernathy, **WWII**, RRR, (**KIA**, Nov. 3, 1944), *L-64684*
107. Bellegarde, Vince. J., Rfn./A/CQMS, **WWII**, RRR
108. Bellegarde, W. A., **WWII**, *L-22221*
109. Bellrose, Albert, Touchwood, **WWII**, SLI
110. Bellrose, George, Touchwood, **WWII**

111. Bennett, George, Lily Plain, **WWI**, en., Prince Albert, Dec. 18, 1915, 53rd Bn., *440427*
112. Bennett, Henry Alexander, Lily Plain, **WWI**, en., Prince Albert, Mar. 19, 1917, Forestry Dep., *2188471*
113. Bennett, Thomas, Lily Plain, **WWI**, en., Prince Albert, Jul. 16, 1917, CFC, *2193049*
114. Berard, Alexander Ambroise, Willow Bunch, **WWII**
115. Berard, Leonard, Willow Bunch, **WWII**
116. Bigman, Alexander, Pte., Battleford, **WWI**, en., Prince Albert, Mar. 3, 1916, 46th Bn. (South SK)/SR/4th CDN Div., FR, (**KIA**, Feb. 6, 1917), *886430*
117. Bird, A., **WWII**, SLI
118. Bird, Benjamin Harold, Cpl., St. Louis/Tiger Hills, **WWII**, SSR, (**KIA**, Nieuwpoort, Sept. 11, 1944), *B440056*
119. Bird, Charlie, Rfn., Foxford, **WWII**, RRR, (**KIA**, D-Day, Jun. 6, 1944), *L-27934*
120. Bird, Clifford, Meadow Lake
121. Bird, Duncan, **WWII**
122. Bird, George J., Meadow Lake
123. Bird, Gustav, **WWII**
124. Bird, Richard
125. Bird, Thomas Vivian, Rfn., Red Deer Hill, **WWII**, RWR, (**KIA**, D-Day, Jun. 6, 1944), *L-105169*
126. Birmingham, Mick, Saskatoon, **WWII**
127. Birmingham, Reg, Saskatoon, **WWII**
128. Birmingham, Roy, Saskatoon, **WWII**
129. Bishop, Albert, Green Lake, **WWII**
130. Bishop, Alcide, Meadow Lake
131. Bishop, Joe A., Green Lake, **WWII**
132. Bishop, Lloyd, Meadow Lake
133. Blondeau, Anthony William, Rfn., Estevan, son of Samuel and Sarah, **WWII**, RRR, FR, (**KIA**, Jun. 10, 1944), *L-100534*
134. Blondeau, Edward, Lebret, **WWII**
135. Blondeau, Edward Gilbert, Bienfait, **KW**, **Suez Crisis**, 20th CDN Field Corps/RCE, *SL-92972*
136. Blondeau, Frederick, Lebret, **WWI**, en., Aug. 1, 1916, Regina, 212th Bn., *261707*
137. Blondeau, James G., Lebret, **WWII**
138. Blondeau, James Hyacinthe, Gnr., Regina **WWII**, RCA, UK/Mediterranean/NW EUR, *L-66568*
139. Blondeau, Joe, Lebret, **WWII**, served in Winnipeg for 4 yrs
140. Blondeau, John Louis, Cpl., Shand, **WWI**, con., Estevan, Nov. 10, 1917, 1st Dep. Bn./SR, *256495*
141. Blondeau, Joseph Clément, Qu'Appelle Valley/Shand, **WWI**, con., Nov. 8, 1917, Estevan, 1st Dep. Bn./SR, *259986*
142. Blondeau, Louis L., Airman 1st Class, Estevan, **WWII**, RCAF, 436th RCAF Sqdn., (**KIA**, Mar. 14, Burma, 1945), *R-270976*
143. Blondeau, Maurice, Fort Qu'Appelle, **WWI**, con., Nov. 6, 1917, Regina, 1st Dep. Bn./SR, *256490*
144. Blondeau, Maurice, Fort Qu'Appelle, **KW**, CASF/129 AA Bty./1st Royal CDN Horse Artillery, *SL-4020*
145. Blondeau, Napoleon, Qu'Appelle
146. Blondeau, Peter, Estevan, **WWI**, en., Apr. 23, 1918, Regina, *2683770*
147. Blondeau, Peter James, Pte., Fort Qu'Appelle, **WWII**, EUR
148. Blondeau, Reuben, Outram/Estevan, **WWII**, (**POW**, Dieppe, Aug. 19, 1942-April 1945)
149. Blondeau, Reuben Israël Urbain (Ben), Snr., Estevan, **WWI**, con., Estevan, Nov. 10, 1917, UK/FR, *25829072*

150. Blondeau, Walter Raymond, Pte., Estevan, **WWII**, SSR, (**WIA**, Dieppe, Aug. 19, 1942; **POW**, released May 16, 1945), *L-13567*
151. Blondeau, W. B., Outram, **WWII**
152. Bloomfield, Frederick, Fir Ridge, **WWI**, en., Oct. 31, 1916, 243rd Bn., (**WIA**, died, Victoria Hospital, Prince Albert, Feb. 6, 1917), *1051377*
153. Bloomfield, Henry, The Pas/Cumberland House, **WWI**, en., Apr. 18, 1916, Winnipeg, 197th OS Bn., *913412*
154. Bloomfield, Simeon, Pte./Rfn., Cumberland House, **WWII**, SSR/RRR, UK/FR/BE/NL/DE, (Combat Stress Reaction)
155. Blyne, Allan, Qu'Appelle Valley, **WWII**
156. Boileau, Alexis, Lebret, **WWII**
157. Boileau, Joseph Rene, Pte., Lebret, **WWI**, 5th Bn./SR, (**KIA**, Sept. 27, 1916), Vimy Memorial, *424091*
158. Boivin, Frank, Touchwood, **WWII**
159. Boucher, Louis Henri, CVSM and Clasp, St. Louis, **WWII**, RCAF, Jun.1941-Mar.1945, CA/Alaska, *J-51339*
160. Boucher, Renald, St. Louis, **WWI**, con., Prince Albert, Nov. 2, 1917, 1st Dep. Bn./SR, *268945*
161. Bourassa, Edward, Meadow Lake
162. Bourassa, Émile, **WWII**
163. Bourassa, Fred, Albertown/Duck Lake, **WWI**, en., Mar. 27, 1917, Saskatoon, 232nd Bn., *1018723*
164. Bourassa, John, Shellwood/Prince Albert, **WWI**, en., Sept. 18, 1915, Camp Hughes, 53rd Bn, en., Mar. 21, 1916, Prince Albert, 188th Bn., *441665*, *886492*
165. Bourassa, Joseph, Meadow Lake, **WWI**
166. Bourassa, Joseph, Prince Albert, **WWI**, *886491*, alias Charley Harris Laourx, 5th Bn., 1st CID/SR, (**KIA**, Aug. 9, 1918), Vimy Memorial, *1051529*
167. Bourassa, Leo, Pte., Meadow Lake, **WWII**, RCA, 1943-45, EUR/UK/FR/DE, *L-107865*
168. Bourassa, Lousaint, Meadow Lake, **WWI**
169. Bourassa, Toussaint, Albertown, **WWI**, 51st Bn./14th Bn., *472190*
170. Bourassa, Wilfred, Meadow Lake
171. Bourassa, William, Albertown, **WWI**, 243rd Bn., *1051146*
172. Bourassa, William, Meadow Lake, **WWI**
173. Bourassa, William John, **WWI**, **WWII**
174. Boxeur (Boxer), Émile Louis, Willow Bunch, **WWII**, Army, Apr. 1942-Nov. 15, 1945, UK/EUR, *L-100151*
175. Boxeur, Louis, Willow Bunch, **WWI**, 233rd Bn. CFNW, *1021257*
176. Boyer, Alan, Cochin, **WWII**
177. Boyer, Albert, Cochin, **WWII**
178. Boyer, Albert, Meadow Lake, **WWI**
179. Boyer, Albert "Hap," Battleford, **KW**, **Peacetime service**
180. Boyer, Albert Jules, Battleford, **WWI**, 232nd Bn., *887806*
181. Boyer, Alcide, Cochin, **WWI**, *3088134*
182. Boyer, Ambroise Meadow Lake, **WWI**
183. Boyer, Ana, Cochin, **WWII**
184. Boyer, Anaclet, Battleford **WWI**, 232nd Bn., *1018083*
185. Boyer, Claude, Cochin
186. Boyer, Edmond Joseph, Batoche, **WWI**, 243rd Bn., *1051130*, **WWII**
187. Boyer, Edward A., **KW**
188. Boyer, Émile, Cochin, **WWII**
189. Boyer, Ernest, Marcelin, **WWI**, 1st Dep. Bn./SR, *3354980*
190. Boyer, Ernest Joseph, Tpr., Bienfait, **WWII**, RCD, UK, EUR, *L-10079*

191. Boyer, Euclide, Pte., St. Laurent, **WWII**, BWRHRC, (**WIA**, Aug. 5, 1944), *L-74738*
192. Boyer, George Charles, Rfn., Yorkton, **WWII**, RRR/RWR, (**KIA**, Jul. 4, 1944), *L-61850*
193. Boyer, George William, AB, Souris Valley/Macoun, **WWII**, RCN, aboard the aircraft carrier, *HMS Nabob* when it was torpedoed in the North Sea on Aug. 22, 1944, *V-40994*
194. Boyer, Homidas (Harry), Springbourne/Duck Lake, **WWI**, 15th Res. Bn., (**KIA**, Sept. 9, 1917), *1051625*
195. Boyer, J. B., Meadow Lake, **WWI**
196. Boyer, Jean-Baptiste, Cochin, **WWII**
197. Boyer, John Baptist, St. Louis, **WWI**, 1st Dep. Bn./SR, *269683*
198. Boyer, John-Baptiste, Duck Lake, **WWI**, 232nd Bn., *887807*
199. Boyer, Joseph, St. Laurent de Grandin, **WWI**, 1st Dep. Bn./SR
200. Boyer, Joseph Earnest, Souris Valley, Estevan, **WWII**
201. Boyer, Lauretta, Cochin, **WWII**, RCAF WD
202. Boyer, Maurice, Cochin, **WWII**, RCAF
203. Boyer, Mick, Cochin, **WWII**
204. Boyer, Nick (Ancelet), Meadow Lake, **WWI**
205. Boyer, Rita, Cochin, **WWII**, RCAF WD
206. Boyer, Tony, Cochin, RCAF, **KW**, 1952-
207. Boyer, Wilfrid (Fred) W., Pte., Bear Lake, **WWI**, 128th Bn./SR/5th CDN Div., (**KIA**, May 14, 1918), *1018696*
208. Brabant, Alexander, Lebret, **WWI**, 128th Bn./SR/5th CDN Div., *781805*
209. Brabant, Allan, Regina, **WWII**
210. Brabant, Clement Henry, Le Ross, **WWI**, 107th/243rd, *718896*
211. Brabant, Frank (Francis), Pte., Balcarres, **WWI**, 195th Bn./SR/5th CDN Div., (**KIA**, Apr. 9, 1917), *908091*
212. Brabant, George, Lebret, **WWI**, 128th Bn./SR/5th CDN Div., *782442*
213. Brabant, George, **WWII**
214. Brabant, Henry, Lebret, **WWII**
215. Brabant, Leo, Lebret, **WWII**
216. Brabant, Napoleon, Katepwa, **WWI**, 217th/229th Bn., *1009512*
217. Brabant, Tobias, Lebret, **WWI**, 128th Bn./SR/5th CDN Div., *781798*
218. Brady, James Patrick Jr., Gnr./Gun signaler, St. Paul, AB/Cumberland House/LaRonge, **WWII**, 50th Bty./4th Medical Reg./RCA
219. Branconnier, Victor, Fish Creek/Batoche, **WWI**, 214th/243rd, *267650*
220. Brass, Ed, Touchwood, **WWII**
221. Brass, Lawrence, Cochin, **WWI**, 232nd, *1018703*
222. Brass, R.A., Pte., **WWII**, WG, *L-13726*
223. Brass, William, Lestock, **WWI**, 249th (SK) Bn., *1069412*
224. Brass, William, Prince Albert, **WWI**, 37th Bn./CDN Field Artillery, *301381*
225. Brass, Wilma
226. Bremner, Peter, Deer Lodge, **WWI**, *3355086*
227. Brown, Bernie, **KW**
228. Brown, David Allen, Red Deer Hill, **WWI**, *441752*
229. Brown, Harvey, **KW**
230. Brown, Percy Victor, MacDowall, **WWI**, *3353012*
231. Buck, Gordon Adam, Pte., The Pas/Cumberland House, **WWI**, 10th (CGR) (Military Police), *3348885*
232. Buck, John Alfred, Prince Albert, **WWI**, 1st Dep./MR, *3348184*
233. Budd, Francis, Pte., Cumberland House, **WWI**, 8th Res. Bn.
234. Budd, George Lloyd, Cumberland House, **WWII**, SSR, (**KIA**, Verrières Ridge, Jul. 20, 1944), *L-39125*

235. Buller, Edward Matheson, Tpr., Saskatoon, **WWII**, 1st Hussars/6th Armoured Reg./ RCAC, (**KIA**, Feb. 26, 1945), *L-103899*
236. Burnouf, Francis Xavier, Pte., Île-à-la-Crosse, **WWII**, *L-106628*
237. Bushey, E., Maple Creek, **WWII**
238. Buskey, John, **WWII**, RCASC, IT, *L-8697*
239. Cadotte, Archibald, Kamsack, **WWI**, 11th Res. Bn., *888012*
240. Cadotte, Joseph, Rfn., Cumberland House, **WWII**, 1st Bn., QORC, **KW**, after Armistice, 1st Rifle Bn./RWR
241. Cadotte, Louis Pierre, Cumberland House, **WWI**, 233rd Bn. (CFNW)/26th (New Brunswick) Bn./178th, *1021158*
242. Caisse, Joseph, Île-à-la-Crosse, **WWI**, 233rd Bn. (CFNW), *1021299*
243. Cameron, James, Mont Nebo, **WWI**, 243rd Bn./28th (NW) Bn., *1051139*
244. Campbell, Joseph Howard, Glen Mary, **WWI**, *234658*
245. Campbell, Theodore Colin, Prince Albert, **WWI**, *204120*
246. Campbell, Thomas Hughes, Prince Albert, **WWI**, 105th Reg. (Bugle Band), *472930*
247. Camponi, Angelo Eugene (Tony), Saskatoon, **KW**
248. Camponi, Clarence, Pte., **WWII**, PPCLI
249. Camponi, Leonard, Saskatoon, CASF, Armoured Reg., **KW**
250. Camponi, Louis, **WWII**, LSH
251. Camponi, Ronald James, Saskatoon, **WWII**, en. underage with fake baptismal records, dis., en. when of age, Japanese Theatre, **KW**, RCAC
252. Camponi, William, Cpl., **WWII**, IT
253. Canada, Charles, Pte., Cumberland House, **WWI**, 233rd Bn. (CFNW), (**KIA**, Dec. 27, 1916), *1021160*
254. Canada, Moise, Cumberland House, **WWII**
255. Caplette, Dennis, Delmas, **WWI**, 232nd Bn., *1018272*
256. Caplette, Eli, Cpl., Meadow Lake, **WWII**, RRR, **KW**, *SL-4508*
257. Caplette, Jean (John) Baptiste, Willow Bunch/Delmas, **WWI**, 65th (SK) Bn., *472196*
258. Caplette, Jean-Marie, Willow Bunch, **WWII**, SSR, (**WIA**, Falaise, Aug. 16, 1944), *L-64581*
259. Caplette, John, Duck Lake, **WWI**
260. Caplette, Joseph Alexander, Welby, **WWI**, 1st Dep. Bn./SR, *268605*
261. Caplette, Lawrence, Meadow Lake
262. Caplette, Paul, Cpl., **KW**, RRR, *SL-4508*
263. Cardinal, François-Xavier, MM, Bunglass, **WWI**, 1st Dep. Bn./SR, *1263581*, *258340*
264. Cardinal, Louis John, Pte./Gnr., Qu'Appelle, **WWII**, RCA, *L-59852*
265. Cardinal, Peter, North Battleford, **WWI**, 188th Bn., *887018*
266. Cardinal, William (Bill), Ituna, **WWII**, May 16, 1941, dis., injured
267. Carey, Lawrence, **WWII**, 5th Field, Ambulance Driver, IT, *L-91515*
268. Caron, Alfred, Batoche, **WWI**, 1st Dep. Bn./SR, *269767*
269. Caron, Anthony, Pte., **WWII**, *L-153049*
270. Caron, F. A., Spr., Saskatoon, **WWII**
271. Caron, I. A., Batoche, **WWII**
272. Caron, Robert, Batoche, **WWI**, 46th Bn. (South SK)/SR/4th CDN Div., *474235*
273. Caron, W. Wilfred, L/Cpl., **WWII**, CDN Provost Corps (Military Police)/SSR, *L-8125*
274. Carriere, Alphonse, Tpr., Cumberland House, **WWII**, Lake Superior Reg. (Motor)/16th/22nd/232nd Bn., SLI
275. Carriere, David Henry, Spr., **WWII**
276. Carriere, Elie, Pte., Meota, **WWI**, 1st Dep. Bn./SR, *256670*
277. Carriere, George, Cochin, **WWII**
278. Carriere, Henry, Cochin, **WWII**, PPCLI, IT
279. Carriere, James, Cumberland House, **WWI**, 1st Dep. Bn./MR, *4670763*
280. Carriere, James Edward, Cpl., Cumberland House, SLI, **WWII**, *L-2880*

281. Carriere, Jonas, Pte., Cumberland House, **WWI**, 1st Dep. Bn./MR, *4070763*
282. Carriere, Joseph Denis, Gnr., Jackfish Lake, **WWII**, RCA, (**KIA**, Jun. 26, 1946), *M-608264*
283. Carriere, Pierre, Sgt./Snr., Cumberland House, **WWII**, SSR, UK/FR/BE, (**WIA**, Orbec, Aug. 23, 1944, Bray Dunes Plage, Sept. 15, 1944), *L-74343*
284. Carriere, Roland, Cochin, **WWII**
285. Carriere, Victor Vernon, Pte., Cumberland House **WWII**, RRC, (**KIA**, Oct. 24, 1944), *H-14906*
286. Carriere, William J., Tpr., Cumberland House, **WWII**, 16th/22nd SLH/RCAC, *L-39119*
287. Chaboyer, Alexandre, L/Cpl., Cumberland House, **WWI**, 22e Bn., UK/FR/BE, *1021171*
288. Chaboyer, Charlie, Pte., Cumberland House, **WWI**, Special Service Coy./Military Div. 10, *3307551*
289. Chaboyer, Cyril, L/Cpl., Cumberland House, **WWII**, RCASC/SLI (MG)/2nd CID, UK/NW EUR
290. Chaboyer, Frank Émile, L/Cpl., Cumberland House, **WWII**, SSR/FMR, UK/NW/EUR, *L-2968*
291. Chaboyer, Patrick, Spr., The Pas/Cumberland House, **WWI**, CRT, *1021153*
292. Chaboyer, Steve, Cumberland House
293. Champagne, John, Touchwood, **WWII**
294. Champagne, Thomas, Touchwood, **WWII**
295. Charette, David, Midnight Lake, **WWI**, 218th Bn., *256032*
296. Charrette, Ed, Cpl., Lebret, **WWII**
297. Charette, John, Rfn., Balcarres, **WWII**, RRR/RWR
298. Charrette, Moses Joseph Arthur, Midnight Lake, **WWI**, 1st Dep. Bn./SR, *260434*
299. Chartier, Ann, Buffalo Narrows, **KW**
300. Chartier, Eugene, Île-à-la-Crosse, **WWI**, 1st Dep. Bn./SR, *3356342*
301. Chartier, Thomas, Buffalo Narrows, **KW**
302. Chartrand, Willow Bunch, **WWI**
303. Chartrand, Alcide (Joe), Big Muddy, **WWII**, First CDN Army/Eighth Army (UK), IT/FR/BE/NL
304. Chartrand, C. J., Cpl., Big Beaver, **WWII**
305. Chartrand, Frank, Meadow Lake, **WWII**, RCASC, Driver
306. Chartrand, Harry A., Pte., Meadow Lake, **WWII**
307. Chartrand, Henry, Meadow Lake
308. Chartrand, Jake, Bengough, **WWII**, (War bride)
309. Chartrand, Joe, Meadow Lake, **WWII**
310. Chartrand, Max, Meadow Lake, **WWII**
311. Chartrand, Peter (Pierre), Willow Bunch/Bengough, **WWI**, 1st Dep./SR, *1263644*
312. Chatelaine, Louis, Meadow Lake, **WWI**, 1st Dep./SR, 260761
313. Chatelain(e), Peter (Sandy) Meadow Lake, **WWI**, 53rd Bn., **WWII**, Res. Army, *441517*
314. Chatelaine, Robert, **WWII**
315. Collins, Alphonse, Meadow Lake, **WWII**, RRR, Truck Driver, EUR
316. Collins, Antoine (Tony), Meadow Lake, **WWI**, 225th Bn./46th Bn. (South SK)/SR/4th CDN Div., (**KIA**, Aug. 15, 1918), *931649*
317. Collins, Edward, Pte., Meadow Lake, **WWI**, CRT, (**KIA**, Aug. 10, 1918), *259420*
318. Collins, Edward James, Broadview, **WWI**, con., 1st Dep. Bn./SR, *259426*
319. Collins, Fred, Rfn., Meadow Lake, **WWII**, RRR, (**WIA**, D-Day, June 6, 1944, returned to the front)
320. Collins, Joseph Alfred (Fred), Rfn., **WWII**, RRR/B Coy., D-Day, *L-74046*
321. Collins, Maxime, PPCLI, **KW**/DE (1950s), CDN Airborne Reg.
322. Collins, Ronald, Meadow Lake, **KW**, PPCLI
323. Cook, Alfred, Spr., Cumberland House, **WWI**, CRT, *4070656*
324. Cook, Colin, Pte., Cumberland House, **WWI**, 1st Dep. Bn./MB/CRT, *4070762*

325. Cook, Daniel, Pte., Cumberland House, **WWI**, 1st Dep./MR, *4070864*
326. Cook, Gilbert Lewis, Rfn., Prince Albert, **WWII**, RRR/RCIC, (**KIA**, Oct. 10, 1944)
327. Cook, Henry, Duck Lake, **WWII**
328. Cook, Howard, Duck Lake, **WWII**
329. Cook, John Henry, Pte., Cumberland House, **WWII**, PPCLI/PVA
330. Cook, Lawrence, Cpl., Cumberland House, **WWII**, RRR, (**WIA**), UK/NW EUR, *L-104964*
331. Cook, Victor, Prince Albert, **WWI**, No.1 Overseas Training/RCASC, *511505*
332. Corrigal, Colin, St. Louis, **WWII**, RCASC
333. Corrigal, Cyprian, **WWII**
334. Corrigal, Harry Allan, Arran, **WWI**, 1st Dep. Bn./MB, *2380231*
335. Corrigal, Joseph Edward, Prince Albert, **WWI**, 230th Btn./CFC, *1013175*
336. Corrigal, Lawrence, Red Deer Hill, **WWI**, 1st Dep. Bn./SR, *4090088*
337. Corrigal, Thomas, Prince Albert, **WWI**, 11th Bn./52nd Reg. (PVA), *22001*
338. Cox, Leonard, St. Louis
339. Cromartie, D. A., Signalman., Birch Hills, **WWII**
340. Cromartie, Peter Andrew, Pte., Prince Albert/Halcro, **WWI**, 188th Bn., (**KIA**, Apr. 26, 1917), *886118*
341. Cromarty, Hilliard, Prince Albert/Birch Hills, **WWI**, 188th Bn./53rd Bn., *886115*
342. Cromarty, N. V., Prince Albert, **WWII**
343. Crow, Joseph, Kamsack, **WWI**, 46th Bn. (South SK)/SR/4th CDN Div./188th Bn., (**KIA**, Mar. 22, 1917), *888014*
344. Cunningham, Stewart, Birch Hills, **WWI**, 1st Dep. Bn., *288604*
345. Cunningham, Vern, Yellow Creek, **WWII**
346. Cuthand, Adam, **WWII**, Radar Technician/Instructor, Labrador, *L-10745*
347. Cyr, Raymond, **WWI**, 192nd Bn., *898276*
348. Cyr, Raymond, Jackfish Lake, AB, **WWII**, RCN, *HMCS Hespeler*, **Peacetime service**, RCN VR
349. Daigneault, Thomas Jr., Île-à-la-Crosse, **WWII**
350. Daniels, Alex J., Pte., Balcarres, **WWII**, IT
351. Daniels, Angus, Pte., File Hills, **WWI**, 217th Bn./229th Bn., *1009517*
352. Daniels, Bill (William) Andrew, Balcarres, **WWII**, Rfn., RRR, (**KIA**, D-Day, Jun. 6, 1944), *L-28053*
353. Daniels, Charles, Pte., Meadow Lake/South Battleford, **WWI**, 243rd Bn./28th (NW) Bn., (**KIA**, Nov. 10, 1918), *718433*
354. Daniels, Ed, Balcarres, **WWII**
355. Daniels, Hector, Pte., Balcarres, **WWI**, CEF, *1263584*
356. Daniels, Henry, Regina Beach, **WWI**
357. Daniels, Joseph Edward, Balcarres, **WWII**, FR
358. Daniels, William, Rfn., **WWII**, RWR
359. Daniels, Victor, **WWII**
360. Danskin, Earl, Traynor, **WWII**
361. Danskin, Ed, Traynor, **WWII**
362. Daze, Albert, Cpl., Lebret, **WWII**
363. Decoteau, Alexander, Pte., Battleford, **WWI**, 49th Bn., BE, (**KIA**, Oct. 30, 1917), *231462*
364. Decoteaux, Alfred, Battleford, **WWI**, 232nd Bn., *887851*
365. Deegan, James, Fort Qu'Appelle, **WWI**, 152nd Bn./Central ON Reg., (**KIA**, May 25, 1916), *925783*
366. Deegan, Peter, Fort Qu'Appelle, **WWI**, *925089*
367. Deese, Harold, Hudson Bay, **WWII**
368. Deguerre, Antoine, Meadow Lake, **WWI**, *1018043*
369. Deguerre, John, Meadow Lake/Battleford, **WWI**, 28th (NW) Bn./232nd Bn., (**KIA**, Oct. 5, 1918), *887812*

370. Deguerre, Joseph, Meadow Lake, **WWI**, 28th (NW) Bn.
371. Deguerre, Joseph Damase, Albertown/Battleford, **WWI**, 232nd Bn., *887852*
372. Deigan, St. Pierre
373. Delaronde, Alec, Meadow Lake
374. Delaronde, Archie, Mont Nebo, **WWII**
375. Delaronde, Étienne, Meadow Lake, **WWI**, 1st Dep. Bn./SR, *259262*
376. Delaronde, Gaspard Louis, Cpl., St. Laurent de Grandin
377. Delaronde, Josh, Meadow Lake
378. Delaronde, Lawrence, Mont Nebo, **WWII**
379. Delaronde, Louis Joseph, Battleford/Meadow Lake, **WWI**, 232nd Bn., *887829*
380. Delorande, Paul Edward, Cpl., Meadow Lake, **WWII**, SLI (MG), (**KIA**, May 18, 1944), *L-110279*
381. Delaronde, Raymond N., Cpl., Meadow Lake, **WWII**, RCR, *L-106008*, **KW**, RCASC
382. Delaronde, Roy N., **WWII**, RRR, *L-106008*
383. Delaronde, Verona, Mont Nebo, **WWII**
384. Delbert, John, Cpl./Sgt., **WWII**, en. Jun. 21, 1940, D. Coys/Support Coy/RRR, D-Day/FR/BE/NL/DE, *L-27775*, M/Sgt./Lt./Cpt., **KW**, **Peacetime service**, dis, Aug. 25, 1969
385. Delorme, Alma, Lebret, **WWII**, RCAF WD
386. Delorme, Amable, Pte., **WWII**, SSR, (**WIA**, Sandhatten, Apr. 30, 1945), *L-55473*
387. Delorme, Daniel, Crooked Lake, **WWI**, 249th (SK) Bn., *1069651*
388. Delorme, James, Yellowgrass, **WWI**, 1st Dep. Bn./SR, *4090364*
389. Delorme, John-Baptiste, Rfn., Prince Albert, **WWII**, RRR, (**KIA**, Jun. 6, 1944), *L-27332*
390. Delorme, Joseph, Crooked Lake, **WWI**, *718703*
391. Delorme, Louis Thomas (Tommy), Sgt./Flight Engineer, Lebret, **WWII**, RCAF/106 RAF Sqdn., (**KIA**, May 30, 1943), *R-70694*
392. Delorme, Paul Henry, Pte., Rocanville, **WWII**, SSR, (**POW**, Dieppe, Aug. 19, 1942-Apr. 20, 1945), *L-27002*
393. Delorme, Thomas, LAC, Lebret, **WWII**, (**KIA**, May 30, 1943)
394. Demarais, Alex, **WWII**
395. Demerais, Alexander, Winton, **WWI**, con., Oct. 27, 1917, 1st Dep. Bn./SR, *260133*
396. Denny, Albert, Lac Pelletier, **WWII**
397. Deschambeault, Joseph Henry, Pte., Cumberland House, **WWI**, RCASC, *1021151*
398. Deschamps, Edward, Montana/Edmonton, AB/Onion Lake, **WWI**, 232nd Bn., *887811*
399. Desjarlais, Edward, Pte., Jasmin, **WWI**, 188th Bn., *888145*
400. Desjarlais, Ernest, Lebret, **WWII**
401. Desjarlais, Ernest, Touchwood, **WWII**
402. Desjarlais, Fred, Lebret, **WWII**
403. Desjarlais, George, Rfn., Lestock, **WWII**, RRR
404. Desjarlais, Henry Ronald (Ron), Fort Qu'Appelle, **KW**, **UN Peacekeeping**
405. Desjarlais, Jimmy, Rfn., Fort Qu'Appelle, **WWII**, RRR, *L-27135*
406. Desjarlais, Joseph, **WWI**, 107th Bn., no records, *718540*
407. Desjarlais, Joseph Ernest Anthony (Tony), Prince Albert, QORC/RCAF, **KW**
408. Desjarlais, J. W., Lebret, **WWII**
409. Desjarlais, Leo, **WWII**
410. Desjarlais, Len
411. Desjarlais, Louis Henry, Pte., Fort Qu'Appelle, **WWII**, RCOC, *L-7443*
412. Desjarlais, Matthew Joseph, Lebret, **WWII**, RRR, (**KIA**, Jun. 6, 1944), *L-27606*
413. Desjarlais, M., Gnr., Battleford, **WWII**
414. Desjarlais, T., Qu'Appelle Valley, **WWII**
415. Desjarlais, Urbain, Lestock, **WWII**
416. Desjarlais, Wilbert, **WWII**, Dieppe

417. Desjardins, Leo Joseph, Spr., **WWII**, en. Saskatoon, May 19, 1942, EUR, dis., Mar. 26, 1946, *L-91640*
418. Desjardins, P.E., **WWII**, SAR, *L-104221*
419. Desmarais, Alex, Lebret, **WWII**
420. Desmarais, Frederick, LaFleche, **WWI**, 1st Dep. Bn./SR, *277639*
421. Desmarais, Joseph Alfred, Neptune, **WWI**, 1st Dep. Bn./SR, *269810*
422. Desmerais Sidney, L/Cpl., Paynton, **WWI**, 232nd Bn., *1018004*
423. Desnomie, George, Balcarres, **WWII**, RRR
424. Dionne, Edmond, Meadow Lake, Spr., **WWII**, RCE, (**KIA**, Jul. 19, 1942), *L-41134*
425. Dionne, Elie Phillip, Alida, **WWI**, 1st Dep. Bn./SR, *258072*
426. Dionne, John, L/Bmdr., Sturgeon Landing, **WWII**, 5th Medium Reg./RCA
427. Dionne, Phillip, Tpr., Sturgeon Landing, **WWII**, Elgin Reg./25th CDN Armoured Delivery Reg./RCAC, (**KIA**, May 1, 1943), *H-100244*
428. Dobie, Doug, Bresaylor, **WWII**, RRR
429. Donald, Johnnie, Prince Albert, **WWI**, en., Dec. 27, 1917, 230th Bn./CFC, *886131*
430. Dorion, Gabriel, Spr., Cumberland House, **WWII**, RCE/4th CAD/RCAC, *L-74438*
431. Dorion, Jean-Baptiste, The Pas/Cumberland House, **WWI**, 233rd Bn. (CFNW)/26th (New Brunswick) Bn., UK/FR/BE, (**WIA**, Passchendaele, gassed, died from war wounds, Jan. 26, 1924), *1021175*
432. Dorion, John Gregory, Cumberland House, **WWI**, 242nd Bn./28th (NW) Bn.,*1069126*
433. Dorion, Thomas, Cumberland House, **WWII**
434. Dorion, William, Cumberland House, **WWII**
435. Dreaver, Alex, **WWII**
436. Dreaver, George, Spr., Regina, **WWI**, 107th Pioneer Bn.
437. Drever, R. A., **WWII**, *L-103954*
438. Dubois, Henry, Coderre/Montana, 1st Dep. Bn./SR, *277403*
439. Dubois, John, Wadena/Lanigan/Batoche, **WWI**, 214th Bn., (**KIA**, Aug. 10, 1918), *267223*
440. Dubois, Marshall, Wadena, 214th Bn., *267099*
441. Ducharme, Alexander, St. Laurent de Grandin, FCB, **WWI**
442. Ducharme, Douglas, Jackfish/Vawn, **WWI**, 232nd Bn., *1018374*
443. Ducharme, Georges Napoleon, South Makwa, **WWII**, **KW**, PPCLI/RCIC (**KIA**, Jan. 12, 1952), *SL-109363*
444. Ducharme, John, Cut Arm Creek/Boissevain, MB, **WWI**, 1st Dep. Bn./MR, *2128944*
445. Ducharme, Joseph, Battleford/Meadow Lake, **WWI**, 232nd Bn./FCB/CEF, *2320396*
446. Ducharme, Percy William, MM, Meadow Lake/Swift Current, **WWI**, 42nd (CDN Infantry) Bn., (**KIA**, Aug. 8, 1918), *441863*
447. Ducharme, Peter William, Midnight Lake, **WWI**, en., Aug. 1915, dis., Feb. 21, 1916, 61st Bn., *472280*
448. Ducharme, Peter, Meadow Lake, **WWI**, 16th Bn., (**KIA**, Aug. 11, 1918)
449. Dufour, Charles, Touchwood, **WWII**
450. Dufour, Mike, Touchwood, **WWII**
451. Dufresne, Harry, Fort Pitt, **WWI**, en., Nov. 29, 1916, 197th Bn., *913794*
452. Dufresne, William, Fort Pitt, **WWI**
453. Dumais, Charles, Duck Lake, **WWII**
454. Dumais, Oscar, Willow Bunch
455. Dumont, Aimé, **WWII**
456. Dumont, Allen, Duck Lake, **WWII**
457. Dumont, August, Carlton, **WWI**, 65th (SK) Bn., *472656*
458. Dumont, David, Sgt., Duck Lake, **WWII**, RR
459. Dumont, David J., Cpl., Meota, **WWII**, RR, *L-27763*
460. Dumont, Gabriel, St. Laurent de Grandin, **WWI**, 1st Dep./SR, *269444*
461. Dumont, George, Duck Lake, **WWII**

462. Dumont, Harris, Pte., Duck Lake, **WWI**, 1st Dep. Bn./SR, *472647*
463. Dumont, Herman, Saskatoon, **WWII**
464. Dumont, J. Louis, Duck Lake, **WWII**
465. Dumont, John Donald, Trp., Lorlie, **WWII**, 6th Armoured Reg./1st Hussars/RCAC, FR, (**KIA**, murdered by the SS, Jun. 11, 1944), *L-36995*
466. Dumont, John Louis, Hoey, **WWI**, 1st Dep. Bn./SR, *276761*
467. Dumont, Joseph, Assiniboia, **WWI**, 1st Dep. Bn./SR, *4090260*
468. Dumont, Lawrence, Duck Lake, **WWII**
469. Dumont, Lewis, Goulee, **WWI**, 1st Dep. Bn./SR, *4090398*
470. Dumont, Louis, Cypress Hills, **WWI**
471. Dumont, Martin, St. Laurent de Grandin, **WWI**, 1st Dep. Bn./SR, *260345*
472. Dumont, Prosper, Duck Lake, **WWII**
473. Dumont, S., Duck Lake, **WWI**
474. Dumont, William A., L/Cpl., Lloydminster, **WWI**, RCAC/16th/22nd/232nd Bn./RRR, *L-39117*
475. Dumont, Willard, Sgt., Maple Creek, **WWII**, SSR, (War bride)
476. Duquette, John O.
477. Durocher, Alexis, Pte., Île-à-la-Crosse, **WWI**, 22e Bn., UK/FR, *1021297*
478. Durocher, Ambroise J., **KW**, PPCLI, *SL-4222*
479. Durocher, John, Meadow Lake
480. Durocher, Stan, Beauval, **WWII**, IT
481. Durskin, Larry
482. Emond, Denis, Meadow Lake
483. Emond, Omer, Meadow Lake
484. Esther, Beatrice, **WWII**
485. Falcon, Angus, Rfn., Meadow Lake, **WWII**, RRR, served: Sept. 1, 1941-Nov. 1945, *L-27236*
486. Falcon, Harvey Victor, Rfn., Battleford, **WWII**, RRR, served: Sept. 1, 1941-Nov. 1945, *L-27153*
487. Falcon, Henry, Rfn., Battleford, **WWII**, RRR, D-Day, *L-27154*
488. Falcon, James, Battleford
489. Falcon, Jean-Baptiste (John) G., **WWII**, SLI (MG), Dunkirk/Dieppe/Africa, (**WIA**), *L-1851*
490. Falcon, Joseph Tobias, **WWII**, Lake Superior Reg. (Motor), *H-45872*
491. Falcon, Willie, Battleford, **WWII**, 4th CAD, Armoured Car Driver for a colonel
492. Falster, Stanley, Touchwood, **WWII**
493. Favel, Harry, Touchwood, **WWII**
494. Favel, Joe, Meadow Lake
495. Fayant, ___, Duck Lake, **WWII**
496. Fayant, Donald Joseph, Sintaluta, **WWII**, **KW**, *SB-13493*
497. Fayant, Elise, Lac Pelletier, **WWII**
498. Fayant, François (Frank), Batoche, **WWI**, 1st Dep. Bn./SR, *269710*
499. Fayant, G., Pte., Batoche, **WWII**
500. Fayant, Joseph, Ituna, **WWI**, 1st Dep. Bn./SR, *256812*
501. Fayant, Joseph, Pte., Balcarres, **WWII**
502. Fayant, Joseph Alexander, Pte./Cpl./Sgt., Sintaluta, **WWII**, RCE/NL, *L-111734*, **KW**, *L-800139*
503. Fayant, Marshall Alexander, Qu'Appelle Valley
504. Fayant, Peter George, Sintaluta, **WWII**, en. underage, Jul. 1942 and served in the RCA Reserves until Sept. 1944, *L-421310*, reen., May 8, 1945, *L-111865*
505. Fayant, Peter Joseph, Sintaluta, **WWII**, **KW**
506. Fayant, William Joseph, Sintaluta, **WWII**
507. Fayant, Wilfrid, Rfn., Indian Head, **WWII**, RRR
508. Ferguson, Ernest, Saskatoon, **WWII**, LSH, welder, **KW**

509. Ferguson, Ernie, Duck Lake, **WWII**
510. Ferguson, Frank, Rfn., North Battleford, **WWII**, RRR, (**KIA**, Dec. 1, 1042), *L-27145*
511. Ferguson, George, Duck Lake, **WWI**, (**WIA**), *886594*
512. Ferguson, Joseph, Wood Mountain, **KW**
513. Ferguson, Leon, Sgt., Duck Lake, **WWII**, WMR/Special Forces, 22nd Reg., IT/NL, PPCLI, *L-54596*, **KW**
514. Ferguson, R. Joseph, **WWII**
515. Ferguson, Walter, Duck Lake, **WWII**
516. Ferguson, William, Touchwood, **WWII**
517. Fiddler, Alexander, Pte., **WWII**, Army, British 8th Army, SIC/IT/UK/EUR, *L-8725*
518. Fiddler, Allan, Kamsack, **WWI**, 197th Bn., *888015*
519. Fiddler, Arthur, **WWII**
520. Fiddler, Clarence, Meadow Lake, **KW**
521. Fiddler, Ernest, Meadow Lake, **WWII**, Flamethrower
522. Fiddler, Frank, Meadow Lake
523. Fiddler, George R., Meadow Lake, **WWII**, RWR, (**WIA**, Jul. 4, 1944, Oct. 6, 1944), *L-105121*
524. Fiddler, Harvey, Touchwood, **WWII**
525. Fiddler, John, Kinistino, **WWII**
526. Fiddler, John Theodore, Rfn., Meadow Lake, **WWII**, RRR, served: 2 yrs, *L-27829*
527. Fiddler, Joseph, Glen Mary/Horseshoe Bend, **WWII**
528. Fiddler, Joseph, Meadow Lake, **WWII**, served: 2 yrs, *L-8174*
529. Fiddler, Lawrence, Meadow Lake, **WWII**, *L-54956*
530. Fiddler, Leona, Meadow Lake, **WWII**, RCAF WD
531. Fiddler, Marion, Kinistino, **WWII**
532. Fiddler, Robert, Meadow Lake, **WWII**, served: 2 yrs
533. Fiddler, Tom, Horseshoe Bend, **WWII**
534. Fiddler, William M. Jr., Meadow Lake, **WWII**, **KW**, served: 20 yrs
535. Fidler, Alex, Glen Mary, **WWI**
536. Fidler, Alexander McLeod, Perdue/Flett Springs/Prince Albert, **WWI**, *1051243*
537. Fidler, A. N., Snr., **WWI**
538. Fidler, Ben, Ethelton, **WWI**, 1st Dep. Bn./SR, *463784*
539. Fidler, Cecil, Rfn., Cumberland House/Flin Flon, **WWII**, RRR, (**KIA**, Aug. 28, 1943), *L-27915*
540. Fidler, George Philip, Batoche, **KW**, **Peacetime service**, PPCLI, en. Regina, Jan. 28, 1952, dis. Mar. 2, 1958, *SL*-4776
541. Fidler, H. R., Mont Nebo, **WWII**
542. Fidler, John, Kinistino, **WWII**
543. Fidler, John D., **KW**
544. Fisher, Armand (Hambone), Pte., Lebret, **WWII**, WMR/PPCLI, *K-3774*, **KW**, PPCLI, Paratrooper, *SK-377*
545. Fisher, Arthur, Touchwood, **WWII**
546. Fisher, Charles William, Batoche, **WWI**, *886595*
547. Fisher, Émile, Spr., Lestock, **WWII**
548. Fisher, Edward Jr., Pte., Fort Qu'Appelle, **WWII**, PPCLI
549. Fisher, Edward Sr., Pte., Fort Qu'Appelle, **WWII**, SSR, UK, *L-13447*
550. Fisher, Émile
551. Fisher, Ernest, Lestock, **WWI**, en., Nov. 11, 1917, 1st Dep. Bn./SR, *4090484*
552. Fisher, Ernest, Duck Lake, **WWII**
553. Fisher, Eugene, Duck Lake, **WWI**
554. Fisher, Eugene, Duck Lake, **WWII**
555. Fisher, George, Touchwood, **WWII**
556. Fisher, Harry J. (Tuppy), Pte., Qu'Appelle Valley, **WWII**

557. Fisher, James, Gnr., Lebret, **WWII**, 5th Anti-Tank Reg./RCA, NL/DE, *L-105051*, **KW**, *SL-105051*
558. Fisher, Jean, Lebret, **WWII**, RCAF WD
559. Fisher, Joe, Lt., Duck Lake, **WWI**
560. Fisher, Joseph, MM, DCM, Duck Lake, **WWI**, *440702*, **WWII**
561. Fisher, Joseph, Rfn., Duck Lake, **WWII**, RRR, served: Sept. 1, 1941-Nov. 1945, *L-27333*
562. Fisher, Jules, Duck Lake, **WWI**, en., Oct. 19, 1915, 65th (SK) Bn., dis., medically unfit, Mar. 14, 1917, *472507*
563. Fisher, Lawrence, Fort Qu'Appelle, **WWII**, (**WIA**, Mook Hill), *L-107944*, **KW**, QORC, served: 1951-54
564. Fisher, Leo, **WWII**
565. Fisher, Marie James, Duck Lake, **WWII**
566. Fisher, Maurice
567. Fisher, Raymond, Lebret, **WWII**
568. Fisher, Velma, Lebret, **WWII**, RCAF WD
569. Fisher, William, Duck Lake, **WWII**
570. Fisher, William, Lebret, **WWI**, **WWII**
571. Flamand, Thomas, Battleford, **WWI**, en., Feb. 2, 1916, 232nd Bn., *887816*
572. Flamand, William James, Battleford, **WWI**, en., Dec. 24, 1915, 232nd Bn., *887815*
573. Flammand, E. J., Regina, **WWII**
574. Flammond, David, Meadow Lake
575. Flammond, Joseph, Rfn., son of Pierre, Meadow Lake, **WWII**, RRR, D-Day, (**KIA**, Jun. 6, 1944), *L-67293*
576. Flammond, J. P., **WWII**, SSR
577. Flamont, John, **WWII**
578. Flett, Wesley John, Pte., Melfort, **WWII**, LER, (**KIA**, Feb. 17, 1944), *K-48239*
579. Fleury, Clément, Duck Lake, **WWI**, en., Aug. 25, 1915, 65th (SK) Bn./46th Bn. (South SK)/SR/4th CDN Div., (**KIA**, Jul. 17, 1920), *472374*
580. Fleury, Conrad René, L/Sgt., Green Lake, **WWII**, RRR, D-Day/NL, (**KIA**, Apr. 22, 1945), *L-27865*
581. Fleury, Owen Jeanor, Meadow Lake/St. Laurent de Grandin, **WWI**, en., Feb. 16, 1918, 1st Dep. Bn./SR, *1263592*
582. Folstrum, Charles, Touchwood, **WWII**
583. Folstrum, Stanley, Touchwood, **WWII**
584. Foster, Jack, Lebret, **WWII**
585. Fosseneuve, Alexander, Pte., Cumberland House, **WWI**, en., Nov. 11, 1917, 1st Dep./MR, *4070663*
586. Fosseneuve, Charles, Gnr., Cumberland House, **WWII**, RCAC/13th Field Reg./RCA, UK/NW EUR, *L-74646*
587. Fosseneuve, Felix A., Pte., Cumberland House, **WWI**, en., May 30, 1918, 260th Bn./CDN Rifles/Siberian Expeditionary Force/10th CGR, *3346877*
588. Fosseneuve, Gordon, Cumberland House, **WWII**, EUR/NL/DE
589. Fosseneuve, John Frank, Gnr., Cumberland House, **WWII**, 13th Field Reg./RCA, UK/NW EUR, *L-74666*
590. Fosseneuve, Pierre Gordon, Gnr., Cumberland House, **WWII**, 13th Field Reg./RCA, *L-74645*
591. Foulds, Frank James, Prince Albert, **WWI**, en., Apr. 20, 1918, 1st Dep. Bn./SR, *259274*
592. Frank, Paul, **WWII**
593. Fraser, Gertrude Clara, Birch Hills, **WWII**, WRCNS, *WC-449*
594. Fulton, Daniel (Mike), Spr., Meadow Lake, **WWII**, 18th Field Coy./RCE, (**KIA**, Jul. 8, 1944), *L-74653*
595. Fulton, Dick, Meadow Lake

596. Fulton, Victor, Meadow Lake
597. Gamble, David
598. Gardiepy, Charles, Duck Lake, **WWII**
599. Gardiepy, Nelson, Duck Lake, **WWII**
600. Gardiepy, Remi, Duck Lake, **WWII**
601. Gardiepy, Romuald, Duck Lake, **WWII**
602. Gardippe, Joseph, North Battleford, **WWI**, 197th Bn., *887044*
603. Gardippi, Noel, Duck Lake, **WWI**, en., Feb. 7, 1916, 65th (SK) Bn., *474016*
604. Gardippy, Edward, Duck Lake, **WWI**, en., Jan. 1915, *424465*
605. Gardipy, Harvey
606. Gardipy, Hilliard
607. Gardipy, Louis
608. Gardipy, Ronald James
609. Gardypie, H., **WWII**, RWR, dis. (sick), Oct. 9, 1944, *L-19843*
610. Gardiner, John, Duck Lake, **WWII**
611. Gardiner, Leo, Pte., Battleford, **WWI**, SR/5th CDN Div., (**KIA**, May 24, 1918)
612. Gaudry, Alfred, Willow Bunch, **WWI**, 233rd Bn. (CFNW), *1021261*
613. Gaudry, Amible, Willow Bunch, **WWI**, 1st Dep. Bn./SR, *260701*, **WWII**
614. Gaudry, Ernest, Willow Bunch
615. Gaudry, Gordon, Willow Bunch, **WWI**
616. Gaudry, Joseph Albert, Willow Bunch, **WWI**, 1st Dep. Bn./SR, *258763*
617. Gaudry, Peter Andrew (P.A.), Pte., Regina, **WWII**, SSR, (**POW**, Dieppe, Aug. 19, 1942-May 12, 1945), *L-12491*
618. Gaudry, Ulderic George, Quantock, **WWI**, 1st Dep. Bn., *3353758*
619. Gautche, Mark
620. Gehl, Daniel, Meadow Lake
621. Gehl, Gerald, Meadow Lake
622. Gerard, Baptiste, Meadow Lake, **WWI**
623. Gerard, John, Green Lake, **WWI**, 46th Bn. (South SK)/SR/4th CDN Div., (**KIA**, Feb. 14, 1917), *472611*
624. Gervais, Arnold Joseph, Makwa, **WWII**, RCASC, *L-41763*, **KW**, *SL-4343*
625. Gervais, Arthur, Meadow Lake
626. Gervais, L., Pte., Loon Lake
627. Gervais, Max, Meadow Lake, **KW**
628. Gervais, Peter, Cochin
629. Gervais, P. J., Pte., Meota
630. Gesard, John, Meadow Lake, **WWI**
631. Giraud, Marcel, **WWII**
632. Gladue, Charles
633. Gladue, Frederick, Rfn., Meadow Lake, **WWII**, RRR, served: Sept. 1941-Nov. 1945, *L-27866*
634. Goodin, Roger, Weyburn, **WWII**
635. Goodin, Tom, Meadow Lake, **WWI**, en., Apr. 1, 1917, 1st Dep. Bn./SR, *4090248*
636. Gordon, Albert, **WWI**, **WWII**
637. Gosselin, Alfred, Willow Bunch, **WWI**, en., May 17, 1918, 1st Dep. Bn./SR, *259963*
638. Gosselin, Robert, Pte., **WWII**, SSR, (**WIA**, Gendringen, Mar. 31, 1945), *L-605485*
639. Gosslin, John, Willow Bunch, **WWII**, RCAF
640. Gouldhawk, Robert Thomas, Mont Nebo, **WWI**, 1st Dep. Bn./SR, *259021*
641. Goulet, Moise A., Cpl., Cumberland House, PPCLI
642. Goulet, Solomon, L/Sgt., Cumberland House, **WWII**, QOCHC (MG), FR/BE/NL/Luxembourg/DE, (**POW**, 11 mos.), *L-106871*

643. Greenleaf, William, Pte., Cumberland House, **WWI**, en., Nov. 11,1916, 78th WG Bn./CFC, *1069129*
644. Grey, Malcolm, Sintaluta, **WWI**, 5th Bn./SR, (**KIA**, Sept. 26, 1916), *105604*
645. Gunn, William (Bill) James, Spr., Swift Current, **WWI**, con., en. Regina, Jun.10, 1918, *277486*
646. Guthrie, Robert Sr., **WWI**
647. Haggerty, Jules, Meadow Lake, **WWI**
648. Haggerty, Julius, Willow Bunch, **WWI**, 1st Dep. Bn./SR, *258092*, **WWII**
649. Halcro, Alfred Charles, Halcro, **WWI**, en., Nov. 11, 1916, 1st SK Dep., *4090087*
650. Halcro, George, Prince Albert, **WWI**, en., Sept. 23, 1914, militia, 11th Bn., *21973*
651. Halcro, Joseph Lawrence, Prince Albert, **WWI**, en., Jul. 1918, 1st Dep. Bn./SR, *3354887*
652. Halcro, L. C., Prince Albert, **WWII**, RWR, sick Jul. 6, 1944, *L-105632*
653. Halcro, Samuel, Meadow Lake, **WWI**
654. Halcro, T. W., Prince Albert, **WWII**
655. Halcrow, Angus, Pte., The Pas/Pelican Narrows, **WWI**, en., Apr. 24, 1915, Prince Albert, 52nd Reg. (PVA)/28th (NW) Bn., (**KIA**, Dec. 25, 1916), *441159*
656. Halcrow, George Cypron, The Pas/Cumberland House, **WWI** en., Aug. 23, 1915, 78th WG Bn./238th Bn./CFC, *1038050*
657. Halcrow, Samuel, Île-à-la-Crosse, **WWI**, 10th Bn./AR, (**KIA**, May 1, 1917), *473220*
658. Hallett, Stanley, Prince Albert, **WWI**, 1st Dep. Bn./SR, *1021134*
659. Hallett, William, Prince Albert/South Battleford, **WWI**, en., Mar. 24, 1916, 188th Bn., *886511*
660. Halliday, Robert Harmon, L/Cpl., Battleford, **WWII**, RWR/RCIC, (**KIA**, Jul. 4, 1944), *L-104342*
661. Hamilton, Gregg, Major, Qu'Appelle Valley, **KW**
662. Hansen, Bill, Saskatoon, **WWII**
663. Harkiss, Ernest Peter, **WWII**
664. Harrington, Alexander, Regina, **WWII**
665. Hayden, Alexander, Rocanville, **WWI**, con., Regina, Nov. 20, 1917, 1st Dep. Bn., *260393*
666. Hayden, David, **WWII**, SSR, (**WIA**, Verrières Ridge, Jul. 19-25, 1944), *L-36945*
667. Heglend, Travis
668. Henderson, Norman, **WWII**
669. Henney, Eric
670. Henney, Jack
671. Henry, Benjamin, Prince Albert, **WWII**, 15th Field Artillery/RCA, UK/FR/NL
672. Henry, George, Prince Albert, **KW**
673. Henry, Harry, Rfn., Prince Albert, **WWII**, RWR, (**WIA**, Apr. 22, 1945), *L-105904*
674. Henry, Joe (Marcel), Prince Albert, **WWII**
675. Henry, Thomas, Prince Albert, **WWII**
676. Henry, Wilfred, Pte., Humboldt, **WWII**, RRR/Highland Light Infantry of CA, served: Sept. 1941-Nov. 1945, *L-24062*
677. Hessdorfer, Cliff, Wakaw, **WWII**, **KW**, *SL-109062*
678. Hessdorfer, Henry, **WWI**
679. Hodgson, Arthur, Saskatoon/Prince Albert, **WWI**, en., Nov. 6, 1915, 54th Bn., (**KIA**, Nov. 16, 1917), Menin Gate, Ieper, BE, *472571*
680. Hodgson, Augustus, Melfort, **WWI**, en., Sept. 21, 1914, 9th Bn./2nd Bn., (**KIA**, Nov. 16, 1917), Menin Gate, Ieper, BE, *18953*
681. Hodgson, James Lawrence Stanley, St. Louis, **WWII**, RRR, (**KIA**, D-Day, Jun. 6, 1944), *L-27966*
682. Hodgson, John Davies, Silver Grove/Prince Albert, **WWI**, en., Mar. 31, 1917, 249th (SK) Bn., *1069759*
683. Hodgson, Lewellyn Victor, Saskatoon/Birch Hills, **WWI**, en., Oct. 21, 1916, 68th/249th (SK) Bn., *472377*
684. Hodgson, William Joseph, Birch Hills, **WWI**, en., Mar. 29, 1915, 52nd Reg. (PVA), *440714*

685. Hourie, Alfred James, Birch Hills, **WWI**, en., Nov. 18, 1916, dis., medically unfit, Jul. 31, 1918, *701161*
686. Hourie, Colin, Melfort/Athelton/Prince Albert, **WWI** en., Aug. 16, 1918, 1st Dep. Bn./SR, *3355996*
687. Hourie, Jerry, L/Cpl., DCM, MacDowell/Lily Plain, **WWI**, en., Mar. 2, 1917, *268115*
688. Hourie, Norman, MacDowell/Lily Plain, **WWI**, 214th Bn., invalided to CA from the CDN Military Hospital, Bramshott, *268104*
689. Hourie, Robert James, Prince Albert, **WWI**, en., Dec. 27, 1915, militia, 188th Bn., *886165*
690. Hourie, W. A. C., **WWII**, SLI, *L-1264*
691. Hurton, Jean, **WWII**, Army
692. Hurton, John, **WWII**, Army
693. Inkster, Andrew, Battleford, **WWI**, en., Apr. 7, 1916, 232nd Bn., *887821*
694. Inkster, J. M., Pte., Paynton
695. Inkster, John Colin, L/Cpl., **WWI**, 31st Bn./AR, (**KIA**, Sept. 1916), *79221*
696. Inkster, Kenneth J., Pte., Weekes, **WWII**, WG, (**POW**, Osaka, **KIA**), *L-2849*
697. Inkster, Robert Henry, Battleford, **WWI**, en., Jan. 24, 1916, 232nd Bn., *887820*
698. Inkster, Rudolph Thomas, Clouston, **WWI**, con., 1st Dep. Bn./SR, Oct. 27, 1917, *260113*
699. Innes, Brian
700. Irvine, Alexander McKenzie, Halcro, **WWI**, en., Dec. 12, 1915, *886176*
701. Irvine, Charles Frederick, Pte., Red Deer Hill, **WWI**, 46th Bn. (South SK)/SR/4th CDN Div., (**KIA**, Mar. 28, 1917), *886525*
702. Irvine, Henry James, Red Deer Hill, **WWI**, en., Oct. 25, 1917, invalided to CA from CDN Military Hospital, (**WIA**, died, Nov. 23, 1918), *269087*
703. Irvine, Stanley Charles, Pte., Halcro, **WWI**, en., Apr. 1, 1916, 46th Bn. (South SK)/ SR/4th CDN Div., *886548*
704. Ionel, John, Spr., Ormiston, **WWII**, 6th Field Coy./RCE, (**KIA**, murdered, Jun. 11, 1944), *B-142277*
705. Isbister, Archie, Mont Nebo, **WWII**, RRR, (**KIA**, D-Day, Jun. 6, 1944), *L-105938*
706. Isbister, Cecil R., Mont Nebo, **WWII**, RCA, FR
707. Isbister, Dick, Mont Nebo, **WWI**
708. Isbister, E. L., Pte., **WWII**, SSR, (**WIA**, Aug. 28, 1945), *L-27519*
709. Isbister, George Robert, Mont Nebo, **WWI**, en., Jun. 28, 1916, 232nd Bn., *1018544*
710. Isbister, Gilbert, Mont Nebo, **WWII**
711. Isbister, James, Touchwood, **WWII**
712. Isbister, Peter, Mistawasis, **WWI**, en., Jun. 24, 1918, 1st Dep. Bn./SR, *3353295*
713. Isbister, R., Cpl., **WWII**, SIC/IT
714. Isbister, Robert Richard, Mont Nebo, **WWI**, en., Mar. 9, 1918, 52nd Reg. (PVA)/1st Dep. Bn./SR, *440727*
715. Isbister, Russell Rudolph, Mont Nebo, **WWII**, RWR, (**KIA**, Jun. 6, 1944), *L-105571*
716. Isbister, Rylie, Battleford, **WWII**
717. Isbister, Thomas Edward, Mont Nebo, **WWI**, en., May 14, 1918, 1st Dep. Bn./SR, *260841*
718. Isbister, Vern Colin (Tony), Rfn., Mont Nebo, **WWII**, RRR/RCIC, (**KIA**, Jun. 8, 1944), *L-27546*
719. Jacobson, Tony Orville, Norquay, **WWII**, Royal Rifles of CA, HK, *L-50094*
720. Janvier, Cheyenne
721. Janvier, Leo, Onion Lake, **WWII**
722. Jeannotte, Joseph J., Cpl., MM, Lebret, **WWII**, SSR, (**POW**, Dieppe, Aug. 19, 1942-May 8, 1945), *L-13201*
723. Jenson, William, Duck Lake, **WWI**
724. Jerome, Joe, Prince Albert, **WWII**, RRR
725. Jerome, Maxwell Joseph, St. Louis, **WWII**, Governor General's Horse Guards/ Armoured Reconnaissance/5th CAD/RCAC, Despatch Rider

726. Jones, William David Thompson, Pte., Cumberland House, **WWI**, 174th QOCHC Bn.
727. Keddie, Eric Thomas, Pte., Cumberland House, **WWI**, 174th QOCHC Bn., *693133*
728. Keddie, Oswald Victor, Cumberland House, **WWI**, en., Aug. 5, 1916, 43rd QOCHC Bn., (**KIA**, Battle of Amiens, Aug. 15, 1918), no known grave, Vimy Memorial, *693112*
729. Keewatin, Maurice, Pte., Balcarres, **WWII**, SSR, (**KIA**, Aug. 28, 1944), *L-64348*
730. Keewatin, Norman
731. Keewatin, Reginald
732. Kelly, Albert, Pte., Fort Qu'Appelle **WWII**, SSR/RCIC, (**KIA**, Jul. 20, 1944), *L-105185*
733. Kelly, A. E., Weyburn, **WWII**, SSR, (**POW**, Dieppe, Aug. 19, 1942-May 10, 1945), *L-12476*
734. Kelly, Fred, Fort Qu'Appelle
735. Kelly, Gordon B., **WWII**, SSR, *L-13155*
736. Kelly, Henry
737. Kelly, James, Cpl., **WWII**, SSR, *L-12189*
738. Kelly, William, Lebret, **WWII**, SSR, Home Service
739. Kennedy, B. G., Duck Lake, **WWI**
740. Kennedy, Fred, Meadow Lake, **WWI**
741. Kennedy, Frederick, Pte., Beauval/Green Lake, **WWI**, 233rd Bn. (CFNW)/14th Bn. (Quebec), (**KIA**, Sept. 27, 1918), *1021293*
742. Kennedy, Herbert Bruce, Pte., Duck Lake, **WWI**, 46th Bn. (South SK)/4th CDN Div., (**KIA**, Sept. 3, 1918), *472295*
743. Kennedy, Joseph
744. Kenndey, Laughlin James, Regina, **WWI**, *2684266*
745. King, Edward, Rfn., Meadow Lake, **WWII**, RRR/RWR, (**WIA**, Sept. 27, 1944), *L-105940*
746. King, Garnet, Meadow Lake
747. King, Rose, Meadow Lake
748. King, Stan, Meadow Lake
749. Klein, Adam, Regina Beach, **WWII**, Army
750. Klein, August, Regina Beach, **WWII**, Army
751. Kline, George
752. Kline, Soloman, Pte., Ituna, **WWII**, CSR, (**KIA**, Jul. 8, 1944), *H-17760*
753. Klyne, A., Balcarres, **WWII**
754. Klyne, Alexander, Regina, **WWII**
755. Klyne, Allan, Balcarres, **WWII**
756. Klyne, Edmond, Estevan, **WWI**, en., Feb. 22, 1918, 1st Dep. Bn./SR, *258548*
757. Klyne, Edmond, Regina
758. Klyne, Frank, Pte., Estevan, **WWI**, en., Nov. 10, 1917, 1st Dep./8th Bn./MR, (**KIA**, Aug. 31, 1918), *257196*
759. Klyne, Fred, Katepwa, **WWI**, en., Mar. 25, 1916, 46th Bn. (South SK)/SR/4th CDN Div., *426978*
760. Klyne, James, Regina, **WWII**
761. Klyne, John, Balcarres, **WWI**, 229th CEF, *1009535*
762. Klyne, John, Regina, **WWII**
763. Klyne, Lawrence, Pte., Big River, **WWII**, Lake Superior Reg. (Motor), (**KIA**, Feb. 19, 1945), *L-106314*
764. Klyne, Lawrence, Balcarres, **WWII**
765. Klyne, Louis, Pte., Qu'Appelle, **WWI**, en., Nov. 19, 1917, 5th Bn./SR/1st CDN Div., (**KIA**, Nov. 12, 1918), *256993*
766. Klyne, Vincent, Balcarres, **WWI**, en., Jul. 29, 1916, 212th Bn./249th (SK) Bn., *261692, 1019541*
767. Knife, Albert
768. Knight, David
769. Krancht, Albert Vancer

770. Krein, Solomon, **WWII**, (**KIA**, July 8, 1944, Caen), *L-17760*
771. Laboucane, Ambroise, Meadow Lake/Mary Lake, **WWI**, en., Mar. 27, 1918, 1st Dep. Bn./SR, *4090353*
772. Laboucane, Émile, Meadow Lake, **WWII**, *L-111210*
773. Laboucane, Louis R., **WWII**, SSR, (**WIA**, Sandhatten, Apr. 30, 1945), *L-107828*
774. Lacerte, Joseph Julian, Willow Bunch, **WWII**
775. Lachance, Ben
776. Ladoux, Peter, Mullingar, **WWI**, en., Dec. 20, 1917, 1st Dep. Bn./SR, *3352857*
777. Lafleur, Fred, Green Lake, **WWII**
778. Lafleur, George, Meadow Lake
779. Lafond, Celestin, Green Lake, **WWI**, en., Jun. 7, 1917, CFC, *2193019*
780. Lafond, Douglas, Battleford, **WWI**, en., Nov. 9, 1917, 1st Dep./SR, *258663*
781. LaFond, Jimmy, Green Lake, **WWII**
782. Lafond, Peter, Mullingar, **WWI**, CFC, *2193019*
783. Lafonde, Alexander (Eddie), North Battleford, **WWII**, (**WIA**, Nov. 1944, leg amputated), *L-74637*
784. Lafontaine, Albert, Touchwood, **WWII**
785. Lafontaine, Fred, Albertown/Duck Lake, **WWI**, en., Oct. 24, 1916, 243rd Bn., *1051361*
786. Lafontaine, Joseph, brother of Leon, Touchwood, **WWI**, en., Winnipeg, Feb. 14, 1916, 107th Bn., *718538*
787. Lafontaine, Joseph, MacDowall, **WWI**, en., Saskatoon, Dec. 11, 1915, 96th Bn., *204056*
788. Lafontaine, Lawrence, Big River, **WWII**, RRR
789. Lafontaine (Lafontine), Leon, brother of Joseph, Lestock, **WWI**, en., Melville, Feb. 17, 1917, 1st CMR/SR, (**KIA**, Sept. 13, 1918), *1069477*
790. Lafontaine, Paul, Touchwood, **WWII**
791. Lafontaine, Pierre, Duck Lake/MacDowall, **WWI**, en., Saskatoon, Mar. 13, 1916, 65th (SK) Bn., *474150*
792. Lafontaine, Victor J., LAC, Qu'Appelle Valley, **WWII**, RCAF, *R-176474*
793. LaFramboise, Edward, Duck Lake, **WWI**
794. Laframboise, Isadore, Maple Creek, **WWI**, en., Dec. 30, 1916, at Maple Creek, 249th (SK) Bn., *1069288*
795. LaFramboise, Joseph, Duck Lake, **WWI**, en., Prince Albert, Feb. 15, 1916, *886392*
796. Laframboise, Patrick, Maple Creek, **WWI**, en., Swift Current, Jan. 26, 1918, 1st Dep. Bn./SR, *258772*
797. Lagimodiere, Harold, Saskatoon, **WWII**, Essex Scottish Reg./Edmonton Reg., *L-102795*
798. Lajour, Albert, Touchwood, **WWII**
799. Laliberte, Abraham, Meadow Lake
800. Laliberte, Alexandre, Green Lake/Beauval, **WWI**, en., Prince Albert, Feb. 7, 1917, 233rd Bn. (CFNW), *1021292*
801. Laliberte, Alex, **WWII**
802. Laliberte, Armand, Meadow Lake, **WWII**, EUR, (War bride)
803. Laliberte, Casey, Meadow Lake
804. Laliberte, Celestin, Green Lake, **WWI**, en., Jun. 9, 1917, CFC, *2193019*
805. Laliberte, Chips, Meadow Lake
806. Laliberte, Clarence, Meadow Lake, **KW**, CDN Airborne Reg.
807. Laliberte, Danny, Meadow Lake
808. Laliberte, Eddy, Meadow Lake, **WWI**, no records, *3086972*
809. Laliberte, Edward Jr., Meadow Lake, **WWII**
810. Laliberte, Émile, Meadow Lake
811. Laliberte, Emilien, Green Lake, **WWI**, con., Prince Albert, Jan. 8, 1918, 1st Dep./SR, *258274*
812. Laliberte, Ernie J., **WWII**, SSR, (**WIA**, Jul. 28, 1944), *L-13162*

813. Laliberte, George, Meadow Lake
814. Laliberte, Johnny, Green Lake, **WWI**, en., Winnipeg, Jun. 30, 1917, FCB, *2320398*
815. Laliberte, Joseph Abraham, Green Lake, **WWII**, RCASC
816. Laliberte, Joseph Victor, **WWI**, en., Regina, Jan. 15, 1918, 1st Dep. Bn./SR, *257767*
817. Laliberte, Jules, Meadow Lake
818. Laliberte, Leon, Green Lake, **WWII**, SSR
819. Laliberte, Magloire, Pte., Île-à-la-Crosse/Lac La Plonge, **WWI**, en., Regina, Jan. 18, 1918, 1st Dep. Bn./SR, *257768*
820. Laliberte, Moses (Moise), Green Lake, **WWII**, RRR
821. Laliberte, Peter, Pte., Green Lake, **WWII**, RCASC, *L-39703*
822. Laliberte, Peter, Green Lake, **WWII**
823. Laliberte, Stanley, LAC, Green Lake, **KW**, RCAF, (**KIA**, Sept. 8, 1952), *61664*
824. Lalibertie, Antoine, Green Lake, **WWI**, en., Feb. 25, 1917, 232rd Bn., *1018702*
825. Lambert, Elmer, Meadow Lake, **WWII**
826. Lambert, Jack J. M., Qu'Appelle Valley
827. Lambert, Louis, Meadow Lake, **WWII**
828. Lamontagne, Fortune, Touchwood, **WWII**
829. Lamotte, Louis, Ponteix, **WWII**
830. Landrie, Agnes, Saskatoon, **WWII**
831. Landrie, Eva, Saskatoon, **WWII**
832. Landrie, Sam, Saskatoon, **WWII**
833. Landrie, Joe, Turtleford, **WWI**, en., Mar. 12, 1918, 1st Dep. Bn./65th (SK) Bn., (**KIA**, Oct. 24, 1918), *4097081*
834. Landry, Arthur, Meadow Lake
835. Landry, Charles, Meadow Lake
836. Landry, George, L/Cpl. Meadow Lake, **WWII**, RRR, D-Day, *L-27886*
837. Landry, Joseph Adelard "Al," Prince Albert, **WWII**, SLI
838. Landry, Stanley Joseph, Pte., Meadow Lake, **WWII**, PPCLI, (**KIA**, Ortona, IT, Dec. 15, 1944), *L-106133*
839. Landry, Thomas Demos, Pte., Meadow Lake, **WWII**, Ortona, IT
840. Laplante, Alexander, Lestock, **WWI**, en., Winnipeg, Mar. 20, 1916, 107th Bn., *718899*
841. Laplante, Alexander, Raymore, **WWI**, en., Feb. 20, 1918, 1st Dep./SR, *258816*
842. Laplante, Gabriel, Duck Lake, **WWI**, en., Oct. 26, 1916, 243rd/5th Bn./SR, (**KIA**, Mar. 12, 1918), *1051371*
843. Laplante, Harry, Touchwood, **WWII**
844. LaPlante, Henry, Titantic, **WWII**
845. Laplante, Izadore, Saskatchewan Landing, **WWI**, en., Swift Current, Jul. 8, 1916, 212th Bn., *261699*
846. Laplante, John Richard, Raymore, **WWI**, con., Saskatoon, Feb. 20, 1917, 1st Dep./SR, *258774*
847. LaPlante, Maurice, Pte., Swift Current, **WWII**, SSR, (**KIA**, May 1, 1945), *L-12938*
848. Laplante, Raymond, Touchwood, **WWII**
849. LaPlante, T. E., Duck Lake, **WWII**
850. LaPlante, Thomas, Lebret, **WWII**
851. LaPlante, Thomas, **WWII**
852. LaPlante, William, Duck Lake, **WWII**, RRR, *L-27875*
853. Lapointe, Émile, Willow Bunch, **WWII**
854. Lapointe, Jules, Willow Bunch, **WWII**
855. Lapointe, Leo, MM, **WWII**, RRR
856. Lapointe, Philip, Willow Bunch, **WWII**, SSR, *L-13021*
857. Lariviere, Gerard Albert, Spr., **WWII**, RCE, (**KIA**, BE, Nov. 20, 1944)
858. Lariviere, Joseph, Fish Creek, **WWI**, en., Vonda, May 1, 1916, 214th Bn., *267915*

859. Lariviere, Joseph Edward, Pte., Fish Creek/Prince Albert, **WWII**, RCASC, (**KIA**, May 16, 1942), *L-8804*
860. Lariviere, Phillip James, Fish Creek, **WWI**, 214th Bn., *718937*
861. Lariviere, Prosper, Rfn., Beauval, **WWII**, RRR, D-Day, *L-27875*
862. La Rocque, Alphonse, Macoun, **WWI**, en., Estevan Jan. 5, 1916, Deserted, Struck off strength, January 26, 1917, *925201*
863. Larocque, Albert, Estevan, **WWI**, en., Weyburn, Feb. 7, 1916, 249th (SK) Bn., Deserted, Struck off strength, September 29, 1916, *925323*
864. Larocque, Albert, Willow Bunch, **WWI**, con.., Estevan Jan. 26, 1918, 1st Dep. Bn./SR, Deserted, Struck off strength, April 27, 1918, *258165*
865. Larocque, Alex, Sgt., Lebret, **WWII**
866. Larocque, Alex, Meadow Lake, **WWII**, Royal CDN Corps of Signals, *B38693*
867. Larocque, Allan Ernest, Lebret, **WWI**, con., Regina, Jun. 8, 1918, 1st Dep. Bn./SR, *277063*
868. Larocque, A. J., Pte., Estevan, **WWII**
869. Larocque, Bill, Lebret, **WWII**
870. Larocque, Clayton, Meadow Lake
871. Larocque, Edwin, Lebret, **WWII**
872. Larocque, Floyd, **KW**
873. Larocque, James (Jimmy), Pte., Lebret, **WWII**, RCASC, *K-10600*
874. Larocque, James Wilfrid, Cpl., Regina, **WWI**, **WWII**, RCOC, (**KIA**, Nov. 7, 1941), *L-22048*
875. Larocque, J., **WWII**, SAR, *L-36280*
876. Larocque, Johnnie, Lebret, **WWII**
877. Larocque, Leo, Lebret, **WWII**
878. Larocque, Maurice, Lebret, **WWII**
879. Larocque, Raymond Joseph, Sgt., Estevan, **WWII**, SSR, (**WIA**, Aug. 1944, Zandfoot, Oct. 23, 1944), *L-12146*
880. Larocque, R. L., Pte., Estevan, **WWII**
881. Larocque, Robert, Cpl., **WWII**, Lebret, SSR
882. Larocque, Roderick
883. Larocque, Scott, Meadow Lake
884. LaRose, Albert George, Tantallon, **WWI**, en., Regina, Jan. 10, 1917, 217th Bn., *276598*
885. LaRose, Ramy (Ramie), L/Cpl. Tantallon, **WWI**, en., Moosomin, Mar. 31, 1916, 217th Bn., *276210*
886. LaRose, John, Saskatoon, **WWII**
887. LaRose, Joseph Edward, Spr., Saskatoon, **WWII**, 5th CAD, *L-74468*
888. Lavaille, Fred, Crooked Lake, **WWI**, en., Indian Head, Feb. 12, 1916, 229th Bn., *1009536*
889. Lavallee, Edward, AB/Swift Current, **WWII**, 47th Division/RCN VR
890. Lavallee, George Joseph, **WWII**
891. Lavallee (Lavalle), Leo, Rfn., Cochin, **WWII**, RRR, BE, *L-100861*
892. Lavallee, Joe, Meadow Lake, **WWII**
893. Lavallee, Joseph Napoleon, Crooked Lake/Marieval, **WWI**, en., Moosomin Apr. 3, 1917, dis., medically unfit, Jul. 10, 1917, *1069706*
894. Lavallee, Martin, Fish Creek, **WWI**, en., Vonda, Apr. 21, 1916, 214th Bn., *267867*
895. Lavallee, Olive, Maple Creek, **WWII**
896. Lavalley, James (Jim), Rfn., Marieval, **WWII**, RRR, 1941-1946, UK/FR/BE/NL/IT, *L-28187*
897. Lavallie, Gabriel, Maple Creek, **WWI**, en., Battleford, Dec. 13, 1916, 232nd Bn., *887828*
898. Lavallie, Harry, Pte., Maple Creek, **WWI**, en., Maple Creek, Feb. 17, 1917, 249th (SK) Bn., *1069496*, **WWII**, VGC, (**KIA**, May 28, 1943), *L-32065*
899. Lavallie, Luglar, MM, Maple Creek, **WWI**, formerly with 27th Light Horse, en., Maple Creek, Jan. 6, 1915, 9th CMR, *114833*

900. Lavallie, Moses, Snr., Maple Creek, **WWI**, en., Winnipeg, Dec. 4, 1916, 233rd Bn. (CFNW)/218th Bn., dis., underage, Feb. 21 1918, *1021268*
901. Lavoie, Meadow Lake, **WWII**
902. Laviolet (Laviolette), Gilds, Duck Lake, **WWII**
903. Leader, Bill, Qu'Appelle Valley, **WWII**
904. Lebarge, Madeline, Cypress Hills, **WWII**
905. Lebarge, Mary, Cypress Hills, **WWII**
906. Lebarge, Roger, Cypress Hills, **WWII**
907. LeBlanc, Antoine
908. Lecaine, Charles, Wood Mountain/Willow Bunch, **WWI**, en., Weyburn, Apr. 17, 1916, 182nd Bn., *925680*
909. Lecaine, Dwayne
910. Ledoux, Gilbert, Pte., North Battleford, **WWII**, SSR, (**KIA**, Jan. 20, 1945), *L-153556*
911. Ledoux, Henry, Duck Lake, **WWII**
912. Ledoux, Isidore Richard, Aldina, **WWI**, en., North Battleford, Mar. 2, 1917, CRT, dis., medically unfit/sick, Dec., 1918, *1018704*
913. Ledoux, Napoleon, Duck Lake, **WWI**, en., Prince Albert, Feb. 26, 1917, 243rd Bn., *1051610*
914. Ledoux, Phillip
915. Légaré, Gideon, Willow Bunch, **WWI**, con., Weyburn, Nov. 3, 1917, 1st Dep. Bn./SR, (**KIA**, Oct., 1918), *3352107*
916. Légaré, Marious, Willow Bunch, **WWI**, en., Edmonton, Oct. 28, 1916, dis., underage (16 yrs, 6 mos.), Dec. 29, 1916, *1021243*
917. Leheureux (L'Heureux), Julien, Cochin
918. Lejour, Albert James, Lestock, **WWII**, SLI, (**KIA**, Dec. 13, 1943), *L-2918*
919. Lejour, Patrick (Patrice), MM, Duck Lake/Battleford, **WWI**, en., Saskatoon, Apr. 10, 1916, *474321*
920. Lejour, Raymond, Duck Lake, **KW**
921. Lejour, Victor, West Prince Albert/Duck Lake, **WWI**, en., Jul. 13, 1916, 29th SLH/243rd Bn., dis. Dec. 14, 1917, *1051080*
922. Lemere, Peter, Lac Pelletier, **WWI**, en. Ap. 25, 1918, *2503805*
923. Lépine, Elie, Onion Lake/Duck Lake, **WWI**, en., Winnipeg, May 25, 1916, 107th Pioneer Bn., *719165*
924. Lespérance, Euphraise, Willow Bunch
925. Lespérance, Rita, Willow Bunch, **WWII**
926. Lespérance, Tony, Wynyard, **WWII**, RCA
927. Lesset, Norbert, Green Lake, **WWII**
928. Letellier, Victor Cecil, Gnr., Steep Creek, **WWI**, en., Prince Albert, Jan. 17, 1916, 44th Bty./RCA, *308697*
929. Letendre, Henry, Batoche, **WWI**, con., Prince Albert, Nov. 2, 1917, 1st Dep. Bn./SR, *269097*
930. Letendre, John, Batoche/Mistawasis, **WWI**, con., Prince Albert, Nov. 2, 1917, 1st Dep. Bn./SR, *258616*
931. Letendre, John, Pte., Lestock, **WWI**, en., Saskatoon, Dec. 6, 1915, 65th (SK) Bn./CDN Labour Corps/4th CDN Labour Bn., dis., physically unfit, Jul. 31, 1918, (**KIA**, Sept. 2, 1918), *472759*
932. Letendre, Samuel John (Sammy), Rfn., DCM, **WWII**, RRR, EUR, *M-31085*
933. Letendre, William John, St. Julien/Batoche, **WWI**, en., Regina, Feb. 19, 1918, *258503*
934. Levaille, John-Baptiste, Crooked Lake, **WWI**, en., Indian Head, Feb. 21, 1916, 229th/249th (SK) Bn., *1009538*
935. Leveille, Napoleon, Willow Bunch/Manor, **WWI**, en., Regina, Jan. 18, 1916, 88th Bn./152nd (Weyburn-Estevan) Bn., (**KIA**, Aug. 11, 1916), *105907*

936. Lewis, Ada, Touchwood, **WWII**, CWAC
937. Lewis, Annie, Touchwood, **WWII**, CWAC
938. Lewis, Donald, Punnichy, **WWI**, con., Regina, May 28, 1918, 1st Dep./SR, *269468*
939. Lewis, Gilbert, Punnichy, **WWI**, con., Melville, Nov. 19, 1917, 1st Dep./SR, *257374*
940. Lewis, Jean, Touchwood, **WWII**, CWAC
941. Lewis, John Norman, Punnichy, **WWI**, en., Winnipeg, May 23, 1916, 107th Pioneer Bn., *719163*
942. Linklater, Edgar, Punnichy, **WWI**, en., Winnipeg, Feb. 14, 1916, 107th Pioneer Bn., *718534*
943. Loftus, Alfred, Touchwood, **WWII**
944. Loftus, John, Touchwood, **WWII**
945. Loftus, Thomas, Touchwood, **WWII**
946. Longman, ___
947. Loyie, George, Onion Lake, **WWI**, en., Battleford, Nov. 17, 1915, 107th Bn., *887076*
948. Lucie, Benjamin, Pte., Horseshoe Bend, **WWII**, BWRHRC, (**KIA**, Oct. 1, 1944), *L-74257*
949. Lucie, Mac, Horseshoe Bend, **WWII**
950. Lucier, John, Shellwood, **WWI**, con., Prince Albert, Mar. 20, 1918, 1st Dep. Bn./4 Coy., *258938*
951. Lucier, Max, Spr., Glen Mary/Prince Albert, **WWII**, RCE, FR/BE/NL/DE, *L-74326*
952. Lucier, Roger, Shellwood, **WWI**, en., Camp Hughes, MB, Sept. 18, 1915, 53rd Bn., *441656*, *1263698*, *258726*
953. Lyons, George, Saskatoon/Birch Hills, **WWI**, en., Saskatoon, Aug. 18, 1915, 65th (SK) Bn., *472324*
954. Lyons, Miles, **WWI**, *2487909*
955. Macauley, Dan Louis, Prince Albert, **WWI**, en., Prince Albert, Mar. 24, 1916, dis., Apr. 15, 1916 by purchase, 188th Bn., *886512*
956. MacIntosh, Mace, Landis, **WWII**
957. Mackie, Wilson Harvey, Goshen/Prince Albert/Eastend, **WWII**, Army
958. Madden, Ora, Pte., MacDowall, **WWII**, RCASC
959. Major, Edmond, Lebret, **WWII**
960. Major, Tommie, Lebret, **WWII**
961. Malbeuf, Alex, Rfn., Meadow Lake, **WWII**, RRR, UK/EUR, *L-39110*
962. Malbeuf, Alfred, Ituna, **WWII**, WG, (**POW**, HK), *L-2182*
963. Malbeuf, Ambrose, Ituna, **WWI**, en., Melville, Mar. 9, 1916, 229th Bn., dis., medically unfit, Jun. 3, 1918, *1009653*
964. Malbeuf, Donald, DCM, Meadow Lake, *M-57020*
965. Malbeuf, Edlore, Meadow Lake, RRR, *L-39110*
966. Malbeuf, Edmond, Ituna, **WWI**, con., Melville, Oct. 23, 1917, 1st Dep. Bn./SR, *257521*
967. Malbeuf, Ernest P., Pte., Ituna, WG, (**POW**, Tokyo, **KIA**), *L-28224*
968. Malbeuf, Eugene, Meadow Lake
969. Malbeuf, Fred, Ituna, **WWII**, WG, (**POW**, Osaka, **KIA**), *L-28212*
970. Malbeuf, Harry, Meadow Lake
971. Malbeuf, Joe, Île-à-la-Crosse
972. Malbeuf, Louis, Ituna, **WWI**, con., Melville, Oct. 30, 1917, 1st Dep. Bn./SR, *257494*
973. Mannix, John, Cochin
974. Marion, Ambroise Louis, Pte., MM, Duck Lake, **WWI**, 46th Bn. (South SK)/SR/4th CDN Div., (**KIA**, May 6, 1917), *472292*
975. Marion, J. A. (Sonny), Meadow Lake
976. Marion, Joseph John, Rfn., Meadow Lake, **WWII**, RRR, served: Sept.1941-Nov. 1945, *L-27871*
977. Martell, Edward, **WWII**, SSR, (**WIA**, Mook Hill, Nov. 24, 1944)
978. Martell, Lawrence, Battleford, **WWII**
979. Martell, Pete, North Battleford, **WWII**
980. Martin, Albert (Joseph), Lebret, RRR

981. Martin, Joseph, Pte., Meadow Lake, **WWII**, RCASC, EUR, *L-8641*
982. Martin, Smyil, RWR
983. Martin, Stanley, Pte. **WWII**, VGC
984. Maryfield (Merryfield), Edith, Pasqua, **WWII**
985. Maurice, François, Île-à-la-Crosse, **WWI**, en., Prince Albert, Feb. 7, 1917, 233rd Bn. (CFNW), dis., medically unfit, Nov. 28, 1917, *1021298*
986. Maurice, John-Baptiste, Pte., Beauval, **WWII**, *L-36717*
987. Mauvieux, Eugene, Duck Lake, **WWII**
988. McAuley, Joseph Richard, Pte., Sturgeon Landing/The Pas/Cumberland House, **WWI**, con., Winnipeg, Jun. 17, 1918, 10th CGR, *2382625*
989. McAuley, Neil, Pte., **WWI**, 1st CMR
990. McAuley, Norman H., La Ronge, **WWII**, en.1941, FR/BE/NL/DE, (War bride)
991. McCallum, Alfred, Meadow Lake, **KW**
992. McCallum, Charles, Pte., Green Lake, **WWI**, en., North Battleford, Feb. 27, 1917, 232nd Bn., *1018699*
993. McCallum, Gilbert, Pte., Île-à-la-Crosse, **WWII**, 16th/22nd /232nd Bn./SLH, *L-39106*
994. McDonald, Campbell, Norquay, **WWII**, 16th/22nd Bn., SLH, *L-36421*
995. McDonald, Roy L., Norquay, **WWII**, 16th/22nd Bn., SLH, *L-36420*
996. McGillis, Felix, Willow Bunch, Gnr., RCA
997. McGillis, Jean-Marie, Willow Bunch, **WWI**, con., Regina, Jun. 28, 1918, 1st Dep. Bn./SR, *3353594*
998. McGillis, Joseph, Willow Bunch, **WWI**
999. McGillis, Joseph Edward, Willow Bunch, **WWII**
1000. McGillis, Joseph Narcisse Armand, Willow Bunch, **WWII**
1001. McGillis, Martin Oscar, Pte., Willow Bunch, **WWII**, SSR,
1002. McGillis, P., L/Cpl., St. Victor, **WWII**, RRR
1003. McGillis, Theophile, Willow Bunch, **WWI**, en., Weyburn, Apr. 11, 1916, 152nd (Weyburn-Estevan) Bn., *925649*
1004. McGillivary, Joe, Fort Pitt
1005. McGillivary, Joseph (Andrew) Sr., L/Cpl./Snr., Cumberland House, RWR, **WWII**, **KW**, PPCLI
1006. McIntosh, Alex, Landis, **WWII**, RCN
1007. McIntosh, Mace, Landis, **WWII**, RCN
1008. McIntosh, Russell, Landis, **WWII**, Army
1009. McKay, Alex, Prince Albert/North Dakota, **WWI**, en., Calgary, Dec. 28, 1915, 97th Bn., *207261*
1010. McKay, Alex, North Battleford, **WWII**
1011. McKay, Alex, Touchwood, **WWII**
1012. McKay, Alice, Regina Beach, **WWII**, CWAC
1013. McKay, Andrew, Regina Beach, **WWII**, Army
1014. McKay, Claude, Touchwood, **WWII**
1015. McKay, Colin, Inkster/Prince Albert, **WWI**, en., Prince Albert, Dec. 18, 1914, 54th Bn., *440537*
1016. McKay, Frederick, Prince Albert/Fort Pitt, **WWI**, en., Prince Albert, Dec. 23, 1915, 188th Bn., *886236*
1017. McKay, George, Pte., Cumberland House, **WWII**, Stormont, Dundas, & Glengarry Highlanders, *H-103868*
1018. McKay, Henry, Prince Albert, **WWII**, SLI
1019. McKay, John, Pte., Cumberland House, **WWI**, 28th (NW) Bn., *3348622*
1020. McKay, John, Sgt., MM, Prince Albert, **WWI**, en., Winnipeg, Nov. 10, 1915, 90th Bn. (Winnipeg Rifles), *186642*
1021. McKay, Lawrence Clarke, Lt., Prince Albert, **WWI**, en., Prince Albert, Dec. 18, 1914, formerly PVA, 53rd/188th dis., Jan. 10, 1916 to take a commission

1022. McKay, Lawrence, Touchwood, **WWII**
1023. McKay, Percival E., Rfn., Cumberland House, **WWII**, 3rd Bn./RRR
1024. McKay, Robert Stanley, Prince Albert, **WWI**, con., Prince Albert, Nov. 3, 1917, 1st Dep. Bn./SR, *258313*
1025. McKay, Rod E., Spr., **WWII**, Cumberland House, RCE, 3rd CID
1026. McKay, Sam, Regina Beach, **WWII**, Army
1027. McKay, Samuel, Dunleith, **WWI**, en., Mar. 1, 1915, 17th Bty./5th Field Artillery Brigade, *86552*
1028. McKay, Samuel, Saskatoon/Onion Lake, **WWI**, en., Saskatoon, Oct. 28, 1915, 46th Bn. (South SK)/SR/4th CDN Div., *472529*
1029. McKay, Victor, Lestock/Prince Albert, **WWI**, 107th Pioneer Bn., *718809*
1030. McKay, Walter, Prince Albert, **WWI**, University of MB, CDN Officer Training Corps, en., Montreal, Apr. 6, 1915, *411110*
1031. McKay, Walter, Touchwood, **WWII**
1032. McKay, Walter Hamilton, Prince Albert, **WWI**, en., Mar. 2, 1915, *440753*
1033. McKay, William, Duck Lake, **WWI**, 52nd Reg. (PVA), 8 mos., RNWMP, en., May 18, 1915, *440627*
1034. McKenzie, Harry, Regina, **WWII**
1035. McKenzie, Leonard, **KW**
1036. McKenzie, Percival (Percy) E., Rfn., Cumberland House, **WWII**, RRR, *L-111030*
1037. McLean, Norman G., Regina, **WWII**
1038. McLeod, Albert Alexander, Gnr., Lorlie, **WWII**, 6th Field Reg./RCA, (**KIA**, Jun. 19, 1945), *L-6264*
1039. McLeod, Albert Edwin, Pte., St. Louis/Red Deer Hill, **WWI**, en., Prince Albert, May 27, 1916, *235150*
1040. McLeod, Gilbert
1041. McNab, Morris, Punnichy, **WWI**, *257304*
1042. McNabb, David, Red Deer Hill, **WWI**, 212th Bn./27th Bn., *261381*
1043. McNevin, Duncan, Dalmeny, **WWI**, *871835*
1044. McNevin, Ronald, Dalmeny, **WWI**, *3355018*
1045. Merasty, Abbe, **WWII**
1046. Merasty, Alex, Meadow Lake, **WWII**
1047. Merasty, Alphonse, Meadow Lake, **WWII**
1048. Merasty Charles Louis, Rfn., Meadow Lake, **WWII**, RRR, D-Day, Jun. 6, 1944, Motorbike Courier, *L-27892*
1049. Merasty, Frank, Meadow Lake, **KW**
1050. Merasty, Frederick Jr., Meadow Lake, **KW**
1051. Merasty, Frederick Sr., Meadow Lake, **WWII**
1052. Merasty, James, Meadow Lake, **WWII**
1053. Merasty, Joseph George, Meadow Lake, **WWII**, **KW**
1054. Merasty, Pat, Meadow Lake, **KW**
1055. Merasty, Peter, Meadow Lake, **WWII**
1056. Merrifield, Edith Hilda, **WWII**, CWAC
1057. Michaud, A., Gnr., North Makwa, **WWII**
1058. Michaud, Rene, L/Cpl., Makwa, **KW**, PPCLI, (**KIA**, Jun. 24, 1953), *SK-13779*
1059. Mirasty, A. S., Rfn., **WWII**, RWR, (**WIA**, Jul. 4, 1944), *L-39164*
1060. Mirasty, Frank
1061. Mirasty, George
1062. Mirasty, Isaac, Lac La Ronge, **WWI**, en., Prince Albert Jan. 28, 1916, 188th Bn., *886229*
1063. Misener, Herschel, L/Cpl., Duck Lake, **KW**, PPCLI
1064. Mitchell, Charles, Cochin
1065. Mitchell, George, Cochin
1066. Mitchell, Harold, Cochin

1067. Mitchell, Tony, Cochin
1068. Moberley, Walter, Duck Lake, **WWI**, en., Wadena, Apr. 14, 1916, formerly South African Constabulary, *267800*
1069. Monkman, Don, St. Louis, **WWII**, RRR
1070. Monkman, Joseph Lee, Rfn., St. Louis, **WWII**
1071. Monkman, Sid, St. Louis, **WWII**, RRR
1072. Monkman, Sydney, Punnichy, **WWI**, *269474*
1073. Montgrand, Adam, Onion Lake/North Battleford, **WWI**, en., North Battleford, Feb. 17, 1917, 232nd Bn., *1018691*
1074. Montour, Denis, Duck Lake, **WWII**, **KW**
1075. Montour, Dineam, Duck Lake, **KW**
1076. Montour, Bernard, Cypress Hills, **WWII**
1077. Montour, Edward, Cypress Hills, **WWII**
1078. Montour, George, **WWI**
1079. Montour, Gilbert, Duck Lake, **WWII**
1080. Montour, Joe, Maple Creek **WWI**, en., Jan. 13, 1918, *257283*
1081. Montour, Lloyd, Cypress Hills, **WWII**
1082. Montour, Louis, Duck Lake, **WWII**, RRR, D-Day
1083. Montour, Maurice, Duck Lake, **WWII**
1084. Montour, Pascal, Duck Lake, **WWI**, con., Prince Albert, Jan. 5, 1918, 1st Dep. Bn./SR, *3352489*
1085. Montour, Sonny, Cypress Hills, **WWII**
1086. Montour, Wilfrid, Duck Lake, **WWII**
1087. Montour, William, **WWI**
1088. Moore, Lloyd George, AB, Regina, **WWII**, RCN, *HMCS St. Croix*
1089. Moran, Charles Joseph, Pte., Fort Qu'Appelle
1090. Moran, Gaspar, **WWII**, 16th/22nd Bn./SLH
1091. Morin, Albert, Meadow Lake, **WWII**, SLI, (**WIA**, IT, Dec. 15, 1943) *L-41532*
1092. Morin, Alexander, Pte., Gnr., Cumberland House, **WWII**, RCASC/RCA, Atlantic Coastal Defence
1093. Morin, Ambroise B., Beauval/Green Lake, **WWI**, en., Prince Albert, Feb. 7, 1917, 233rd Bn. (CFNW), *1021296*
1094. Morin, Armand, **WWII**
1095. Morin, Bernard, Green Lake, **WWII**
1096. Morin, Charlie, Green Lake, **WWII**
1097. Morin, Charles, Spr., Sturgeon Landing, **WWII**, RCE
1098. Morin, Cyril, Green Lake (Lac Vert), **WWI**, con., Regina, Jun. 13, 1918, 1st Dep./SR, *4090521*
1099. Morin, Don, Meadow Lake, **KW**
1100. Morin, Edward, Meadow Lake
1101. Morin, Edwin, Meadow Lake, **WWII**, 3rd CID, *L-74917*
1102. Morin, Eugene, Pte., Green Lake, **WWI**, **WWII**, WMR, (**KIA**, Nov. 18, 1944), *L-74409*
1103. Morin, Eugene, Meadow Lake, **KW**
1104. Morin, Felix, Pte., Big River, **WWII**, SSR, (**KIA**, Jul. 4, 1946), *L-66314*
1105. Morin, Frederick, South Battleford, **WWI**, Special Service, *1018328*
1106. Morin, Fred, Meadow Lake, **KW**
1107. Morin, Gaspar, Shell River, **WWI**, en., Prince Albert, Jul. 20, 1916, 243rd Bn., *1051107*
1108. Morin, Gaspard, son of Jean-Marie and Marguerite, Green Lake, **WWII**
1109. Morin, George, Green Lake, **WWII**
1110. Morin, Gilbert, Meadow Lake
1111. Morin, Isidore, Green Lake/Big River, MM, **WWI**, en., Saskatoon, Mar. 14, 1917, 232nd Bn., *1018714*
1112. Morin, Jeremi, Meadow Lake
1113. Morin, Jean-Baptiste, Willow Bunch, **WWI**, con., Jan. 15, 1918, 1st Dep. Bn./SR, *259546*

1114. Morin, John, Lebret, **WWII**
1115. Morin, John-Baptiste, Chellwood/Green Lake, **WWI**, en., Mar. 27, 1917, Saskatoon, No. 6 Forestry Dep., *2188480*
1116. Morin, Jean-Baptiste Gaspard, Shell River, **WWI**, en., Edmonton, Feb. 7, 1917, 233rd Bn. (CFNW), *1021294*
1117. Morin, John-Baptiste, Rfn., Meadow Lake, **WWII**, RRR, served: Sept. 1941-Nov. 1945, North Africa/IT, *L-27831*
1118. Morin, John James, Green Lake, **WWII**
1119. Morin, Joseph, Meadow Lake
1120. Morin, Jules J., Meadow Lake, Pte., **WWII**, *L-41465*
1121. Morin, Lawrence, **WWII**
1122. Morin, Leonard, **WWII**
1123. Morin, Louis, Lebret, **WWII**
1124. Morin, Napoleon W., Rfn., Cumberland House, **WWII**, RWR/16th/22nd Bn./SLH, (**POW**, **KIA**, murdered, Abbaye d'Adrenne, Jun. 11, 1944), *L-39126*
1125. Morin, Napoleon, Fort Pitt
1126. Morin, Napoleon, Green Lake, **WWII**
1127. Morin, Norbert, Meadow Lake, **WWI**, en., Winnipeg, Jun. 29, 1917, FCB, *2320400*
1128. Morin, Norman Joseph, Rfn., Meadow Lake, **WWII**, RRR, (**POW**, **KIA**, murdered by 12th SS Panzer Div., Jun. 9, 1944), *L-74212*
1129. Morin, Paul, Meadow Lake, **WWI**, en., Winnipeg, Jun. 29, 1917, FCB, *2320399*
1130. Morin, Paul, Shell River, **WWI**, con., Regina, Jul. 11, 1918, 1st Dep. Bn./SR, *3355145*
1131. Morin, Peter, Green Lake, **WWII**
1132. Morin, Peter, Prince Albert, **WWI**, en., Prince Albert, Mar. 4, 1916, dis., Jul. 4, 1916, medically unfit, *886432*
1133. Morin, Peter Hyacinthe, Meadow Lake, **WWI**, en. underage, reen. when of age, served in: CA
1134. Morin, Ralph, Green Lake, **WWI**
1135. Morin, Ralph, Green Lake, **WWII**
1136. Morin, Raphaël, Green Lake, **WWI**, en. North Battleford, Feb. 27, 1917, 232nd Bn., *1018698*
1137. Morin, Robert, Meadow Lake
1138. Morin, Sangadore Joseph, Rfn., CD and 2 Bars, **KW** after Armistice, Cpl./M/Cpl, 2nd Bn./QORC/RCASC/Logistics Branch, (CDN Forces Base Moose Jaw)
1139. Morin, Stanley, Meadow Lake, **KW**, *SL-44285*
1140. Morin, Vilmor, Meadow Lake
1141. Morin, Vital, Eldred/Green Lake, **WWI**, en. Prince Albert, Mar. 1, 1917, 232nd Bn., *1018701*
1142. Morin, Vital Arthur, Pte., Île-à-la-Crosse, **WWII**, RRR, (**POW**, 1945), *L-101467*
1143. Morin, William, Mullrany/Willow Bunch, **WWI**, con., Regina, Jun. 15, 1918, 1st Dep. Bn./SR, *3352522*
1144. Morris, Andrew William, Punnichy, **WWI**, en., Winnipeg, Feb. 14, 1916, 107th Pioneer Bn., dis., Dec. 22, 1916, *718535*
1145. Morris, Burns, Touchwood, **WWII**
1146. Morris, Frederick Earl, Meadow Lake/Punnichy, **WWII**, QOCHC, (**KIA**, Apr. 30, 1941), *L-18192*
1147. Munroe, George
1148. Munroe, John
1149. Munroe, Michael
1150. Munroe, William
1151. Murray, Charlie, Meadow Lake
1152. Murray, Clarence Paul, Meadow Lake, **WWII**, **KW**, RCAMC/RCASC, Ambulance Driver
1153. Murray, James, Meadow Lake
1154. Murray, Joseph Patrick (Pat), Meadow Lake, **WWII**, CFC, Forester/RCE, Welder

1155. Myette, H. J., **WWII**
1156. Nabess, Joe, Regina Beach, **WWII**, Army
1157. Nabess, Joseph G., **WWII**
1158. Nabess, Lionel, Pte., **KW**, PPCLI
1159. Nabess, Louis, Pte., Tpr., Cumberland House, SLI/16th/22nd Bn./SLH, *L-39127*
1160. Nabess, Victor, Pte., Cumberland House, Lake Superior Reg. (Motor), SLI (MG), (**POW**), *L-2965*
1161. Nabis, George, Rfn., Regina Beach, **WWII**, RRR, D-Day, *L-28172*
1162. Nabiss, Nora, Regina Beach, **WWII**
1163. Natamogan, Jimmy, Pine House, **WWII**
1164. Nault, Alexander Damase, Stony Lake/Jackfish Lake, **WWI**, *260549*
1165. Nault, Allen, Cochin
1166. Nault, Denis, Cochin
1167. Nault, Ernest A., Rfn., Meadow Lake, **WWII**, RRR, served: Sept. 1941-Nov. 1945, UK/FR/NL/DE, *L-27868*
1168. Nault, Joe, Meadow Lake, **WWII**, SLI, IT/NL
1169. Nault, Larry, Cochin
1170. Nault, Napoleon, Pte., Stony Lake (Jackfish Lake), **WWI**, 232nd/5th Bn./SR/1st CDN Div., (**KIA**, Nov. 10, 1917), Menin Gate, Ieper, BE, *108298*
1171. Nault, Wallace, Cochin
1172. Nault, William M., Rfn., Meadow Lake, **WWII**, RRR, served: Sept. 1941-Nov., 1945, *L-27869*
1173. Nelson, Edward John, Prince Albert, **WWI**, en., Prince Albert, Mar. 27, 1916, 188th Bn./46th Bn. (South SK)/SR/4th CDN Div., *886526*
1174. Ness, John, Meota/Prince Albert, **WWI**, con., North Battleford, Oct. 16, 1917, 1st Dep. Bn./SR, *3353268*
1175. Nicholas, Archie Hubert, Pte., Duck Lake, **WWII**, LER/22e Reg., *L-74088*, **KW**
1176. Nicholas, Robert F., Duck Lake, **KW**, RRC, *SL-4727*
1177. Nickelson, J. G., Touchwood, **WWII**
1178. Nofield, Ernest, Touchwood, RCAF
1179. Nofield, William, Touchwood, **WWII**, RCAF
1180. Nokusis, Archibald
1181. Nokusis, Maurice Edward, Rfn., Lorlie, **WWII**, RRR, (**KIA**, Aug. 7, 1944), *L-64734*
1182. Nolin, Alexander, Cochin, **WWII**
1183. Nolin, Edward, Cochin, **WWII**
1184. Nolin, Joseph Charles, Onion Lake, **WWI**, en., Winnipeg, Mar. 6, 1916, 107th Bn., dis., medically unfit/sick, Aug. 2, 1918, *718721*
1185. Nolin, Louis Toussiant Alexander, Meota, **WWI**, en., Saskatoon, Aug. 3, 1915, 65th (SK) Bn., *472330*
1186. Nolin, Louis, Cochin, **WWII**, CA
1187. Nolin, William, Duck Lake/Onion Lake, **WWI**, en., Winnipeg, Mar. 11, 1916, 197th Bn., *913115*
1188. Norris, John James, Sgt., Regina, **WWI**, 52nd (New ON) Bn./MR/3rd CDN Div., (**KIA**, Sept. 27, 1919), *105092*
1189. Norwest, Henry Louis (Louie), Pte., MM and Bar, Prince Albert, **WWI**, en. Sept. 8, 1915, Calgary, 50th Bn., (**KIA**, Aug. 18, 1918), *435684*
1190. O'Hare, H. A., Maple Creek, **WWII**
1191. Orth, Dale G., Leask, **WWII**, RRR
1192. Ouelette, Alfred, **WWII**
1193. Ouelette, Ted, Lebret, **WWII**
1194. Ouellette, Ambroise, Battleford
1195. Ouelette, Buster, Saskatoon, **WWII**
1196. Ouellette, Flavan Isrial, Maple Creek, **WWI**, en., Maple Creek, Feb. 9, 1916, 209th Bn., *252252*

1197. Oullette, Flavien, Aldina, **WWI**, con., Prince Albert, Jan. 15, 1918, 1st Dep. Bn./SR, *4090203*
1198. Ouellette, Gabriel, Titanic (Duck Lake), **WWI**, con., Prince Albert, Dec. 28, 1917, 1st Dep. Bn./SR, *1263723*
1199. Ouellette, Israël, Duck Lake, **WWI**
1200. Ouellette, James, Duck Lake, **WWI**, en., Saskatoon, Jan. 5, 1917, 243rd Bn., *1051562*
1201. Ouellette, James Oliver (J. O.), Pte./Cpl., Prince Albert, **KW**, PPCLI/RCIC, (**KIA**, May 21, 1952), UN Cemetery at Busan, *L-800199*
1202. Ouellette, Jean B. (Chip), Battleford, **WWII**
1203. Ouellette, Joe, Meadow Lake, **WWI**, con., Regina, Feb. 21, 1918, 1st Dep./SR, *4090278*
1204. Ouelette, Leonard, Prince Albert, **KW**, PPCLI
1205. Ouellette, Louis A., Rfn., Battleford, **WWII**, RWR
1206. Ouellette, Oliver, brother of W. J., Saskatoon, **WWII**, IT
1207. Ouellette, Paul, Saskatoon, **WWII**
1208. Ouelette, Tom, Duck Lake, **WWI**
1209. Ouellette, Wallace, Battleford
1210. Ouellette, William, Battleford, **WWI**
1211. Ouellette, William, Duck Lake, **WWI**
1212. Ouellette, W. J., Sgt., Saskatoon, **WWII**, SLI, UK/SIC/IT, (**KIA**, Dec. 28, 1943)
1213. Ouellette, Xavier, Battleford, **WWI**, *3293567*
1214. Ouellette, Xavier Frank, Duck Lake, **WWII**, CA
1215. Pagé, Cecilia, Lebret, **WWII**, RCAF WD
1216. Pagé, Ernest, Lebret, **WWII**
1217. Paget, Ernest, Fort Qu'Appelle, **WWII**, RCOC, *L-7464*
1218. Paget, Isadore, St. Paul, Minn/Jasmin, **WWI**, en., Regina, Nov. 8, 1915, 10th Bn., *115694*
1219. Pambrun, Frank, Battleford, **WWI**, en., Battleford, Apr. 29, 1916, 232nd Bn., *1018208*
1220. Pambrun, George, Cpl., Meadow Lake, **WWII**
1221. Pambrun, Henry Alfred, Battleford, **WWI**, en., Battleford, Apr. 12, 1916, 232nd Bn., *1018144*
1222. Parenteau, George John, Pte., Duck Lake, **WWII**, *L-154053*
1223. Parenteau, Gustav, St. Julien/Duck Lake, **WWI**, en., Duck Lake, Oct. 21, 1916, 243rd Bn., *1051350*
1224. Parenteau, G. O., **WWII**, SSR, arrived in FR, Jul. 7, 1944, *L-36836*
1225. Parenteau, James, Fort Pitt, **WWII**
1226. Parenteau, Joseph, Frog Lake/Duck Lake, **WWI**, en., Lloydminster, Dec. 15, 1916, *913777*
1227. Parenteau, Lawrence, Fort Pitt, **WWII**
1228. Parenteau, Louis, Fort Pitt, **WWI**, no records, *3288431*
1229. Parenteau, Michael, Duck Lake, **WWI**, con., Regina, Jun. 1, 1918, 1st Dep. Bn/SR, *269987*
1230. Parenteau, Osias, Saskatoon, **WWI**, 1st Dep. Bn./SR, *258430*
1231. Parenteau, Pat, **WWII**
1232. Parenteau, Robert Frederick, Fort Pitt, **WWII**, WG, *L-41404*
1233. Parenteau, Samuel, Duck Lake/Frog Lake, **WWI**, en., Regina, May 11, 1918, 197th Bn., *2684428*
1234. Parenteau, Tom, Fort Pitt, **WWII**
1235. Parenteau, Victor, Fort Pitt, **WWII**
1236. Parenteau, Walter Joseph, Pte., **WWII**, WG, (**KIA**, Dec. 19, 1942), *L-2858*
1237. Parenteau, Wilfrid, Fort Pitt, **WWII**
1238. Parisian, Raymond, Qu'Appelle, **WWII**, SSR, (**KIA**, Aug. 28, 1944), *L-13253*
1239. Parisien, Albert, Lebret, **WWII**
1240. Parisien, Alfred, Regina, **WWII**
1241. Parisien, Charles
1242. Parisien, Fred, Lebret, **WWII**
1243. Parisien, Frederick, Regina, **WWII**
1244. Parisien, George, Katepwa, **WWI**, en., Indian Head, Feb. 6, 1916, 249th (SK) Bn., *1009545*
1245. Parisien, George, Regina, **WWII**

1246. Parisien, John, Regina, **WWII**
1247. Parisien, Leo, Fort Qu'Appelle, **WWII**
1248. Parisien, Modest, Lebret, **WWI**, en., Melville, Jan. 15, 1917, 249th (SK) Bn., *1069338*
1249. Parisien, Morris, Lebret, **WWII**
1250. Parisien, Norman, Regina, **WWII**
1251. Parisien, Roy, Pte., Qu'Appelle Valley, **WWII**
1252. Parisien, Stanley, Regina, **WWII**
1253. Parisien, Terry, Regina, **WWII**
1254. Parisien, Vincent, Lebret, **WWII**
1255. Parisien, William John
1256. Parks, Herb
1257. Paul, Ambroise, Duck Lake, **WWII**
1258. Paul, Arthur, Duck Lake, **WWII**
1259. Paul, Bernard, Duck Lake, **WWII**
1260. Paul, C. A., Balgonnie, **WWII**
1261. Paul, Donald, Duck Lake, **WWII**
1262. Paul, Édouard, Duck Lake, **WWII**
1263. Paul, Edward, Onion Lake, **WWII**
1264. Paul, Edwin, Onion Lake, **WWII**
1265. Paul, Émile, Duck Lake, **WWII**
1266. Paul, Frank, Pte., Cumberland House, **WWI**, 233rd Bn. (CFNW)
1267. Paul, Frank, Cumberland House, **WWII**
1268. Paul, Henri, Duck Lake, **WWII**
1269. Paul, Israël, Duck Lake, **WWI**, con., Regina, Aug. 15, 1918, 1st Dep. Bn./65th (SK) Bn., *3355931*, **WWII**
1270. Paul, James, Duck Lake, **WWII**
1271. Paul, John, Onion Lake, **WWII**
1272. Paul, John Robert, DCM, Cpl., Duck Lake, **WWII**, Army
1273. Paul, Joseph Jean-Marie, Duck Lake, MM,**WWI**, en., Saskatoon, Dec. 10, 1915, 65th (SK) Bn./CFC, *472793*
1274. Paul, Joseph (Jos) Robert, Duck Lake, **WWI**, en., Saskatoon, Apr. 6, 1916, 46th Bn. (South SK)/SR/4th CDN Div., *474286*, **WWII**, Rfn., RRR, served: Sept. 1941-Nov. 1945, *L-27944*
1275. Paul, Marcel, Duck Lake, **WWII**, **KW**
1276. Paul, Michael, Duck Lake, **WWII**
1277. Paul, Peter, Rfn., **WWII**, RRR, (**KIA**, Aug. 28, 1944), *L-2922*
1278. Paul, William, Duck Lake, **WWI**, en., Prince Albert, Jul. 9, 1917, CFC, *2193044*
1279. Pechow, W., **WWII**
1280. Pederson, John, Pte., Moose Jaw, **KW**, 25th Field Dressing Station (near North Korea), *SL-4138*
1281. Pelletier, Alexander, Lestock, **WWI**, en., Winnipeg, Feb. 14, 1916, 107th Pioneer, Bn., *718542*
1282. Pelletier, Alfred, Crooked Lake, **WWI**, en., Indian Head, Feb. 21, 1916, 217th Bn., *1009546*
1283. Pelletier, Antonie, Touchwood, **WWII**
1284. Pelletier, Charles, Lebret, **WWI**
1285. Pelletier, Daniel, Lestock, **WWI**, en., Melville, Oct. 24, 1916, 249th (SK) Bn., *1069042*
1286. Pelletier, Dan, Gnr./Sgt., Yorkton, **WWI**, 217th Bn., Oct. 24, 1916-Apr. 10, 1919, **WWII**, 16th/22nd SLH/VGC, served: Jul. 4, 1940-Mar. 22, 1941, Jul. 12, 1943-Nov. 6, 1945
1287. Pelletier, Darcy
1288. Pelletier, Edward, Lebret, **WWI**
1289. Pelletier, Felix, Qu'Appelle Valley
1290. Pelletier, George J., Rfn., Lebret, **WWII**, RRR, *L-28024*
1291. Pelletier, George M., Lebret, **WWII**
1292. Pelletier, Harry Paul

1293. Pelletier, Harvey, Yorkton
1294. Pelletier, Ivan, **WWI**
1295. Pelletier, James (Jim), Lebret, **WWII**
1296. Pelletier, John, L/Cpl., Touchwood, **WWII**, La Reg. De Maisonneuve, (**KIA**, Jul. 25, 1944), *L-19377*
1297. Pelletier, Joseph Jr., Rfn., Lebret, **WWII**, RRR, (**KIA**, Jun. 6, 1944), *L-28017*
1298. Pelletier, Joseph Armand, **WWII**
1299. Pelletier, Joseph Louis Henry
1300. Pelletier, Louis Jean, **WWII**, RCA
1301. Pelletier, Michael J., Rfn., Lebret, **WWII**, RRR, 2nd CID
1302. Pelletier, Paul, Cpl., MM, Fort Qu'Appelle, **WWI**, **WWII**, 46th Bn. (South SK)/SR/4th CDN Div.
1303. Pelletier, Paul, Lestock, **WWI**, en., May 8, 1916, 217th Bn., *276284*
1304. Pelletier, Paul, Pelly Agency
1305. Pelletier, Paul, Touchwood, **WWII**
1306. Pelletier, Peter, Pte., Lebret, **WWII**, RCA, NL/BE
1307. Pelletier, Sandy, Pelly Agency, **WWI**
1308. Pelletier, Scotty
1309. Pelletier, T., Gnr., Qu'Appelle Valley
1310. Pelletier, William Henry, Lestock, **WWII**, RRR, *L-33115*
1311. Pelltier, Anton, Rfn., **WWII**, Div. 10/RRR, (**KIA**, D-Day, Jun. 6, 1944), Bretteville-sur-Laize Canadian War Cemetery, FR, *L-74285*
1312. Pelltier, Peter Clément, Qu'Appelle Valley
1313. Pelly, Edward, Pte., Cumberland House, **WWI**, 10th CGR, *3348886*
1314. Pelly, Isaac, Pte., Cumberland House, **WWI**, 1st Dep./MR, *3348443*
1315. Pelly, Joseph Adam, Pte., Cumberland House, **WWI**, 10th CGR, *3348444*
1316. Pelly, Simon, Pte., Cumberland House, **WWI**, 78th WG Bn./CFC, *913748*
1317. Peltier, Charles, Katepwa, **WWI**, en., Indian Head, Mar. 18, 1916, 217th Bn., *1009550*
1318. Peltier, Harry
1319. Peltier, Henry Clément, Cpl., Katepwa, **WWI**, en., Indian Head, Feb. 5, 1916, 217th Bn., dis., medically unfit, Apr. 28, 1917, *1009503*
1320. Peltier, James, Regina
1321. Peltier, Jim C., Lebret, **WWII**
1322. Peltier, John(nie), Gnr., Lebret, **WWII**, 17th Field Reg./RCA, (**KIA**, IT, May 21, 1944), *L-35034*
1323. Peltier, John
1324. Peltier, P. C., Gnr., Lebret, **WWII**
1325. Peltier, Peter, Katepwa
1326. Petch, Franklyn Charles, Meadow Lake, L/Cpl., 1st Bn., Winnipeg, *K85493*
1327. Pete, Nick, Duck Lake, **WWII**
1328. Petit (Samuel), Alice, Duck Lake, **WWII**, CWAC, Runner/Orderly, *W-120519*
1329. Petit, Alfred, Duck Lake, **WWI**, en., Prince Albert, Mar. 1, 1917, 243rd Bn., *1051611*, **WWII**
1330. Petit, Claude, CM, SOM, CD, Duck Lake, **KW**, PPCLI, **Peacetime service**
1331. Petit, Donat (Don), Duck Lake, **WWII**, RRR, **KW**
1332. Petit, Ernest, St. Laurent de Grandin, **WWI**, con., 1st Dep. Bn./SR, *269989*
1333. Petit, Jean-Marie, Duck Lake, **WWI**, **WWII**, WMR
1334. Petit, Marcel, Duck Lake, **WWII**, **KW**
1335. Petit, Murray, Cpl., Duck Lake, **KW**, PPCLI
1336. Petit, Norris, Duck Lake, **KW**, PPCLI
1337. Petit, Pierre, Cudworth, **WWI**, con., Prince Albert, Dec. 4, 1917, 1st Dep. Bn./SR, *1263512*
1338. Petit, Tommy, Duck Lake, **WWII**
1339. Piché, Alexander, Chellwood/Duck Lake, **WWI**, en., Mar. 19, 1917, 232nd Bn., *1018719*

1340. Pichette, Andrew, Delmas, **WWI**, con., North Battleford, Oct. 26, 1917, 1st Dep. Bn./SR, *276953*
1341. Pilon, Bob, Duck Lake
1342. Pilon, Edgar, Duck Lake, **WWII**
1343. Pilon, Edmond, Batoche, **WWI**, con., Regina, Aug. 16, 1918, 1st Dep./SR, *3355871*
1344. Pilon, Ernie, Duck Lake
1345. Pilon, Hermond, Duck Lake, **WWII**
1346. Pilon, Reo, Duck Lake, **KW**
1347. Plante, Charles, Battleford, **WWI**, en., Battleford, Dec. 9, 1915, 232nd Bn., *887835*
1348. Pocha, Augustus Adolphus, Prince Albert, **WWI**, en., Prince Albert, Apr. 6, 1917, Forestry Dep., *2188497*
1349. Pocha, George Milton, Spr., Prince Albert, **WWI**, en., Calgary, Nov. 2, 1917, 1st Dep. Bn./AR, *2621898*
1350. Pocha, Gilbert, Prince Albert., **WWI**, en., Prince Albert, Jul. 3, 1915, 65th (SK) Bn., *473016*
1351. Pocha, Henry George, Kirkpatrick, **WWI**, en., Prince Albert, Mar. 29, 1916, 188th Bn., dis., Aug. 21, 1916, *886537*
1352. Pocha, Hillyard Charles, Kirkpatrick, **WWI**, en., Prince Albert, Feb. 24, 1916, *886420*
1353. Pocha, Jesse James, Prince Albert, **WWI**, en., Prince Albert, Mar. 6, 1916, 188th Bn., *886440*
1354. Pocha, John, Prince Albert, **WWI**, en., Prince Albert, Dec. 15, 1915, 188th Bn., *886251*
1355. Pocha, John Robert, Prince Albert, **WWI**, con., Calgary, Sept. 28, 1918, 1st Dep. Bn./AR, *3215170*
1356. Pocha, Roderick James, Prince Albert, **WWI**, en., Shorncliffe, Jul. 16, 1915, 9th Res. Bn., (**KIA**, Jun. 5, 1916), *424209*
1357. Pocha, R. R., Rfn., MacDowall, **WWII**
1358. Pocha, Roy, Pte., **WWII**, SSR, landed in FR, Jul. 8, 1944, (**WIA**, Orbec, Aug. 22, 1944), *L-105601*
1359. Poirier, Wilfrid, **WWII**, RRC, *L-154297*
1360. Poitras, Albert, Lebret, **WWII**
1361. Poitras, Alexander, Pte., Meadow Lake/Moosimin, **WWII**, RCASC, D-Day/UK/FR/BE/NL/DE, *L-36741*
1362. Poitras, Edward Joseph, Pte., Lebret/Fort Qu'Appelle, **WWII**, SSR, (**KIA**, Dieppe, Aug. 19, 1942), *L-13147*
1363. Poitras, Ernest, Meadow Lake
1364. Poitras, Fred, Lebret, **WWII**
1365. Poitras, George, Lebret, **WWII**, SSR, (**WIA**, Dieppe, Aug. 19, 1942)
1366. Poitras, George, Meadow Lake
1367. Poitras, J. A., Tpr., Lebret
1368. Poitras, James G., Pte., Fort Qu'Appelle, **WWII**, SSR
1369. Poitras, John, Lebret, **WWII**
1370. Poitras, John, Meadow Lake
1371. Poitras, John, Touchwood, **WWII**
1372. Poitras, John-Baptiste, Fort Qu'Appelle, **WWI**, con., Melville, Dec. 18, 1918, 1st Dep. Bn./SR, *259167*
1373. Poitras, Joseph, Jackfish Lake, **WWI**, en., Saskatoon, Jan. 4, 1916, 65th (SK) Bn., *472924*
1374. Poitras, Joseph G., **WWII**, SSR, (**WIA**, Dieppe Aug. 19, 1942) *L-13493*
1375. Poitras, Joseph Martial, Sgt., Lebret, **WWII**, RCASC, *L-7439*
1376. Poitras, Leo, Lebret, **WWII**
1377. Poitras, Leon, Jack Fish Lake,**WWI**, con., North Battleford, Oct. 20, 1917, 1st Dep. Bn./SR, *276954*
1378. Poitras, Louis, Meadow Lake, **WWII**, SLI, *H-42313*
1379. Poitras, Michael, Qu'Appelle Valley, **WWI**
1380. Poitras, Modeste, Lebret, **WWII**
1381. Poitras, Morris Joseph, Spr., Lestock, **WWII**, 1st CID/RCE, UK/SIC/IT/FR/NL/DE

1382. Poitras, Norman, Lebret, **WWII**
1383. Poitras, Pat, Qu'Appelle Valley
1384. Poitras, Val, Meadow Lake, **WWII**
1385. Poitras, Victor, **WWII**
1386. Poitras, Vital, Meadow Lake, **WWII**
1387. Powless, Peter J., Sgt., Qu'Appelle Valley, **WWII**
1388. Pratt, Earl, Touchwood, **WWII**
1389. Pratt, Glen, Touchwood, **WWII**
1390. Pratt, Harvey Edward, Pte., Birch Hills, **WWII**, en., Oct. 15, 1939, first contingent of CDN Army to go EUR, dis., at war's end, 1945, *L-1704*
1391. Pratt, Kenneth Wilfred, Punnichy, **WWII**, RWR, (**KIA**, Jun. 7, 1944), *L-105301*
1392. Pratt, Leslie
1393. Pratt, Vern, Touchwood, **WWII**
1394. Pratt, William, Regina Beach, **WWII**, Army
1395. Price, William Joseph (Joe) E., Sgt., Fishing Lake, **WWII**, RCE, served: May, 1940-Oct.1945
1396. Primeau, Alexander, Spr., Prince Albert, **WWI**, en., Prince Albert, Aug. 3, 1915, 107th Bn., *886248*
1397. Primeau, Ernest
1398. Primeau, Frederick, MacDowall/Duck Lake, **WWI**, en., Saskatoon, Feb. 5, 1917, 214th Bn., *268109*
1399. Primeau, Joseph, **WWII**, CFC
1400. Primeau, Norman
1401. Prince, A., Gnr., Abernethy, **WWII**
1402. Pritchard E., Pte., Baljennie, **WWII**
1403. Pritchard, Edward, Patch Grove, **WWI**, con., Regina, Sept. 10, 1918, 1st Dep./SR, *3356237*
1404. Pritchard, Frederick Alexander, Battleford, **WWI**, en., Battleford, Jan. 3, 1916, 232nd Bn., *887837*
1405. Pritchard, Harry, Welby, **WWI**, con., Melville, Nov. 29, 1917, 1st Dep./SR, *257548*
1406. Pritchard, Ralph, Battleford, **WWI**, en., Dec. 6, 1915, Battleford, 232nd Bn., *887838*
1407. Pritchard, William Patrick, Bresaylor
1408. Pruden, Alexander, Meota, **WWI**, en., North Battleford, Mar. 9, 1916, 188th Bn., *887185*
1409. Pruden, Archie, Cochin, **WWII**, (War bride)
1410. Pruden, Charles, Cochin, **WWII**
1411. Pruden, Clayton, Wynyard, **WWII**
1412. Pruden, Edward, Cochin, **WWII**
1413. Pruden, James Joseph, Big River, **WWII**, BWRHRC, (**KIA**, Jul. 25, 1944), *L-74300*
1414. Pruden, Joseph, Prince Albert, **WWI**, en., Prince Albert, Sept. 21, 1916, 243rd Bn., dis., Dec. 14, 1916, *1051263*
1415. Pruden, Laurence, Cochin, **WWII**, (War bride)
1416. Pruden, Leo, Pte., Wynyard, **WWII**, CDN Infantry Corps, served: CA, 4½ yrs, *L-53495*
1417. Pruden, William, **WWII**
1418. Quinney, Lawrence, **WWII**
1419. Racette, Albert, **WWII**
1420. Racette, Allen, Rfn., Katepwa, **WWII**, RRR, DE
1421. Racette, Fred, **WWII**
1422. Racette (Rascette), George, Prongua, **WWI**, en., Battleford, Feb. 18, 1916, 232nd Bn., dis., medically unfit, Jul. 4, 1917, *887840*
1423. Racette, George Frank Allen, Rfn., Katepwa, **WWII**, Regina
1424. Racette, Henry, Indian Head, **WWII**
1425. Racette, Maurice, Gnr., Indian Head, **WWII**
1426. Racette, Norman, Qu'Appelle Valley, **WWII**, Royal Military College, Kingston, ON,

Officer Training/Payroll
1427. Racette, Peter, Katepwa, **WWII**, SSR, UK/FR, *L-13696*
1428. Racette, R. J., Pte., Regina, **WWII**, (**WIA**)
1429. Racette, Stanley, Lebret, **WWII**, SSR, NL/DE, *L-13695*
1430. Racette, Toby, Balcarres, **WWII**
1431. Racette, Zacre (Zacharie), Duck Lake, **WWI**, en., Prince Albert, May 3, 1916, 297th Bn., *886596*
1432. Rainville, Jules, L/Sgt., Willow Bunch, **WWII**, SSR, (**KIA**, May 2, 1943), *L-12916*
1433. Rall, Charlie, **WWI**
1434. Ranger, Amédée, Duck Lake, **KW**
1435. Ranger, Jean-Baptiste (John), MM, Batoche, **WWI**, en., Saskatoon, Apr. 1, 1916, 65th (SK) Bn., *474236*
1436. Raymond, Bud, Meadow Lake
1437. Raymond, George, Meadow Lake, **KW**
1438. Raymond, Peter, Pte., Île-à-la-Crosse, **KW**, *SM-17870*
1439. Rayon, Graham, Pelly Agency, **WWI**
1440. Read, Frederick W., Cpl., **WWII**, en. Jan. 22, 1942, 4th Division/RCASC, FR/BE/NL/DE, *L-74365*
1441. Read, Landon W., Cpl., **WWII**, en. Jan. 22, 1942, SLI (MG), SIC/IT/FR/BE/NL/DE, *L-74362*
1442. Red Head, Frederick, Prince Albert
1443. Regan, William, Meadow Lake, **WWII**, SLI, SIC/IT, Malaria, *L-2908*
1444. Richard, Jean-Baptiste, Pte., Cumberland House, **WWI**, en. Jun. 23, 1916, 223rd Bn., *1021152*
1445. Richard, Roger Victor, **WWI**, 52nd (New ON) Bn./MR, (**KIA**, Oct. 14, 1916), *2379844*
1446. Richards, Harvey William, Pte., PPCLI
1447. Richards, Henry, Gnr., RCA
1448. Richards, Walter G., Rfn., RWR
1449. Richardson, Allan, Pte., Battleford, **WWI**, en. April 14, 1916, Battleford, (**WIA**), *1018154*, **WWII**, VGC, India/CA
1450. Richardson, Arthur Alphonse, Pte./Tpr., Maidstone, **WWII**, 2nd CDN Armoured Brigade, Despatch Rider, (**KIA**, March 1, 1944 in UK, Buried in Sheffield, England), *L-36855*
1451. Richardson, Lawrence, Pte., Maidstone, **WWII**, RRR, (**WIA**, D-Day, June 6, 1944)
1452. Richardson, Marjory, Pte., Maidstone, **WWII**, CWAC, Calgary
1453. Risdale, Robert, Meadow Lake
1454. Risdale, Stanley, Meadow Lake
1455. Rivard, Joseph Louis, Harp Tree/Willow Bunch, **WWII**, en. Regina, Mar. 5, 1942, dis. Oct. 24, 1945, SLI, UK/EUR/IT/SIC, *L-65639*
1456. Roberts, Fred, Lebret, **WWII**
1457. Robertson, Andrew James, Duck Lake, **WWI**, en., Prince Albert, Nov. 3, 1915, 188th Bn., *886258*
1458. Robertson, Russell J., Tpr., Cumberland House, **WWII**, FGH
1459. Robillard, Alex, Regina Beach, **WWII**, Army
1460. Robillard, August, Fort Qu'Appelle, **WWI**, en., Regina, Aug. 1, 1916, 212th Bn., *261706*
1461. Robillard, August, Lebret, **WWII**
1462. Robillard, Edward, Lebret/Fort Qu'Appelle, **WWI**, en., Regina, May 22, 1917, *276432*
1463. Robillard, Edward, Touchwood, **WWII**
1464. Robillard, Fred, Saskatoon, **WWI**, en., Saskatoon, Nov. 6, 1917, 1st Dep. Bn./SR, *258403*, *1263623*
1465. Robillard, Hilliard, Mont Nebo, **WWII**, RRR, served: Sept. 1941-Nov. 1945, **KW**, *K-76403*
1466. Robillard, J. M., Gnr., Regina, **WWII**
1467. Robillard, Joe, Mont Nebo, **WWII**, RRR, served Sept. 1941-Nov. 1945, *L-27047*, **KW**
1468. Robillard, Lenard, Regina Beach, **WWII**, Army

1469. Robillard, Leonard, Touchwood, **WWII**
1470. Robillard, Maurice, Touchwood, **WWII**
1471. Robillard, Peter, Saskatoon, **WWI**, con., Saskatoon, Nov. 5, 1917, 1st Dep. Bn./SR, *258443*
1472. Robillard, Robert, Rfn., Mont Nebo, **WWII**, RRR, D-Day, *L-27363*
1473. Robillard, Rose (Lucy), **WWII**
1474. Robinson, A.W., Saskatoon, **WWII**
1475. Robinson, Christopher
1476. Robinson, Colin Richard
1477. Robinson, Glen, Touchwood, **WWII**
1478. Robinson, John George
1479. Robinson, Richard, Cumberland House, **WWII**
1480. Robinson, Russell, Cumberland House, **WWII**
1481. Robinson, William Riley, **WWII**
1482. Roi (Roy) Oscar, Green Lake, **WWI**, en., Saskatoon, Mar. 19, 1917, 232nd Bn., *1018724*
1483. Ross, Daniel, Green Lake, **WWII**, **KW**, *SL-4273*
1484. Ross, "Dutch," Prince Albert, **WWII**
1485. Ross, Ed, **WWII**
1486. Ross, Emil, **WWII**
1487. Ross, Ernest, Duck Lake, **WWI**, 1st Dep. Bn./AR/3rd Dep. Bn./QC Reg., *3213330*
1488. Ross, Fred, Hubbard, **WWI**, con., Regina, Nov. 4, 1918, 1st Dep./SR, *3356476*
1489. Ross, Harold, Cpl., Fort Qu'Appelle, **WWII**, 1st Bn./PPCLI, NL/DE, *L-11843* (1943-46), **KW**, PPLCI, (1951-54), Parachuter and Jumper, dis. after contracting malaria, *SL-11843*
1490. Ross, John W., L/Cpl., CIC
1491. Ross, Louis, Gnr., Moose Jaw, **WWII**
1492. Ross, Norman, **WWI**
1493. Ross, Roman, Lorlie, **WWI**, en., Regina, Feb. 12, 1918, 1st Dep. Bn./SR, *58324*, **WWII**, VGC, (**KIA**, Jan. 26, 1946), *L-32371*
1494. Ross, Robert, Pte., Meadow Lake/Saskatoon, **KW**, 48th Highlanders of CA, (**KIA**, Jun. 23, 1953), *SL-5030*
1495. Ross, Sam, Meadow Lake
1496. Ross, Victor, Pte., Green Lake, **WWII**, WG, HK, (**KIA**, Dec. 25, 1941), *L-2855*
1497. Ross, William, Dog Lake, **WWI**, 1st Dep. Bn./AB Reg., *4100782*
1498. Ross, William, Meadow Lake, **WWII**
1499. Ross, William Delore, Balcarres, **WWI**, en., Indian Head, Feb. 13, 1916, 229th Bn., *1009551*
1500. Rouzault, John, Ponteix, **KW**
1501. Roy, Louis, Pte., Beauval, **WWII**, SLI, UK/North Africa/SIC/IT, *L-74678*
1502. Roy, Oscar, Green Lake, **WWI**
1503. Sabiston, David Hamilton, Touchwood, **WWII**, RWR
1504. Sabiston, James, Bankend
1505. Sabiston, William Wallace George, Cpl., Milday Park, **WWII**, RWR, (**KIA**, Jun. 26, 1944), *L-41504*
1506. Sahyes, Edward, Cumberland House, **WWI**, con., Winnipeg, May 30, 1918, 1st Dep. Bn./SR, *4070660*
1507. Salter, Charles, Fort Pitt
1508. Salter, Edwin, Fort Pitt
1509. Samson, Ed, Onion Lake, **WWI**
1510. Samuel, Hector, Duck Lake, **WWII**
1511. Samuel, Thomas, Duck Lake, **WWII**
1512. Samuel, Thomas Sr., Duck Lake, **WWI**
1513. Samuel, William, Duck Lake, **WWII**, 16th/22nd Bn./SLH/Calgary Tank Reg.
1514. Sanderson, E., Swift Current, CMR
1515. Sanderson, George Archibald P., Shellbrook, **WWI**, en., Oct. 3, 1915, 44th Bn., *308664*

1516. Sanderson, George Henry, Kilwinning, **WWI**, en., Prince Albert, Mar. 27, 1916, 188th Bn., *886521*
1517. Sanderson, James, Prince Albert, **WWI**, en., Prince Albert, Jan. 3, 1916, 188th Bn., *886290*
1518. Sanderson, John Jack, Wakaw, **WWII**
1519. Sanderson, Norman George, MM, Lily Plain, **WWI**, en., Leask, Feb. 5, 1917, 5th Bn./SR/1st CDN Div., *1018690*
1520. Sanderson, Owen, St. Catherine's Settlement/Prince Albert, **WWI**, en., Dec. 21, 1914, 53rd Bn., *440599*
1521. Sanderson, Thomas Scott, Prince Albert, **WWI**, *154802*
1522. Sanderson, William, Muskeg Lake/Lily Plain, **WWI**, en., North Battleford, Feb. 23, 1917, 232nd Bn., *1018697*
1523. Sanderson, William Charles, Prince Albert, **WWI**, en., Prince Albert, Feb. 21, 1916, 46th Bn. (South SK)/SR/4th CDN Div., (**KIA**, Dec. 4, 1917), *886407*
1524. Sangret, August, Rfn., Battleford, **WWII**, RCIC, (Hanged for murder, Apr. 29, 1943), *L-27572*
1525. Sangrey, Percy, **KW**
1526. Sanregret, Bruno, Meadow Lake
1527. Sanregret, George, Duck Lake, **WWI**, con., Edmonton, Dec. 5, 1917, 1st Dep./AR, *3207598*
1528. San(s)regret, Harry, **KW**, *SL-4274*
1529. Sanregret, Harvey, Meadow Lake, **KW**
1530. Sanregret, John, Meadow Lake, **WWII**, (**POW**)
1531. Sanregret, William John, Pte., Meadow Lake
1532. Sansgret, Napoleon, Battleford, **WWI**, en. Battleford, Mar. 17, 1916, 232nd Bn., dis., medically unfit, Jun. 7, 1917, *887853*
1533. Sauvé, Jean-Baptise, Duck Lake, **WWII**
1534. Sauvé, Joseph, Duck Lake, **WWII**, CIC
1535. Sayer, Arthur, Bresaylor
1536. Sayers, Cecil, Bresaylor/Battleford
1537. Sayers, Douglas Harris, Bresaylor, RRR, FR/DE, POW Guard, 1945-46, *L-109106*
1538. Sayers, Edgar, Bresaylor
1539. Sayers, George Walter, Pte., Battleford, **WWII**, WG, (**POW**, Dec. 22, 1942, died in prison camp from pellagra), *L-2862*
1540. Sayers, Gordon, Bresaylor
1541. Sayers, Harris, Bresaylor
1542. Sayers, Henry, Bresaylor
1543. Sayers, Henry Peter, Bresaylor
1544. Sayers, James, Breslayor
1545. Sayers, Joseph A., Bresaylor, **WWII**
1546. Sayers, Leonard, Bresaylor
1547. Sayers, Sidney, Bresaylor
1548. Sayers, Stanley, Bresaylor
1549. Sayers, Walter G., Bresaylor
1550. Sayers, Walter Peter, Bresaylor, **WWI**, en., Saskatoon Jun. 7, 1917, 77th Dep. Bty. Bn./CFA, *1250771*
1551. Sayers, William Clayton, Bresaylor, **WWII**, after 1945 guarded prisoners at Medicine Hat, *L-110883*
1552. Sayese, Baptiste, **WWII**
1553. Sayese, Edward, Cumberland House, **WWI**
1554. Sayese, Gabe, **WWII**
1555. Sayese, James Alvin, Cpl./Rfn., Prince Albert, **WWII**, RRR, (**KIA**, Aug. 14, 1944), *L-86831*
1556. Sayese, Lawrence, Pte., Horseshoe Bend, **WWII**, 16th/22nd Bn./SLH/LER
1557. Sayese, William, Cpl., Cumberland House, **WWII**, Royal CDN Postal Corps
1558. Sayhes, Edward, Cumberland House, **WWI**, 1st Dep. Bn./MR, *40/0660*

1559. Sayhes, Edward T., Pte., Cumberland House, **WWI**, 52nd (New ON) Bn., **WWII**, VGC
1560. Sayhese, Edward, Fort Pitt
1561. Sayies, Baptiste, Spr., Cumberland House, **WWII**, RCE/WG
1562. Schoenthal, Walter, Regina
1563. Scofield, Ralph Earl, Margo, **WWII**, RCAF
1564. Scott, Morrison, **WWII**
1565. Settee, Alexander, Cumberland House/The Pas, **WWI**, en., The Pas, May 19, 1917, No. 5/CFC, *1288762*
1566. Settee, Alexander, Fus., Cumberland House, **WWII**, PLF, 11th Ind. MG Coy., IT, (**KIA**, Sept. 3, 1944), *L-2963*
1567. Settee, Henry, Pte., Cumberland House, **WWI**, en. Jul. 2, 1916, Winnipeg, 217th Bn./28th (NW) Bn., *913589*
1568. Settee, Jean-Baptiste, Pte., Cumberland House, **WWII**, SLI (MG)
1569. Settee, Nathan, Fsr., Cumberland House, **WWII**, PLF (MG)/SLI (MG), *L-2970*
1570. Settee, Thomas, Pte., The Pas/Cumberland House, **WWI**, en., The Pas, Nov. 18, 1916, trans. from 249th (SK) Bn./Special Service Coy., Military Div. 12, Dec. 28, 1916, *1069067*
1571. Settee, Thomas, Fort Pitt
1572. Settee, Thomas, Rfn., Prince Albert, **WWII**, RRR, (**WIA**, D-Day, June 6, 1944), *L-24026*
1573. Shatilla, Alex, Meadow Lake
1574. Shortt, A. Raynor, Saskatoon, **WWII**, Army
1575. Shortt, James Williard, Saskatoon, **WWII**, Army
1576. Shortt, Marie Agnes, Saskatoon, **WWII**, CWAC
1577. Simpson, George, Regina Beach, **WWII**, RCAF
1578. Sinclair, ___, Cpl., MM, **WWII**, RWR, (**WIA**, Oct. 7, 1944), *L-104383*
1579. Sinclair, Alexander, Green Lake, **WWI**, con., Regina, Jun. 13, 1918, 1st Dep. Bn./SR, *3352256*
1580. Sinclair, C. A., Maple Creek, **WWII**
1581. Sinclair, David, Prince Albert, **WWI**, en., Saskatoon, Mar. 29, 1917, 249th (SK) Bn., *1069637*
1582. Sinclair, Douglas, Touchwood, **WWII**
1583. Sinclair, Edward, Touchwood, **WWII**
1584. Sinclair, Elie Victor, L/Sgt., Lebret, **WWII**, RRR, (**KIA**, Jun. 9, 1944), *L-27721*
1585. Sinclair, Garnet, Rfn., **WWII**
1586. Sinclair, John, Maple Creek, **WWII**
1587. Sinclair, John, Touchwood, **WWII**, Stretcher Bearer
1588. Sinclair, Peter, Touchwood, **WWII**
1589. Sinclair, Raymond, Touchwood, **WWII**
1590. Sinclair, Raymond J., Clouston, **WWII**
1591. Sinclair, William, Pte., Weyburn, **WWI**, 28th (NW) Bn./SR, (**KIA**, Jun. 30, 1920), *781534*
1592. Sinclair, William Douglas, Tpr., Punnichy, **WWII**, RCD, IT, (**KIA**, Apr. 11, 1944), *L-53793*
1593. Slater, Charlie, Fort Pitt, **WWII**, RCAF, 20 yrs service with NATO: FR/DE
1594. Slater, Edwin, Fort Pitt, **WWII**, 34th Coy./RCE, UK/FR
1595. Slater, James, Fort Pitt, **WWI**, dis., overage
1596. Slater, Tommy James Jr., Fort Pitt/Bresaylor, **WWI**, en. Camp Hughes, MB, Oct. 4, 1916, 197th Bn., *913740*
1597. Smith, Andrew
1598. Smith, Daniel
1599. Smith, Fred, Pte., The Pas/Fort Qu'Appelle, **WWI**, con., The Pas, Nov. 5, 1917, 1st Dep./MR, *2381304*
1600. Smith, Joe, 1st Bn., CSR
1601. Spence, Charles, Herbert/Red Deer Hill/Birch Hills, **WWI**, 243rd Bn., *1051306*
1602. Spence, David

1603. Spence, Edwin Stanley, Maidstone, **WWI**, con., Regina, Jun. 20, 1918, 1st Dep. Bn./SR, *3352882*
1604. Spence, Gordon Raymond, Pte., Delisle, **WWII**, *L-103931*
1605. Spence, K. D.
1606. Spence, Lloyd
1607. Spence, Raymond, Red Deer Hill, **WWI**, en., Prince Albert, May 27, 1916, 203rd Bn., *235148*
1608. Spence, Reginald, Red Deer Hill, **WWI**, en., Prince Albert, Apr. 20, 1916, 203rd Bn., *234801*
1609. Spence, William J., Gnr., Duck Lake, **WWII**, SLI/1st CID/MG Bn., *L-2272*
1610. Standinghorn, Norman, MM, Battleford, **WWI**, en., Battleford, Dec. 6, 1915, 232nd Bn., *887842*
1611. St. Cyr, Robert, Titanic, **WWI**, con., Prince Albert, Jan. 5, 1918, 1st Dep. (SR), *258629*
1612. Stevens, Carl Lloyd, Prince Albert, RCAF
1613. Stevens, Oswald Hilliard, Rosthern, RCAF
1614. Stevens, Philip, Glen Mary/Fenton, **WWI**, en., Winnipeg, June 16, 1915, 43rd Bn., (MR), (**KIA**, Oct. 8, 1916, Battle of the Somme), *153294*
1615. Stevens, William Hillyard, Lily Plain, **WWI**, en., Prince Albert, Apr. 20, 1915, 52nd Reg. (PVA), **WWII**, served in EUR in both wars, *441190*
1616. Stevens, William Walter, Brancepeth, **WWI**, en., Calgary, Apr. 26, 1915, 56th Bn., *446051*
1617. St. Denis, Alex, Lebret, **WWI**, con., Regina, Mar. 8, 1918, 1st Dep./SR, *4090296*
1618. St. Denis, Ernest, Duck Lake, **WWII**
1619. St. Denis, Patrick, Willow Bunch, **WWI**, con., Regina, 1st Dep./SR, dis., Dec. 6, 1918, *258630*
1620. St. Denis, Raoul Oliver, Duck Lake, **WWI**, en., Duck Lake Oct. 22, 1916, 243rd Bn., *1051490*
1621. St. Dennis, Victor, Duck Lake, **WWI**, en., Saskatoon, Aug. 14, 1915, 65th (SK) Bn., *472296*
1622. St. Germain, Edward, Regina, **WWII**
1623. St. Germain, Émile, Pte., St. Laurent de Grandin, **WWII**, La Reg. de la Chaudière, (**KIA**, Oct. 21, 1944), *L-74784*
1624. St. Germain, John, Regina, **WWII**
1625. St. Germaine, J., Pte., father of T. E. St. Germaine, Fort Qu'Appelle, **WWII**
1626. St. Germaine, Thomas E., Pte., Fort Qu'Appelle, **WWII**, en. April 15, 1941,WG, HK
1627. Stone, William, Touchwood, **WWII**
1628. Sutherland, Malcolm Arnold S., Hoey, **WWI**, en., May 15, 1916, 214th/5th Bn./SR/1st CDN Div., *268013*
1629. Swain, John, Battleford/Duck Lake, **WWI**, en., Battleford, Dec. 10, 1915, 232nd Bn., *887844*
1630. Swan, Alex, Lebret, **WWII**
1631. Swanson, Edward, Pte., Balcarres,**WWI**, en., Regina, Oct. 24, 1914, 28th (NW) Bn., *73849*
1632. Tait, Andrew, Fort Qu'Appelle, **WWII**, RRR, (**KIA**, Jul. 4, 1944), *L-105060*
1633. Tanner, Lawrence, **WWII**, RCN
1634. Tanner, Leo Cyril, Prince Albert, **WWII**, Army, EUR
1635. Tanner, Wesley, Lindsay, **WWII**, Army, EUR
1636. Tanner, William, Meadow Lake/Prince Albert, **WWI**, dis., underage, 14 yrs, **WWII**, RCASC, *L-8175*
1637. Tate, Leslie J., Tpr., MacDowall, **WWII**, British Columbia Reg., (**KIA**, Aug. 2, 1944), *L-36731*
1638. Taylor, Allan Bentley, Brancepeth, **WWI**, con., Prince Albert, Oct. 25, 1917, *257893*
1639. Taylor, E. D., Spr., Bresaylor
1640. Taylor, Fred Marigold, Paynton, **WWI**, con., North Battleford, Nov. 27, 1917, 1st Dep. Bn./SR, dis., Feb. 11, 1919, *257896*
1641. Taylor, James Curtis, Yorkton, **WWI**, en., Winnipegosis, MB, Sept. 6, 1915, 79th Bn./5th Bn./SR/1st CDN Div., *150634*
1642. Thomas, Angus, Cpl., Cumberland House, **WWII**, RCASC, 3rd CID, *L-74437*
1643. Thunder, Joe, Batoche, MM, **WWI**, en., Jan. 17, 1916, 128th (NW) Bn., *781920*
1644. Toranzo, Malcolm

1645. Tourond, Arthur Joseph, Batoche, **WWI**, en., Edmonton, Jul. 3, 1916, 22e Bn., (**WIA**, Aug. 27, 1918), *1021144*
1646. Tourond, Isidore, Regina, **WWI**, con., Regina, Jan. 5, 1918, 1st Dep. Bn./SR, *258569*
1647. Tourond, Urbain, Jasmin, **WWI**, en., Melville, Mar. 28, 1916, 229th Bn., *1009752*
1648. Traill, Allan Dougal, Prince Albert, **WWI**, en., Prince Albert, Aug. 2, 1915, *204325*
1649. Traill, Harry, Prince Albert/Big River, **WWI**, en., Prince Albert, Nov. 4, 1916, 243rd Bn., *1051386*
1650. Traill, Wesley, Prince Albert, **WWII**, SSR, *L-86777*
1651. Traill, William McKay, Captain, Prince Albert, **WWI**, 243rd Bn., Prince Albert, 1916
1652. Trotchie, Clarence Joseph, Saskatoon, **WWII**, RCAC, en. in 1941 at 17, dis., underage, reen., April 23, 1942, *B-85244*
1653. Trotchie (Askwith), Dorothy, Saskatoon, **WWII**, RCAF WD, *W-310805*
1654. Trotchie, Irvin, Saskatoon
1655. Trottier, Joe, Muskeg Lake/Duck Lake, **WWI**, en., North Battleford, May 23, 1916, 232nd Bn., *1018311*
1656. Trottier, Joe (Joseph), Val Marie, **WWI**
1657. Trottier, John, Val Marie/Swift Current, **WWI**, con., Regina, Apr. 20, 1918, 1st Dep./SR, *4090385*, **WWII**, VGC
1658. Trottier, Lloyd, Val Marie, **WWII**
1659. Trottier, Peter, **WWII**
1660. Trottier, Samuel, Lloydminster, **WWI**, en., Winnipeg, Mar. 31, 1916, 197th Bn., *913474*
1661. Turner, Leslie, **WWII**
1662. Turner, Joe, **WWII**
1663. Turner, Joseph Edward, Big River/Glen Mary, **WWI**, en., Mar. 15, 1916, 188th Bn., *886474*
1664. Turner, Wilfrid Lawrence, Coxby/Birch Hills, **WWI**, con., Prince Albert, Oct. 27, 1917, 1st Dep. Bn./SR, *268775*
1665. Umpherville, Andrew, MM, Glen Mary, **WWI**, en. Jul. 20, 1916, Prince Albert, 28th (NW) Bn./SLI, *1051115*
1666. Umpherville, Angus Arthur, Glen Mary/Horseshoe Bend, **WWII**, Hastings and Prince Edward Reg., IT, (**KIA**, IT, Hitler Line, May, 14, 1943)
1667. Umpherville, Bud Oliver, Rfn., Glen Mary/Horseshoe Bend, **WWII**, RRR, served: Sept. 1941-Nov. 1945, *L-27955*
1668. Umpherville, Charles (Charlie) Peter, Glen Mary, **WWII**, 1st CID/MG Bn./SLI, *L-2952*
1669. Umpherville, Colin, Rfn., Horseshoe Bend, **WWII**, RRR, (**KIA**, Nov. 15, 1942), *L-27957*
1670. Umpherville, F. S.
1671. Umpherville, Gordon, Glen Mary/Horseshoe Bend, **WWII**
1672. Umpherville, Henry James, Glen Mary/Horseshoe Bend, **WWI**, con., Prince Albert, Nov. 10, 1917, 1st Dep./SR, *257850*
1673. Umpherville, Henry John, Glen Mary/Horseshoe Bend, **WWII**, RCASC/5th RCD, SIC/IT/UK, *L-53875*
1674. Umpherville, Hilmer, Horseshoe Bend, **WWII**
1675. Umpherville, (Horace) Walter, Cumberland House/Glen Mary/Horseshoe Bend, Spr., **WWI**, en., The Pas, Jul. 1, 1916, RCE/233rd Bn. (CFNW)/26th (New Brunswick) Bn., *1021174*
1676. Umpherville, J. E., Sgt., Glen Mary/Horseshoe Bend, **WWII**, RRR, D-Day, *L-27956*
1677. Umpherville, Jerry, Pte., Glen Mary/Horseshoe Bend, **WWII**, Seaforth Highlanders of CA, (**KIA**, IT, Sept. 17, 1944), *L-106905*
1678. Umpherville, John, **WWII**
1679. Umpherville, Ken, Sedley, **WWII**, QORC, **KW**, PPCLI
1680. Umpherville, Peter Charles (Charlie), Pte., Glen Mary/Horseshoe Bend, **WWII**, 1st CID/MG Bn./SLI, *L-2952*
1681. Umpherville, Robert Maxwell, Pte., Glen Mary/Horseshoe Bend, **WWII**, Hastings & Prince Edward Reg., (**KIA**, May 17, 1944 in IT), *L-110317*

1682. Umpherville, Roderick, Glen Mary/Horseshoe Bend, **WWII**, Lorne Scots (Peel, Dufferin, Halton Reg.)
1683. Umpherville, Walter, Glen Mary, **WWII**
1684. Umpherville, William, Glen Mary/Horseshoe Bend, **WWII**
1685. Vandal, Gabriel, Debden, **WWI**, con., Prince Albert, Nov. 17, 1917, 1st Dep. Bn./SR, *258198*
1686. Vandal, Norbert, Duck Lake, **WWI**, en., Saskatoon, Sept. 4, 1916, 243rd Bn., (41 yrs, 8 mos.), *1051239*
1687. Vandale, Albert John, Nutana, **WWI**, en., Saskatoon, Nov. 2, 1915, 65th (SK) Bn., *472551*
1688. Vandale, D. J., LAC, Saskatoon, **WWII**
1689. Vandale, Edward, **WWII**, *R-877331*
1690. Vandale, Ernie, **WWII**
1691. Vandale, Frank, Rfn., Duck Lake, **WWII**, RRR, served: Sept. 1941-Nov. 1945, *L-27772*
1692. Vandale, H., **WWII**
1693. Vandale, James Howard, Nutana, **WWI**, en., Saskatoon, Feb. 22, 1916, 65th (SK) Bn., *474058*
1694. Vandale, Joseph R., **WWII**, SLI, *L-2873*, *B-801685*
1695. Vandale, Norman
1696. Vandale, Oliver, **WWII**
1697. Vandale, William, Duck Lake, **WWII**
1698. Vandale, William, Pte., Saskatoon, **WWI**, (43 yrs, 10 mos.), en. Jun. 15, 1916, Winnipeg, 197th Bn., dis., medically unfit, Dec. 14, 1916, *913548*
1699. Vandale, William Alfred, Pte., Nutana, **WWI**, en., Saskatoon, Dec. 31, 1915, 65th (SK) Bn./46th Bn. (South SK)/SR/4th CDN Div., (**KIA**, Feb. 13, 1917), *472896*
1700. Venne, Joseph Alvin, Marcelin, **WWI**, *1263522*
1701. Venne, Robert, Batoche/Battleford, **WWI**, con., Saskatoon, Jan. 3, 1918, 1st Dep. Bn./SR, *260280*
1702. Vermete, Daniel J., Lindsay, **WWI**, en., Prince Albert, Nov. 3, 1915, *886302*
1703. Vermette, A. C. C., Rfn., Loon Lake, **WWII**, RRR
1704. Vermette, Earl H., Pte., Prince Albert, **WWII**, WG, (**POW**), *L-2867*
1705. Vermette, George, Prince Albert, **WWI**, en., Prince Albert, Jun. 9, 1916, 233rd Bn. (CFNW), *1021117*
1706. Vermette, Henry, Pte., Regina, **WWII**, RCOC, *L-7182*
1707. Vermette, John, Prince Albert, **WWI**, en., Prince Albert, Jun. 7, 1916, *1021116*
1708. Vermette, Louie Robert, Prince Albert, **WWI**, en., Prince Albert, Jun. 9, 1917, *2403203*
1709. Vermette, Louis Ernest John, Prince Albert, **WWI**, en., Prince Albert, Feb. 14, 1916, 15 yrs. Sent to EUR when 19 yrs old. RCAMC Training Dep., *886390*
1710. Vermette, U. L., **WWII**, WG, *L-2860*
1711. Venne, Marie Beatrice, Regina, **WWII**, RCAF WD
1712. Villebrun, Charlie, Meadow Lake
1713. Villebrun, George Alexander, Green Lake, **WWI**, en., Prince Albert, Jun. 9, 1917, CFC, *2193018*
1714. Villebrun, Oscar, Meadow Lake
1715. Villeneuve, François-Xavier (Frank), Cpl., Cochin, Meota Roll of Honour, **WWII**, SLI (MG)
1716. Villeneuve, Henry Edward, Strongfield, **WWI**, en., Wadena, Feb. 25, 1916, 214th Bn., *267226*
1717. Villeneuve, Serve, Pte., Cochin, **WWII**, SLI (MG)
1718. Vizena, Louis, Pte., St. Louis, **WWI**, en., Selkirk, MB, Dec. 14, 1915, (**KIA**, Oct. 10, 1918), *721173*
1719. Vizena, Paul (William), St. Louis, **WWI**, con., Saskatoon, Jul. 5, 1918, 1st Dep. Bn./SR, *3355718*
1720. Vizena, William Hector, Pte., St. Louis, **WWI**, en. Wakaw, May 5, 1916, (**KIA**, Aug. 30, 1918), *267962*
1721. Walker, Norman Stanley, Balcarres, **WWII**, RRR, (**KIA**, Jul. 8, 1944), *L-28050*
1722. Wady, Glen, Touchwood, **WWII**

1723. Warner, S. G., L/Cpl./L/Sgt., **WWII**, 4th Armoured Brigade Coy, Driver/Orderly/ Room Clerk, (**WIA**, broken leg, 1943, hernia, Apr. 1944), *L-64369*
1724. Wells, John, Battleford/Saskatoon, **WWI**, en., Battleford, Dec. 13, 1915, *887845*
1725. Welsh, Douglas, L/Sgt., Broadview, **WWII**, SSR, (**KIA**, 23 Jul., 1944)
1726. Welsh, Joe, Lebret,**WWII**
1727. Wheeler, John Jr., **KW**, CASCF/Sniper Bn./PPCLI
1728. Wheeler, John Sr., **KW**, CASCF/Sniper Bn./PPCLI
1729. White, Louis, Battleford, **WWI**, 5th Bn./SR/1st CDN Div., (**KIA**, Sept. 1, 1918), *1018731*
1730. Whiteford, Clifford, Lac Pelletier, **WWII**
1731. Whiteford, Delphine, Lac Pelletier, **WWII**
1732. Whiteford, Jim, Big River, **WWII**
1733. Whiteford, Pearl, Lac Pelletier, **WWII**
1734. Whitford, Alfred Thomas, North Battleford/Birch Hills, **WWI**, en., Battleford, Jul. 31, 1915, 65th (SK) Bn./46th Bn. (South SK)/SR/4th CDN Div., (**KIA**, Sept. 2, 1918), *472204*
1735. Whitford, Andrew, Lily Plain, 1st Dep. Bn./SR, *260790*
1736. Whitford, Cyrus D., **WWII**, SSR, (**WIA**, Brecht) *L-103302*
1737. Whitford, David, Pte., Piapot, **WWI**, en., Jan. 25, 1917, 1st CMR/SR/249th (SK) Bn., (**KIA**, Sept. 29, 1918), *1069388*
1738. Whitford, David, Pte., **WWII**, SSR, (**KIA**, Jul. 23, 1944), *L-39121*
1739. Whitford, Harold, Battleford, **WWII**, RCASC, (**KIA**, Nov. 21, 1944), *L-8036*
1740. Whitford, James, **WWII**
1741. Whitford, John, Birch Hills, **WWI**, con., Prince Albert, Mar. 3, 1917, 1st Dep. Bn./SR, *268841*
1742. Whitford, Norman, Prince Albert, **WWII**
1743. Whitford, Wilfrid, Saskatoon/Birch Hills, **WWI**, en., Saskatoon, Oct. 15, 1916, 65th (SK) Bn./46th Bn. (South SK)/SR/4th CDN Div., (**KIA**, Apr. 12, 1917), *L-8036*
1744. Wills, Charles, Fort Pitt
1745. Wilson, Charlie Thomas, Pte., The Pas/Cumberland House, **WWI**, con., Winnipeg, Jul. 30, 1918, 10th CGR, *3348442*
1746. Wilson, Harvey, Mackie, **WWII**
1747. Woodman, Edgar Percy, Prince Albert, **WWI**, en., Prince Albert, Oct. 23, 1914, 28th (NW) Bn., *73527*
1748. Woodman, Frederick Thomas, Prince Albert, **WWI**, en., Prince Albert, Apr. 1, 1916, 188th Bn., *886547*
1749. Woodman, Joseph Charles, Prince Albert, **WWI**, en., Prince Albert, Dec. 18, 1916, 230th Bn., CFC, *1013027*
1750. Woodman, William Hector, Prince Albert, **WWI**, en., Big River, Mar. 28, 1916, 188th Bn., *886555*
1751. Work, Peter, **WWII**
1752. Young, Lewis E., Pte., Meadow Lake, **WWII**, WG, (**POW**, **KIA**, Japanese POW camp, May 7, 1944), *H-41770*
1753. Young, R. R., Tpr., Meadow Lake, **WWII**
1754. Young, Stanley, Pte., Cumberland House, **WWII**, SLI (MG)
1755. Young, Thomas Miles, Brancepeth, **WWI**, con., Regina, June 1, 1918, 1st Dep. Bn./SR, *276991*
1756. Young, Zaccheus, Cumberland House/The Pas, **WWI**, No. 49 Coy./CFC, *2487917*, **WWII**, VGC
1757. Zibreski, Mike, Pte., Cumberland House, **WWII**, PPCLI

Endnotes

1 Desmond Morton, "Foreword" in Patricia Burns, *They Were So Young: Montrealers Remember World War II*. Montreal: Véhicule Press, 2002: 17.

2 For a detailed look at Canada's war effort during the Second World War, see Jeffrey A. Keshen, *Saints, Sinners and Soldiers: Canada's Second World War*. Vancouver: The University of British Columbia Press, 2004.

3 It had been a long-held historical canon that the Canadians were inefficient soldiers in World War II and only learned to be an effective fighting force through their long struggle to liberate Western Europe. However, historians are now starting to see the Canadians as an effective, well-trained, and efficient fighting force from the moment they landed in Normandy. See Terry Copp, *Fields of Fire: The Canadians in Normandy*. Toronto: The University of Toronto Press, 2003.

4 English-speaking Canadians had the highest recorded enlistment during the Second World War. French Canadians, Acadians, and "ethnic" Canadians had lower enlistment ratios largely because they did not identify with Britain to the same extent as people of British ancestry. Therefore, Québec and Saskatchewan had the lowest enlistments in Canada because they respectively had the largest populations of people of non-British descent. See Serge Bernier, "Participation des Canadiens Français aux combats: evaluation et tentative de quantification," *Association Québécois d'histoire politque*, Vol. 3, No. 3/4 (1994): 23.

5 Dave Hutchinson, *Remembrances: Interviews with Métis Veterans*. Saskatoon: Gabriel Dumont Institute, 1997: 89. As a postscript, a Canadian War Crimes Tribunal sentenced Meyer to death, but this was commuted to a life sentence and later, after less than a decade in prison, freedom, but not before being made an advisor to the Canadian Forces. See: Patrick Brode, *Casual Slaughters and Accidental Judgments: Canadian War Crimes Prosecutions, 1944-1948*. Toronto: The University of Toronto Press, 1997; and Howard Margolian, *Conduct Unbecoming: The Story of the Murder of Canadian Prisoners of War in Normandy*. Toronto: The University of Toronto Press, 1998.

6 "Canada's Windtalkers," *The Globe and Mail*. June 13, 2002.

7 Many, if not most, Métis veterans, like other veterans such as those in the the Merchant Marine, did not receive any benefits following the war's conclusion. In theory, all veterans were supposed to receive benefits; in practice, this was not the case. To see how the benefits system was supposed to work, consult Peter Neary and J.L. Granatstein, Eds., *The Veterans Charter and Post-World War II Canada*. Montreal and Kingston: McGill-Queen's University Press, 1998; and Douglas Kovatch, "Lack of Justice For Metis Vets," *New Breed Magazine*, Christmas 1999: 16-17.

8 Bryan A. Cyr, *Métis Veterans of Manitoba: From Buffalo to Battlefields*. Winnipeg: Manitoba Métis Federation, 2009.

9 Métis Veterans Memorial Monument Project (Gabriel Dumont Institute). *http://www.gdins.org/veteransmonument*.

10 Manon Lamontagne et al., *The Voice of the People: Reminiscences of Prince Albert's Early Citizens 1866-1895*. Prince Albert: Prince Albert Historical Society, 1985: 169.

11 Stewart A. G. Mein, *Up the Johns! The Story of the Royal Regina Rifles*. North Battleford: Senate of the Royal Regina Rifles, 1992: 5.

12 *Ibid.*

13 Julia Harrison, *Metis: People Between Two Worlds*. Vancouver: The Glenbow-Alberta Institute in Association with Douglas & McIntrye, 1985: 16.

14 "Why Are So Many Metis Enlisting?," Saskatoon *Phoenix*, September 16, 1916.

15 "Soldiers of World War One," Library and Archives Canada (LAC), *http://www.collectionscanda.ca.*

16 Pierre Vandale, "Going to War," *Towards a New Past Volume II: Found Poems of the Métis*. Regina: Government of Saskatchewan, Department of Culture and Youth, 1975: 2.

17 Darren R. Préfontaine, "Remembering Madame Josephte Tourond and the 1885 Resistance," *The New Nation: La novel naayson*, Summer 2010: 16.

18 LAC, *http://www.collectionscanada.ca.*

19 Joe Maurice, "Soldiers from Ile-a-la-Crosse," *Found Poems of the Métis*: 11.

20 Information on the military contribution of Cumberland House residents has been researched and provided by the late Claude Goulet, formerly with the Canadian Forces.

21 Norm Christie, *The Canadians at Mount Sorrel, June 2nd-June 14th, 1916. For King & Empire: Volume VIII*. Ottawa: CEF Books, 2000: 12.

22 Owen Sanderson, *Remembrances*: 123.

23 Victor Wheeler, *The 50th Battalion in No Man's Land*. Ottawa: CEF Books, 2000: 193.

24 Z.M. Hamilton to Flying Officer Stewart, Air Force Recruitment Headquarters, Regina, July 10, 1940. Saskatchewan Archives Board (SAB): R1260 V.16.

25 Wheeler, *op. cit.*: 5.

26 Paul Pelletier, *Remembrances*: 103.

27 Norm Christie, *The Canadians at Ypres, 22nd-26th April, 1915. For King & Empire: Volume I*. (Revised Edition). Ottawa: CEF Books, 2005: 1.

28 "Interview with Lester Stevens: 8th Battalion," Oral Histories of the First World War: Veterans 1914-1918. LAC, *http://www.collectionscanada.gc.ca/first-world-war/interviews/025015-1130-e.html.*

29 Dan Pelletier, *Remembrances:* 99-100.

30 Angus Brown and Richard Gimblett, *In the Footsteps of the Canadian Corps: Canada's First World War 1914-1918*. Ottawa: Magic Light Publishing, 2006: 32.

31 Eddy Lambrecht, *Gas Clouds Over Flanders: The Second Battle of Ypres*. York, England: G.H. Smith and Sons, 2005: 5.

32 Christie, *The Canadians at Ypres*: 1.

33 *Ibid.*

34 *Ibid.*

35 "Owen Sanderson," *op. cit.*: 123.

36 Captain George B. McKean, *Scouting Thrills*, New York: The Macmillan Company, 1919: v.

37 *Ibid.*: 4.

38 *Ibid.*

39 *Ibid.*: 6.

40 *Ibid.*: 7.

41 Sue Ferguson, "A War Scout's Honor: A hero's forgotten story sheds new light on Canada's role in ending the First World War," *Maclean's*, September 8, 2003.

42 Michael Gravel with Darren Préfontaine, "François-Xavier Cardinal: Unknown Métis War Hero," *New Breed*, March-April 2005: 20-21.

43 James Kirk, of Summerside, Prince Edward Island quoted in Tim Cook, *At the Sharp End Canadians Fighting the Great War, 1914 to 1916*. Toronto: Penguin Group, 2007: 467.

44 *Ibid.*: 468.

45 Christie, *The Canadians at Mount Sorrel*: 20.

46 Tim Cook, *Shock Troops*, Toronto: Penguin Group, 2008: 60.

47 Quoted in Cook, *Ibid.*: 77.

48 *Ibid.*: 141.

49 *Ibid.*: 148.

50 Nigel Cave, *Vimy Ridge*, Barnsley, South Yorkshire: Pen & Sword, 2009: 123.

51 Dan Pelletier, Veterans' Interviews, Gabriel Dumont Institute (GDI).

52 Cook, *Shock Troops*: 80.

53 Cave, *Vimy Ridge*: 101.

54 *Ibid.*: 169.

55 *Ibid.*: 110.

56 10th Brigade Infantry Brigade, Report on Minor Raid Carried out by the 46th Canadian Infantry Battalion, February 19, 1917. War Diary of 46th Canadian Infantry Battalion, February 1 to February 28, 1917, Appendix no. VIII. LAC, *http://www.collectionscanada.ca/e/e045/e001112102.jpg*.

57 *Ibid.*: 2.

58 War Diary or Intelligence Summary of 46th Canadian Infantry Battalion, February 17, 1917. LAC, *http://www.collectioncanada.ca/e/e045/e001112092.jpg*.

59 Dan Pelletier, *op. cit.:* 100.

60 War Diary of 5th Canadian Mounted Rifle Battalion, 3rd Canadian Division, from 1st April to 30th April, 1917. Volume 19: 9. LAC, *http://www.collectionscanada.ca/e/e040/e000979411.jpg*.

61 Cook, *Shock Troops*: 144.

62 Cave, *Vimy Ridge*: 146.

63 Cook, *Shock Troops*: 293.

64 *Ibid.*: 159.

65 Médéric McDougall, "Grandfather and Grandmother," *Towards a New Past*: 5.

66 Virginia McKay and Jean Carriere et al., History and Culture Report — Cumberland House. R.M. Bone fonds, University of Saskatchewan Archives. MG 240 Box 2 I. Northern Sask. Housing Needs Survey. A. General files. Cumberland House. Historical material — 1930-1958, 1969-1974 — folder 2. Database ID: 16176: 53.

67 Paul Pelletier (03), Veterans' Interviews, GDI.

68 Mary Jacobson, "There Was a Sickness," *Towards a New Past*: 12.

69 William Sayese, Cumberland House, Interview by Mike Tymchak, 1975: 26.

70 McKay et al., *History and Culture Report*: 53.

71 *Ibid.*: 42.

72 Alex Bishop, interview by Mike Tymchak, April, 1975: 22.

73 Edward King, *The Life and Times of Edward King*. Meadow Lake: Self-Published, 2000: 19.

74 "Métis Support for Gardiner (1934)," Saskatchewan Archives Board (SAB) R33.2, III, 37 (1-5-3).

75 Z.M. Hamilton to Flying Officer Stewart.

76 James G. Gardiner, Minister of the Department of National War Services, to Z. M. Hamilton, Secretary, Saskatchewan Historical Society, dated at Ottawa, 6th May, 1941. SAB.

77 Muriel Stanley Venne, Ed., *Our Women in Uniform*. Edmonton: Institute for the Advancement of Aboriginal Women: 5.

78 "Metis Answer Call of Country to War," Regina *Leader-Post*, March 9, 1941.

79 *Ibid.*

80 *Ibid.*

81 "24 Metis Enlist in Armed Forces," Regina *Leader-Post*, March 9, 1942.

82 "Metis Compile Soldier List," Regina *Leader-Post*, September 18, 1942.

83 Martin Aubichon and Lloyd Bishop, in conversation with Cathy Littlejohn, November, 10, 2001.

84 John Cuthand, "The War Years: Norman McAuley," *New Breed Magazine*, November 1983: 23.

85 Edward King, *Remembrances*: 63-64.

86 *Ibid.*: 63.

87 "Eugene Desjarlais," in Fred Shore and Lawrence Barkwell, Eds., *Past Reflects to the Present: The Métis Elders' Conference*, Winnipeg: Manitoba Métis Federation, 1997: 147.

88 Claude Adams, in conversation with Cathy Littlejohn, May, 2001-December, 2001.

89 Rose Fleury, "Friends," *Found Poems*: 17.

90 Adelaide Ranger (translated in part), "Away We Go," *Found Poems*: 8.

91 Adelaide Ranger (translated in part), "Obliged,"*Ibid.*: 27.

92 Rose Fleury, "All the Work," *Found Poems*: 16.

93 Adelaide Ranger, "She Waited for Him," *Found Poems*: 9.

94 Meota History Book Committee, *Footsteps in Time: Meota, Prince, Wing, Russell, Fitzgerald, Vyner, St. Michael, Jackfish Creek, Ness, Lavigne, Cochin, Murray Lake, Scentgrass, Glenrose, Moosomin, Saulteaux, and Metinota*. Meota: Meota History Book Committee, 1980: 228.

95 Information obtained at Meadow Lake Legion Branch #76, April 23, 2007.

96 Métis National Council, *Towards a Métis Database, Elders' Workshop Report*, May, 1990.

97 *Ibid.*

98 Sayese, interview by Tymchak: 14-18 and 29-30.

99 Charles Pilon, "Why Duck Lake Went To War," *Found Poems*: 7.

100 Médéric McDougall, "Why His People Went to War," *Found Poems*: 20.

101 Roderick Bear, Veterans' Interviews, GDI.

102 Euclide Boyer, *Remembrances:* 17.

103 *Ibid.*: 17-18.

104 "Quit Free Northland For Army," Regina *Leader-Post*, June 18, 1941.

105 Regina *Leader-Post*, September 18, 1943.

106 Ed White, "The War for Recognition," *Western People,* November 5, 1998: 8-9.

107 Sayese, interview by Tymchak, no pp.

108 Euclide Boyer, Veterans' Interviews, GDI.

109 William Carriere, Veterans' Interviews, GDI.

110 Joe McGillivary, Veterans' Interviews, GDI.

111 Aimé Dumont, "Yeah, He Was a Soldier," *Found Poems*: 15.

112 Sayese, interview by Mike Tymchak, no pp.

113 *Ibid.*

114 Regina *Leader-Post*, November 13, 1941.

115 Euclide Boyer, Veterans' Interviews, GDI.

116 See R. Scott, "Of Pure European Descent and the White Race:" Recruitment Policy and Aboriginal Canadians, 1939-1945," *Canadian Military History*, Vol. 5. [Spring 1996], No. 1: 8-15.

117 "Saskatchewan Men Heros in Air Blitz," Regina *Leader-Post*, July 26, 1941.

118 Saskatchewan Soldiers Use Pitchforks … Help Farmers in England Harvest Crops," Regina *Leader-Post*, July 11, 1941.

119 *Ibid.*

120 Brereton Greenhous, *C Force to Hong Kong: A Canadian Catastrophe, 1941-1945*, Toronto: Dundurn Press, 1997: 22.

121 *Ibid.*

122 *Ibid.*: 21.

123 Larry Laliberte, "The War Years: Joe Amyotte," *New Breed Magazine*, November 1983: 23.

124 Dr. Jean Martin, Special Projects Historian, Directorate of History and Heritage, National Defence Headquarters provided the information on the enlistees, survivors, and those who died. These documents are files 92/226, 145.2W3065 (D1), and 593.065 (D4).

125 Alfred Malbeuf, Veterans' Interviews, GDI.

126 B. Dobrucki, B. Letter to the editor, "Devil's Brigade Was Aptly Named," *National Post*, December 22, 2006, A19.

127 Regina *Leader-Post*, July 23, 1942.

128 *Ibid.*

129 Greenhous, *C Force to Hong Kong*: 120.

130 *Ibid.*

131 *Ibid.*: 121-122.

132 *Ibid.*: 121.

133 Alfred Malbeuf, Veterans' Interviews, GDI.

134 Maurice Blondeau, Veterans' Interviews, GDI.

135 *The Windsor Daily Star,* August 20, 1942.

136 "A Chronology of Canadian Military History — Dieppe, 1942," Canadian War Museum, *http://www.warmuseum.ca.*

137 J. L. Granatstein and Desmond Morton. *Bloody Victory: Canadians and the D-Day Campaign, 1944*. Toronto: Lester Publishing Limited, 1994: 11.

138 "Metis Compile Soldier List," Regina *Leader-Post*, September 18, 1942.

139 *The Fort Qu'Appelle Times,* "Military Medal Awarded," *The Fort Qu'Appelle Times*, November 9, 2004: B6.

140 Mary Rose Boyer, "A Métis Family Legacy: Five Men Who Went to War," *New Breed Magazine*, Summer-Fall, 2007: 20.

141 Rocanville History Committee, *Where the Prairie Lily Blows, A History of Rocanville and District.* Vol. 2. Rocanville: Rocanville History Committee, 1997: 610.

142 *Ibid.*: 611.

143 Regina *Leader-Post*, July 24, 1945.

144 Quoted in Terry Copp, (Ed.) *A Nation at War, 1939-1945. Essays from Legion Magazine*. Waterloo: The Laurier Centre for Military Strategic and Disarmament Studies, 2004: 54.

145 *Ibid.*: 55.

146 Dobrucki, *op. cit.*

147 Mark Zuehlke, *Ortona*, Toronto: Douglas & McIntyre, 1999: 320.

148 Archie Nicolas, Veterans' Interviews, GDI.

149 Willow Bunch Historical Society, *Poplar Poles and Wagon Trails: A Mosaic of Willow Bunch R.M. #42*. Willow Bunch, SK: Willow Bunch Historical Society, 1998: 102.

150 "Wounded come home from the Italian front," Regina *Leader-Post*, April 17, 1944.

151 Leona Poitras "Morris Joseph Poitras: Metis War Veteran," *New Breed Magazine*, November 1988: 15.

152 "Wounded come home from Italian Front," *op. cit.*

153 *Ibid.*

154 Bill Barry with Doug Chisholm and Beth Parsons, *Age Shall Not Weary Them: Saskatchewan Remembers its War Dead*. Regina: People Places Publishing, 2005: 357.

155 "Veterans Return," Saskatoon *Star-Phoenix*, April 24, 1945.

156 Dobrucki, *op. cit.*

157 "Devils get their due as US honours Canadian Soldiers," *The National Post*, August 16, 2006.

158 *Ibid.*

159 Granatstein and Morton, *Bloody Victory*: 24-25.

160 *Ibid.*: 25.

161 David Dumont, Veterans' Interviews, GDI.

162 Charles Fosseneuve, Veterans' Interviews, GDI.

163 "32 Now Listed Killed," Regina *Leader-Post*, August 26, 1942.

164 "Saskatchewan Soldiers are Back from Overseas," Saskatoon *Star-Phoenix*, April 16, 1945.

165 White, "The War for Recognition": 8.

166 Fort Pitt Historical Society, *Fort Pitt History Unfolding*. Frenchman Butte: Fort Pitt History Society, 1985: 646.

167 Darren R. Préfontaine, "Honouring Métis Veterans," *New Breed Magazine*, Fall 2005: 2.

168 Joe McGillivary, Veterans' Interviews, GDI.

169 Brode and Margolian. *Casual Slaughters and Accidental Judgments.*

170 Kathy Hodgson-Smith, "Solomon Goulet: Métis Veteran," *New Breed Magazine*, November-December, 2002: 15.

171 William A. Dumont, Veterans' Interviews, GDI.

172 Joe McGillvray, Veterans' Interviews, GDI.

173 Vital Morin, Veterans' Interviews, GDI.

174 "The War for Recognition": 8-9.

175 Regina *Leader-Post*, January 15, 1945.

176 Peter Pelletier, Veterans' Interviews, GDI.

177 Charles Fosseuneuve, Veterans' Interviews, GDI.

178 David Dumont, Veterans' Interviews, GDI.

179 Euclide Boyer, Veterans' Interviews, GDI.

180 "Crossing the Leopold," in Copp, *A Nation at* War, 156.

181 Gordon Brown and Terry Copp, *Look to Your Front … Regina Rifles: A Regiment at War: 1944-45*. Waterloo: Laurier Centre for Military Strategic and Disarmament Studies, 2001: 216.

182 Quoted in Bresaylor Heritage Museum Association Inc., *Bresaylor Between the Battle and the North Saskatchewan Rivers, 1882-1992*. Battleford: Marian Press Ltd., 1992: 460.

183 *Ibid.*

184 Vital Morin, Veterans' Interviews, GDI.

185 *Ibid.*

186 "Regina Men Now Liberated," Regina *Leader-Post*, May 7, 1945.

187 Cuthand, "The War Years: Norman McAuley," 23.

188 Peter Pelletier, *Remembrances*: 106.

189 Vital Morin, Veterans' Interviews, GDI.

190 White, "The War for Recognition": 8-9.

191 Rose Fleury, "Who Came Back," *Found Poems*: 18.

192 Archie Nicolas, Veterans' Interviews, GDI.

193 Charlie Fosseneuve, Veterans' Interviews, GDI.

194 William Carriere, Veterans' Interviews, GDI.

195 The details of Prosper Lariviere's case were shared by his son and step-grandson.

196 David Dumont, Veterans' Interviews, GDI.

197 King, *The Life and Times of Edward King*: 68.

198 Euclide Boyer, Veterans' Interviews, GDI.

199 Archie Nicolas, Veterans' Interviews, GDI.

200 Alfred Malbeuf, Veterans' Interviews, GDI.

201 William A. Dumont, Veterans' Interviews, GDI.

202 Hill's Happenings, "People and the Cypress Hills," *Hills' Happenings*, Ed. 5: 6-7.

203 Meota History Book Committee. *Footsteps in Time*: 228.

204 Weins, Alfred. *Our Roots, La Ronge*. La Ronge: La Ronge Heritage Committee: 1981: 86-87.

205 Médéric McDougall, "Helping Out his Brother After the War," *Found Poems*: 24.

206 Médéric McDougall, "Settling Down After the War," *Found Poems*: 23.

207 Euclide Boyer, Veterans' Interviews, GDI.

208 Sayese, interview by Mike Tymchak, no. pp.

209 Alfred Malbeuf, Veterans' Interviews, GDI.

210 Greenhous, *C Force to Hong Kong*: 148.

211 Charlie Umpherville, Veterans' Interviews, GDI.

212 Cathy Littlejohn, In conversation with Claude Adams, June 25, 2001.

213 McKay et al, History and Culture Report: 49.

214 Robert Alexander Innes, *The Social-Political Influence of the Second World War Saskatchewan Aboriginal Veterans, 1945-1960*. MA Thesis. Saskatoon: University of Saskatchewan, 2000: 75.

215 McKay et al, History and Culture Report: 49.

216 *Ibid.*: 49-50.

217 *Ibid.*

218 *Ibid.*

219 *Ibid.*

220 Weins, *Our Roots*: 86-87.

221 King, *The Life and Times of Edward King*: 93.

222 "Ferguson, Leon J. "Fergie," (WWII & Korea), in *2012 Military Service Recognition Book*. Regina: The Royal Canada Legion, Saskatchewan Command, 2012: 113.

223 Claude Petit, Veterans' Interviews, GDI.

224 "Chronology of the Canadian Advance in Korea," Veterans Affairs Canada, *http://www.veterans.gc/eng*.

225 Courtney, *Patricias in the Korean War*: 2-3.

226 Ron Camponi, Veterans' Interviews, GDI.

227 Courtney: 100.

228 Harold Ross, *Remembrances*: 121.

229 Norris Petit, *Remembrances:* 113.

230 *Ibid.*

231 Maurice Blondeau, Veterans' Interviews, GDI.

232 Ron Camponi, Veterans' Interviews, GDI.

233 Claude Petit, *Remembrances*: 109.

234 Joe McGillivary, *Remembrances*: 87.

235 Hap (Albert) Boyer, *Fiddling Métis Style*. Liner Notes. CD. Saskatoon: Turtle Island Music, 2006.

236 Leon Ferguson, *Remembrances*: 46.

237 Alexandrine Nicolas, Interview, July, 11, 1973, GDI Oral History Collection.

238 David C. Bercuson, *The Patricias*: *The Proud History of a Fighting Regiment.* Toronto: Stoddart Pub. Co., Ltd., 2001: 299.

239 "Our Man in Korea," *New Breed Magazine*, November-December, 1993: 16.

240 Alex Bishop, interview by Mike Tymchak, April, 1975, no. pp.

241 National Métis Veterans Association, National Métis Veterans Association Final Report, December 2001.

242 *Ibid.*

243 *Ibid.*

244 Donna Pinay, "In Recognition of our Veterans," *New Breed Magazine*, November 1988: 3.

245 Carriere, John V., Statement for Pierre Carriere, Regimental number L74343 from for Agnes Carriere, wife of Pierre Carriere to National Métis Veterans Association. November 15, 2001.

246 Wilfred John Henry, *Remembrances*: 58.

247 Pinay, "In Recognition of Our Veterans": 2.

248 *Ibid.*: 2.

249 *Ibid.*: 3.

250 *Ibid.*: 4.

251 *Ibid.*

252 *Ibid.*: 3.

253 Vital Morin, testimony, *Standing Senate Committee on Aboriginal People*, June 16, 1994.

254 *Minutes of the Proceedings of the Standing Senate Committee on Aboriginal Peoples*, November 15, 1994.

255 *Minutes of the Proceedings of the Standing Senate Committee on Aboriginal Peoples*, November 16, 1994.

256 *Ibid.*

257 National Métis Veterans Association, *Final Report National Métis Veterans Association*, December 2001: 19.

258 Métis Veterans Launch Class Action Lawsuit, January 8, 2004, CBC Digital Archives, *http://www.cbc.ca/archives/categories/war-conflict/veterans/continuing-the-fight-canadas-veterans/metis-veterans-launch-class-action-lawsuit.html.*

259 Leon Ferguson, Veterans' Interviews, GDI.

260 Wilfred John Henry, *Remembrances*: 58.

261 Jean-Rodrique Paré, *Post-Traumatic Stress Disorder and the Mental Health of Military Personnel and Veterans*. Publication No. 2011-97-E, Ottawa: Library of Parliament, October 14, 2011: 1. Parliament of Canada, *http://www.parl.gc.ca/Content/LOP/ResearchPublications/2011-97-e.pdf.*

262 *Ibid.*: 2.

263 Quoted in Paré, *Post-Traumatic Stress Disorder*: 2.

264 *Ibid.*: 4.

265 Boyer, "A Métis Family Legacy": 26-27.

Photograph Credits

A note about the images used in this book: Many individuals and institutions provided images of Métis soldiers and Canadians at war for this book. The author and the Gabriel Dumont Institute would like to thank every person and institution for providing this visual catalogue of the Métis and Canada's war experiences. For this book, GDI was able to use a large body of Métis soldier and veteran images in its substantial archival collection, which has been built because of the generous support from veterans like the late Edward King and dedicated community people such as Lawrence Arnault, the late Mary Rose Boyer, and the late Claude Goulet. Since the 1990s, the Institute has collected dozens of Métis soldier and veteran images. GDI has therefore made a conscience effort to include as many images of Métis soldiers as possible in this book. Suffice it to say, it is impossible to thank every person in this book who has provided Métis soldiers or veterans' images to the Institute over the past twenty or so years. Therefore, if you feel that an acknowledgment or credit is required for any image used in this book please contact Darren Préfontaine at 306.657.5711 or at *metismuseum@gdi.gdins.org*. Please send him any corrections for erroneous information that appear in the book as well. The Institute will ensure that all future printings of this book will contain the updated information.

Cover Image Collage: *Juno Beach Centre* (Rob Piercy); *Beny-sur-Mer Cemetery*; *Maple Leaves* (Wikipedia Commons); *World War One Soldiers' Silhouette* (Over the Top Tours). **Page I**: *Mother of Canada Statue, Vimy Ridge Memorial* (Cathy Littlejohn). **Page II**: *Claude Goulet (Left) and Unknown Veteran Batoche* (Cathy Littlejohn). **Page 1**: *Métis Scouts attached to the International Boundary Commission* (Saskatchewan Archives Board/ SAB, R-B635). **Page 2**: *Patrice Fleury, Métis captain of scouts during the 1885 Resistance* (SAB, S-B321). **Page 3**: *Surveyors (Scout) Corps during the 1885 Rebellion, probably at Qu'Appelle, SK* (SAB, S-B5767). **Page 4**: *"D" Squadron, 22nd Saskatchewan Light Horse Officers, Battleford, Saskatchewan, 1911* (NA-299-8); *Twenty-seventh Light Horse, Camp Sewell?, Manitoba. [ca. 1911]*(Glenbow Archives/GB, NA-5155-3). **Page 5**: *22nd Saskatchewan Light Horse, Training at Camp Sewell, Manitoba, May 1912* (NA-326-1); *Military Parade, Battleford, Saskatchewan, 1914* (NA-1138-10); *Military Parade, Battleford, Saskatchewan, 1914* (NA-1138-11); *Voluntary Expedition Force, Battleford, Saskatchewan, August 16, 1914* (GB, NA-1138-12). **Page 6**: *George Loyie*; *Robert Guthrie Sr* (GDI Archives). **Page 7**: *Joseph Victor Daniels, France, 1914* (GB, NA-4584-1). **Page 8**: *Joe McGillis, Métis [ca.1914-1918]* (NA-2365-105); *Army Training, Western Canada* [ca.1914-1918] (GB, NA-2597-16). **Page 9**: *Officers of 28th Battalion. Canadian Expeditionary Force* [ca.1914-1918] (GB, NA-2642-58). **Page 10**: *Alfred Petit*; *Clément Fleury*; *Jean-Marie Paul*; *Jules Fisher*; *Patrick Lejour*; *S. Dumont*; *Thomas Samuel Sr.*; *William Jenson* (Duck Lake History Committee); *Robert Caron* (Cindy LaPlante). **Page 11**: *Tom Ouellette (Right) and R. Joseph Ferguson (Duck Lake)*; *Napoléon Ledoux; Ralph Morin, Oscar Roy, Charles McCallum, and George Villebrun*; *Peter Sandy (1889-1956) and Louis Chatelaine*

(1898-1986); *George and William Montour*; *Joseph Robert Paul and Unknown* (GDI Archives). **Page 12**: *William John Bourassa* (Yvonne Gariepy); *Alexander Sinclair*; *Baptiste Gerard, Peter Morin, Paul Morin, and Norbert Morin*; *Frederick Kennedy* (GDI Archives). **Page 13**: *Norbert and Ralph Morin*; *Norbert Morin*; *Peter Hyacinthe Morin*; *William Bourassa* (GDI Archives). **Page 14**: *Henry Settee, (Centre), Angus Sayese (Left) and Henry Sayese (Right), 1918* (GDI Archives). **Page 15**: *William John Bourassa, WWI Attestation Papers* (Yvonne Gariepy). **Page 16**: *Joseph Victor Laliberte*; *Julius Haggerty, Gaudry, and Chartrand, Willow Bunch* (GDI Archives); *232nd Battalion, Canadian Expeditionary Force recruits, North Battleford, Saskatchewan, 1916* (GB, NA-2499-4). **Page 17**: *Tenth battalion, Canadian Expeditionary Force, Valcartier, Quebec, 1914* (NA-5279-2); *Army camp, Regina, Saskatchewan, 1918* (NA-3229-36*); Men on the troop ship "Olympia", sailing to England during the First World War. [ca.1917-1918]* (PA-3756-7); *Soldiers travelling in box car in France, during the First World War [ca. 1917-1918]* (GB, NA-479-15). **Page 18**: *Village of St. Julien, France, 1915* (GB, NA-2880-1); *Joseph LaRose and Sons: Wilfrid (Joseph's Left), Ramie (Uniform), William John, Albert George (Moustache), Pool Room, Tantallion, SK* (Lynn LaRose). **Page 19**: *Owen Sanderson* (GDI Archives); *Shell bursting in a trench, injuring an unidentified member of the 5th Battalion, C. E. F.* (Library and Archives Canada/LAC, PA-000742); *Essex Farm, Flanders Fields. Inside of Canadian Trench* (Rob Waywood). **Page 20**: *German shell bursting near advanced dressing station [ca.1914-1918]* (GB, NA-4025-17); *Case of trench feet suffered by unidentified soldier, 1917* (LAC, PA-149311). **Page 21**: *A trench on the Canadian front showing "funk holes"* (PA-001326); *Canadian Pioneers laying trench mats over mud. Battle of Passchendaele. November 1917* (PA-002156); *Draining Trenches. 22nd Infantry Battalion (French Canadian). July 1916* (LAC, PA-000396). **Page 22**: *Scouts and snipers (8th infantry Battalion), June 1916* (LAC, PA-00059). **Page 24**: *Daniel Pelletier* (GDI Archives); *Unidentified Canadian Soldier with burns caused by mustard gas, ca. 1916-1918* (LAC, C-080027). **Page 25**: *Nurses en route overseas, Winnipeg, Manitoba, 1915* (GB, NA-3233-6); *St. Julien Memorial, Brooding Soldier* (Rob Waywood). **Page 26**: *Gas helmet drill, 92nd Highlanders, August 15, 1916* (LAC, PA-022718). **Page 28**: *Daniel Pelletier and Toby MacKenzie* (GDI Archives); *World War One Soldiers' Silhouette* (Over the Top Tours). **Page 29**: *A Scene on the battlefield near Coucelette. October, 1916* (PA-000689); *"No Man's Land" in front of Canadian lines, Courcelette, France, October 1916* (PA-000786); *Canadian soldiers returning from trenches during the Battle of the Somme, France, Nov. 1916* (LAC, PA-000832). **Page 30**: *A machine gun emplacement on the crest of Vimy Ridge and the men who drove the Germans from it during the Battle of Vimy Ridge, April 1917* (PA-001101); *Canadian machine gunner dug in shell holes in Vimy advance. April 1917* (LAC, PA-001079). **Page 31**: *Dan Pelletier* (GDI Archives); *Wounded prisoners [ca.1914-1918]* (GB, NA-4025-18). **Page 32**: *Bringing Canadian wounded to the Field Dressing Station. Vimy Ridge. April 1917* (PA-001024); *29th Infantry Battalion advancing over "No Man's Land" through the German barbed wire and heavy fire during the Battle of Vimy Ridge, April 1917* (LAC, PA-001020); *Vimy Ridge Canadian Trenches* (Cathy Littlejohn). **Page 33**: *Vimy Ridge Canadian Trenches* (Cathy Littlejohn); *Vimy Ridge, Grange Subway* (Rob Waywood). **Page 34**: *Shrapnel bursting over our troops in the act of digging themselves in at Vimy Ridge. April, 1917* (LAC, PA-001131). **Page 35**:

Patrice (and Alexandrine) Lejour (GDI Archives); *The Canadian Light Horse going into action at Vimy Ridge. April 1917* (LAC, PA-001111). **Page 36**: *Tank advancing with Infantry at Vimy. April 1917* (PA-004388); *Happy Canadians who captured Vimy Ridge returning to rest billets on motor lorries. May 1917* (PA-001353); *View over the crest of Vimy Ridge showing the village of Vimy, which was captured by Canadian troops. May 1917* (LAC, PA-001446). **Page 37**: *Vimy Ridge, Canadian Cemetery No. 2*; *Vimy Ridge, Canadian Cemetery No. 2. Unknown Canadian Soldier Grave* (Rob Waywood). **Page 38**: *Mud and barbed wire though which the Canadians advanced during the Battle of Passchendaele. November 1917* (PA-002165); *Personnel of the 16th Canadian Machine Gun Company holding the line in shell holes during the Battle of Passchendaele. November 1917* (PA-002162); *A Canadian sleeping in the front line. February, 1918* (LAC, PA-002468). **Page 40**: *Ruben Blondeau* (GDI Archives); *Pat St. Denis* (Ron Rivard). **Page 41**: *Graves of Unknown Canadian Soldiers* (Cathy Littlejohn). **Page 42**: *Menin Gate, Last Post Ceremony* (Rob Waywood). **Page 43**: *Grave of C. Cunningham* (Cathy Littlejohn). **Page 46**: *Edward King, 1943* (GDI Archives); *Second World War recruitment poster, Canada* [ca. 1940-1945] (GB, Poster-125). **Page 47**: *Second World War Recruitment Poster, Canada.* (GDI Archives). **Page 48**: *Personnel of the Canadian Women's Army Corps (C. W. A. C) disembarking from a troopship at Naples, Italy, 22 June 1944* (LAC, PA-108175); *Window display promoting Canadian Women's Army Corps [ca. 1943]* (GB, NA-4784-6); *Dorothy Trotchie (Askwith)*; *Edith Hilda Merrifield* (GDI Archives); *Alice Petit* (Duck Lake History Committee). **Page 50**: *John Amyotte*; *James G. and Edward Poitras, South Saskatchewan Regiment, Winnipeg, 1941*(GDI Archives). **Page 51**: *Charles Arnault*; *Peter Laliberte*; *Fred Merasty, Unknown, and Dan Ross*; *New Recruits, Meadow Lake, June 25, 1940. The men in the back row are: Rfn. A.E. Speer (L-27877), Rfn. G. Landry (L-27886), E.A. Nault (L-27868), Rfn. W.M. Nault (L-27869), Rfn. A. Hein (L-27830), F. Gladue (L-27866), Rfn. P. Lariviere (L-27675), Rfn. W.J. Shaw (L-27883), H. Lang (L-278__), and Rfn. Cullen (L-278__). The men in the front row are: Rfn. J.O. Beaudry (L-27867), Rfn. A. Spenst (L-27873), J.B. Morin (L-27831), Rfn. J.J. Marion (L-27871), Rfn. C.L. Merasty (L-27892), D.T. Moloney (L-27828), Rfn. E. Frisky (L-278__), Rfn. C.R. Fleury (L-27865), J.T. Fiddler (L-27829), Rfn. A. Falcon (L-27236), and Rfn. G. Whelan (L-27876). The Métis men were Landry, both Naults, Gladue, Lariviere, Beaudry, Morin, Marion, Merasty, Fleury, Fiddler and Falcon* (GDI Archives). **Page 52**: *Bill (William) Sayese*; *Lawrence Sayese*; *Stanley Bear, Lawrence Quinney, Charlie Umpherville*; *Unknown, Lawrence and Joe Fiddler, and Unknown* (GDI Archives). **Page 53**: *Donat (Don) Petit* (Claude Petit); *Israël Paul* (GDI Archives); *20th Field Brigade, Royal Canadian Artillery, Edmonton, Alberta, June 1939* (GB, NA-4638-41). **Page 54**: *Leon and R. Joseph Ferguson* (GDI Archives); *Hermond and Edgar Pilon*; *Marcel Petit* (Duck Lake History Committee); *James Paul*; *Arthur Paul*; *Bernard Paul and Marie-Rose Sauvé*; *Ambroise and Donald Paul*; *Alice (Petit) Samuels and Jean-Marie Petit* (GDI Archives). **Page 55**: *Edward King, 1946*; *Army Platoon, North Bay, ON, Basic Training* (GDI Archives). **Page 56**: *E Troop, A Battery at AL Canadian Artillery Training Centre*; *Mounting Guard, Saskatchewan Horse, A Coy, Ottawa, Sept. 1941*(GDI Archives). **Page 59**: *Wilfred John Henry* (GDI Archives). **Page 63**: *Privates James G. and Edward Poitras, South Saskatchewan Regiment, Winnipeg,*

Manitoba [ca. 1941] (NA-4712-2); *Private J.P. Flammond, Private James G. Poitras, Winnipeg, Manitoba [ca. 1940-1945]* (NA-4712-3); *John Howse, Métis, while attending basic camp, Grande Prairie, Alberta, 1943* (GB, NA-5197-9). **Page 67**: *King George VI inspecting 3rd Field Regiment, Royal Canadian Artillery at Aldershot, Hants, February 1940* (NA-4638-15); *Troops in action, southern England, March 1940* (GB, NA-4638-18); *Unidentified member of the Regina Rifle Regiment, England, September 1941* (PA-130245); *An unidentified member of the Regina Rifle Regiment, England, 30 March 1943* (LAC, PA-191315). **Page 68**: *Infantrymen of "C" Company, Royal Rifles of Canada, disembarking from H.M.C.S. Prince Robert, Hong Kong, 16 November 1941* (LAC, PA-114820). **Page 69**: *Victor Ross* (GDI Archives). **Page 71**: *Maurice Blondeau* (GDI Archives); *Lieutenant-Commander Fred Day and officers of the auxiliary anti-aircraft ship H.M.C.S. Prince Robert with liberated Canadian prisoners-of-war at Shamshuipo Camp, Hong Kong, August 1945* (PA-151738); *Canadian and British Prisoners in Hong Kong waiting to be liberated by a landing party from HMCS Prince Robert, 30 August 1945* (LAC, PA-114811). **Page 72**: *Landing craft en route to Dieppe France, during Operation Jubilee, 19 August 1942* (PA-171080); *Canadian Dead litter the Dieppe Beach among Ruined and Abandoned Tanks* (C017291); *German Soldiers Keep Canadian Prisoners of War under Surveillance as they are led through Dieppe* (LAC, PA-200058). **Page 73**: *Edward Joseph Poitras* (GDI Archives). "At Dieppe: Pte. Edward Joseph Poitras, of the S.S.R. killed [August 19, 1942] in the raid on Dieppe. Pte. Poitras was born at Lebret, educated there and later farmed at Avonhurst. In 1940 he married Alice McDougall, enlisted that year, and reached England in 1941 with reinforcements for the unit. Pte. Poitras was among the first Metis casualties of the war. Up the present time 71 [Saskatchewan] Metis are listed as having joined the forces." Regina *Leader-Post*, September 14, 1942. **Page 74**: *Walter Blondeau* (GDI Archives). **Page 75**: *Saskatoon Light Infantry Crest* (Ron Rivard); *Joseph Martial Poitras* (GDI Archives). **Page 78**: *A jeep ambulance of the Royal Canadian Army Medical Corps (R. C. A. M. C.) bringing in two wounded Canadian soldiers on the Moro River front south of San Leonardo di Orona, Italy, 10 December 1943* (LAC, PA-180097); *Archie Nicholas* (GDI Archives). **Page 79**: *Joseph Louis Rivard* (Ron Rivard); *Louis Roy* (GDI Archives). **Page 80**: *Charles Umpherville, Italy* (GDI Archives); *Signore Tomasso, an Italian barber, cuts the hair of Private R. J. Tims of the Anti-Aircraft Support Company, Saskatoon Light Infantry (M.G.), watched by Private Tommy Bear, Ortona, Italy, 10 January 1944* (LAC, PA-177097). **Page 81**: *Thomas Bear Gravesite* (Veterans Affairs Canada, 2222655_1). **Page 82**: *Forcemen of the First Special Service Force boarding a Douglas C-47 aircraft during parachute training at Fort William Harrison, Helena, Montana, United States, August, 1942* (PA-183755); *Canadian Soldiers aboard a troopship arriving at Greenock, Scotland, 31 August 1942* (PA-132775); *Unidentified Forceman of the First Special Service Force during a winter training exercise, Blossburg, Montana, United States, January 1943* (PA-183753); *Major-General E.G. Weeks, Major-General in charge of Administration, talking with personnel of No.1 Canadian Special Service Battalion, which is being disbanded, Aldershot, England, 9 January 1945* (LAC, PA-206723). **Page 83**: *Personnel of the First Special Force being briefed before setting out on a patrol, Anzio beach-head, Italy, 20 April 1944. Lt. H. Rayner of Toronto in the foreground* (PA-128986); *Members of the First Special Service Force* *preparing a meal, Anzio beach-head, Italy, late April 1944* (LAC, PA-128973). **Page 84**: *Paratroopers of the 1st Canadian Parachute Battalion in a transit camp staging area prior to D-Day, England, ca. 1-5 June 1944* (LAC, PA 114599). **Page 85**: *Infantrymen in a Landing Craft Assault (LCA) going ashore from H. M. C. S. Prince Henry off the Normandy beachhead, France, 6 June 1944* (PA-132790); *Reinforcements going ashore from a LCA from H.M. C. S. Henry off the Normandy bridgehead, June 1944* (LAC, PA-190123). **Page 86**: *Infantrymen of the Regina Rifle Regiment en route to France studying a map of Courseulles-sur-Mer, France, ca. 8-10 June 1944* (PA-132799); *Personnel of the Regina Rifles Regiment aboard a landing craft en route to NAN Green Beach, Courseulles-su-Mer, France, 6 June 1944* (PA-205113); *Unidentified Canadian soldiers landing on Juno Beach, Courseulles-sur-Mer, France, 6 June 1944* (LAC, PA-132655). **Page 87**: *Joseph Alfred Collins* (GDI Archives); *Unidentified infantryman of "D" Company, Regina Rifle Regiment on guard duty in forward post, Normandy, France, 10 June 1944* (LAC, PA-131423); *M.E. (Maurice Edward) Nokusis, Bény-Sur-Mer Canadian War Cemetery, France* (Cathy Littlejohn). **Page 89**: *Private G. O. Parenteau of the South Saskatchewan Regiment, Rocquancourt, France, 11 August 1944* (LAC, PA-128089). *Joseph McGillivary* (GDI Archives). **Page 91**: *Canadian Street Patrol in France, WWII. Canadian Army Overseas Photo* (GDI Archives); *Infantrymen of the Regina Rifle Regiment and a   rider firing into a damaged building, Caen, France, 10 July 1944* (LAC, PA-132727); *Peter Pelletier* (GDI Archives). **Page 92**: *Charles, Gordon and Frank Fosseneuve, 1942*; *David Dumont* (GDI Archives). **Page 94**: *Sapper, W. H. Lindstom, 2nd Field Company, Royal Canadian Engineers (R.C.E.) sweeping for mines and road blocks near Kappellen, Belgium, 5 October 1944* (LAC, PA-116748). **Page 95**: *Avro Lancaster in flight* (LAC, PA-145613); *Leo Belanger* (GDI Archives). **Page 96**: *German prisoners guarded by infantrymen of the South Saskatchewan Regiment, Hoogerheide, Netherlands, 15 October 1944* (PA-137142); *A Sherman Vc Firefly tank of The Fort Garry Horse near the Beveland Canal, Netherlands, ca. 29 October 1944* (PA-166849); *Unloading of sacks of Christmas mail at 2nd Canadian Corps Post Office, Canadian Postal Corps (C. P. C.), Oss, Netherlands, 6 December 1944* (LAC, PA-137934). **Page 97**: *Conrad Fleury* (GDI Archives). **Page 98**: *Regimental Aid Party treating an infantryman of the South Saskatchewan Regiment who was wounded by sniper fire while crossing a canal north of Laren, Netherlands, 7 April 1945* (PA-167193); *Regimental Aid Party of the South Saskatchewan Regiment resting on the southern bank of canal north of Laren, Netherlands, 7 April 1945. (L-R): Privates Vic Aubichon, Emile Guerin, Lionel Drouin, Eric Hebert.* (LAC, PA-167196); *Rfn. William Andrew Daniels.* Regina *Leader-Post*, August 7, 1944. "Killed: Rfn. William Andrew Daniels, son of Mr. and Mrs. Angus Daniels, has been reported killed in action in France. He was born at Balcarres Jan. 8. 1920, enlisted in the Regina Rifles May 19, 1941, and went overseas in August, 1941. Besides his parents there are four sisters and six brothers. Two of the brothers, Ptes. Alex J. and Joseph, are in active service overseas, Alex in Italy, and Joseph in France, and a third, Pte. Edward, has returned to Canada after two and half years overseas"; *John Belanger* (GDI Archives): *Canadian Soldiers Display a German Flag. Lieut. Ken Bell, photographer, Xanten (Germany), 9 March 1945* (LAC, PA-137461). **Page 99**: *Vital Morin, 1945* (GDI Archives). **Page 100**: *Pte. John Charette.* Regina *Leader-Post*, October 4, 1944.

"Wounded: Pte. John Charette, son of Mr. and Mrs. L. Charette of Balcarres has been reported wounded in France. He enlisted with the Regina Rifles in 1941, went overseas with the unit in September of that year, was later attached to the Winnipeg Rifles. He was with the Algonquin regiment when wounded"; *Rfn. A. Folster, Pte. R. J. Racette and Pte. G. W. Sherman.* Regina *Leader-Post*, October 4, 1944. "Invalided Veterans Return: Wounded in action in the invasion of France were, left to right, Rfn. A. Folster, Prince Albert; Pte. P. J. Racette, Regina, and Pte. G. W. Sherman, Regina. They were with a group of invalided veterans of the France and Italy campaigns which returned to Regina Tuesday night"; *Pte. T. E. St. Germaine.* Regina *Leader-Post*, January 6, 1942. "Hong Kong Defenders: Pte. T. E. St. Germaine, Qu'Appelle. Brief sketches of three more Saskatchewan men who figured in the defence of the Hong Kong garrison: … Pte. T. E. St. Germaine, 20, of Qu'Appelle, is son of Pte. J. St. Germaine who is serving with the army overseas. T. E. St. Germaine joined the Winnipeg Grenadiers at Winnipeg, April 5, 1941"; *Sgt. Raymond Joseph La Rocque.* Regina *Leader-Post*, September 10, 1944. "Wounded: Sgt. Raymond Joseph La Rocque, 22, son of Pte. A. J. La Rocque and Mrs. La Rocque, Estevan, was wounded in action in France Aug. 27. He joined the S.S.R. in 1939 at the age of 17, and went overseas in December, 1940. He was in the Dieppe raid. Besides his parents, he has wife and son in England, his eldest brother, Robert, with the S.S.R. in France, a younger brother, Richard, at home, and five sisters"; *Sgt. W. J. Ouelette.* Saskatoon *Star-Phoenix*, January 28, 1944. "Died for His Country: Sgt. W. J. Ouelettte. 24 years of age, who was killed in action in Italy, December 28, according to information received by his parents, Mr. and Mrs. C. Ouelette, 1200 Broadway. Enlisting in the Saskatoon Light Infantry at the outbreak of the war in 1939, Sergeant Ouelette went overseas with his unit in December the same year. He was wounded in Sicily on August 4, last year and was flown to North Africa for treatment. He had been back in action again for about a month when he lost his life. Born in Hanley in 1919, he came to Saskatoon with parents the following year. He attended St. Mary's School. A brother, Oliver, is with the Canadian Forces in Italy"; *Rfn. J. C. Wright, Paddockwood*; Pte. E. Pritchard, Baljennie; Pte. C. W. Reid, Regina and Hemingford, Que.; Gnr. A. Prince, Abernethy. Regina *Leader-Post*, April 16, 1945."Home again: The men shown above were among a group of veterans who arrived in Regina from overseas. Sunday night: Left to right: Rfn J. C. Wright, Paddockwood; Pte. E. Pritchard, Baljennie; Pte. C. W. Reid, Regina and Hemingford, Que.; Gnr. A. Prince, Abernethy." **Page 101**: *Peter Pelletier* (GDI Archives). **Page 103**: *Norm Henderson and Nathan Settee* (GDI Archives). **Page 104**: *Charles Fosseneuve* (GDI Archives). **Page 105**: *Saskatoon Light Infantry parades on 21st Street. Saskatoon Light Infantry parades on 21st Street East from the CN Station to Kiwanis Park for the homecoming ceremony. Crowds and cards line street. October 3, 1945. Photographer: Hillyard, Leonard A.* (B-138); *Light Infantry returning at end of World War II. Men of the Saskatoon Light Infantry, 1st Battalion, parade down 21st Street on their return from the war. Photographer: Hillyard, Leonard A.* (Saskatoon Public Library, B-1737); *1939-45 Service Medal (Back and Front), Joseph Alexander Fayant* (GDI Archives). **Page 106**: *Prosper Lariviere,*

Discharge Certificate, WWII (Alcide Lariviere). **Page 107**: *Euclide Boyer* (GDI Archives). **Page 108**: *Alfred Malbeuf, Right* (GDI Archives). **Page 109**: *Hospital Ship, Oranje*; *William Dumont* (GDI Archives). **Page 112**: *Alfred Malbeuf*; *Charles Umpherville* (GDI Archives). **Page 113**: *Charles Umpherville, Discharge Certificate, November 13, 1945* (GDI Archives). **Page 114**: *James Lavalley* (GDI Archives). **Page 115**: Alex *Morin, Councillor, A28 Fur Conservation Block, Cumberland House, Saskatchewan, 1949* (PA-2218-388); *Edward Sahyes, Cumberland House, SK, 1951* (PA-2218-483); *Pierre Carriere, Cumberland House Legion Branch President, Cumberland House, SK, 1949* (GB, PA-2218-387). **Page 117**: *Volunteers for the Korean War, 27th Brigade, Regina Rifles, Hanover, Germany, 1950. Bottom Left: Sgt. Martin Aubichon (M), ___ Hill (Prince Albert) (M), ___ Prosper (Duck Lake), Boyer (M) (Prince Albert), ___ Lacombe (Regina); Second Left: _____ (Prince Albert), ___ Greyeyes (M) (Duck Lake), _____, Fisher (M)(Lebret), ___ Lariviere (*Île-*à*-la-Cross *or Beauval); Third Left: _____ Anderson (Prince Albert area), ____ Desjarlais (M) (Fort Qu'Apelle), _____, ___ Runs (Duck Lake), ___Holbett (Duck Lake), ___(Black) (M) (Beardy's First Nation); Top Right: ___(Morin) (M) (Meadow Lake), ___Laliberte (M) (Green Lake), ____, ____, ___Beauchense, ___Callaghen, ____* (Lois Dolby); *Joseph and Lawrence Fiddler (Ptes.), and Unknown*; *Joseph George Merasty* (GDI Archives). **Page 118**: *Albert Morin, Back Row, 2nd from Left. Saskatoon Light Infantry*; *Alexander Poitras*, *Alexander Malbeuf*; *Charles Aubichon*; *Albert Merasty with son Peter*; *Joseph Flammond*; *Leonard Morin* (GDI Archives). **Page 119**: *Lawrence Morin, Group of Soldiers*; *Louis Nolin*; *Ralph Aubichon and J.-B. (Jean-Baptiste)(Chip) Ouelette*; *Alfred Malbeuf, Right*; *Roy L. McDonald (Norquay)* (GDI Archives). **Page 120**: *Victor (and Justine) Daniels*; *Wilfrid Poirier*; *Alfred Ouellette*; *Alphonse Collins*; *Alphonse Merasty and Alex Bear*; *Armand Morin and Peter Laliberte*; *John-Baptiste Maurice*; *Joseph Martin; Louis Blondeau* (GDI Archives). **Page 121**: *Louis Poitras and Unknown Man*; *Ora Madden*; *Ralph Aubichon*; *John Buskey*; *Max Lucier (Centre)* (GDI Archives). **Page 122**: *Leo Pruden*; *Louis Laboucane*; *Peter Laliberte*; *Raymond Delaronde (Pte.) and Edward King (Pte.), Meadow Lake, SK, 1943*; *Solomon Krein*; *Vital Poitras*; *Stan Durocher and Charles Umpherville; William Tanner* (GDI Archives). **Page 123**: *Jules J. Morin; Lawrence Carey*; *John Fiddler*, *John Flamont and mother, Alice*; *Emile Laboucane*; *H. J. Myette*; *Harold Ross* (GDI Archives). **Page 124**: *George Pambrun*; *Dan Pelletier*; *Gaspard Morin*; *Cyprian Corrigal*; *Ernest Joseph Boyer* (GDI Archives); *Métis Soldiers [ca. 1940-1945]* (NA-4712-1); *Frank Howse (John Nelson?), Métis, while serving in Army, 1943* (GB, NA-5197-10); *Vital and Alex (Alexander) Poitras (Ptes.)* (GDI Archives). **Page 125**: *Edwin, Leon, and Norbert Morin*; *Leo Bourassa* (GDI Archives*); Rose, Edward, Patsy, Elmer, and Pat Parenteau* (May Henderson); *James Willard Shortt* (Nora Cummings). **Page 127**: *Ambroise J. Durocher*; *Daniel Ross, Stanley Morin, Harry Sanregret, and Unknown Man*; *Edward G. Blondeau*; *Eli Caplette (Cpl.)*; *Eugene Morin and Stanley Laliberte*; *Fred Merasty and Dan Ross*; *Cliff Hessdorfer, circa 1942*; *Joseph Fayant*; *Harry Sanregret, Stanley Morin and Arnold Gervais* (GDI Archives). **Page 128**: *Leon Ferguson*; *Maxime Collins and Clarence Laliberte*; *Raymond Delaronde (Pte.) and William M. Fiddler Jr. (Pte.), 1951*; *Ronald Collins*; *Leon Ferguson, Ft. Lewis, Washington, 1951; William Jr. and Clarence Fiddler (with parents and siblings)* (GDI Archives). **Page 129**: *Claude Petit (Left), with Bren Gun, Mountain Training on the way to Korea, Jasper,*

Alberta; *Claude Petit, Saskatchewan Order of Merit recipient* (Claude Petit); *Cpl. Len Camponi, a veteran of 14 months' service in the Far East war theatre as a member of "C" Squadron, Lord Strathcona's Horse, found to his surprise that his newly arrived replacement as crew commander of the tank "Calvados" was none other than his brother, Cpl. Ron Camponi, of "B" Squadron, who to Len's further amazement and delight was accompanied by younger brother Tony. This image appeared on the cover Legion Magazine, August 1952* (LAC, e011061845). **Page 130**: *Frontlines, Korean War, 1952* (NA-5117-2); *Handing out rations in the front lines, Korea, 1952* (NA-5117-13); *Soldiers of the Princess Patricia's Canadian Light Infantry, Korea, March 17, 1953* (GB, NA-5117-6). **Page 131**: *Ron Camponi*; *Maxime Collins and Unknown Soldier* (GDI Archives); *Private John J. Wheeler, 1st Battalion P. P. C. L. I and his son John with sniper rifle at Korean front, 20 February 1952* (LAC, PA-128444); *Unknown and Eugene Morin; Unknown Métis Soldier*; *Unknown Métis Soldier and Another Soldier; Unknown Métis Soldiers* (GDI Archives). **Page 132**: *Harold Ross*; *Norris and Claude Petit (Top Left) on Leave*; *Norris Petit* (GDI Archives). **Page 133**: *Royal Canadian Army Service Corps trucks taking supplies along a mountain road north of Pusan, January 1951*(LAC, PA-133339). **Page 134**: *Particias on Patrol, February 1951*(PA-115034); *PPCLI Personnel on Patrol* (LAC, PA-115564); *Joseph McGillivary* (GDI Archives); *Albert "Hap" Boyer (With fiddle), Brian Cyr (maroon jacket), Claude Adams (Legion blazer)* (Cathy Littlejohn). **Page 135**: *Leon Ferguson* (GDI Archives). **Page 136**: *Claude Petit with other Korean War Veterans, Korean War Anniversary Thank You Banquet, 2010* (Claude Petit); *Clarence Fiddler*; *Maurice Blondeau, Unknown, and Claude and Norris Petit*; *Korea Volunteer Force Medal (Back and Front), Joseph Alexander Fayant*; *Korean War Service Medal (Back and Front), Joseph Alexander Fayant* (GDI Archives). **Page 137**: *United Nations Korean War Medal (Front and Back), Joseph Alexander Fayant*; *Bobby (Robert) Morin with Grandmother Maria (Gaspard) Morin, 1960s*; *Edward King, 1950s, Regina Rifles* (GDI Archives); *Claude Petit (Left), Canadian Army, PPCLI, Germany, 1964* (Claude Petit); *Wilber Fisher*; *Janet Blaze*; *Claude Goulet and Roy Fosseneuve*; *Norris Petit and Son*; *Leon Ferguson, Prince Albert, 1971* (GDI Archives). **Page 139**: *Duck Lake Métis Veterans, Late 1950s*; *Cliff Hessdorfer* (GDI Archives). **Page 140**: *Charles Umpherville*; *Claude Adams and Max Lucier* (GDI Archives). **Page 142**: *Wilfred John Henry* (GDI Archives). **Page 143**: *Edward King*; *Vital Morin* (GDI Archives). **Page 144**: *Cliff Hessdorfer, Frank Tomkins, Leon Ferguson, and Charles Umpherville*; *Métis Veterans, Prince Albert Métis Fall Festival, 1998. Left to right in the back row are: Claude Goulet, Nathan Setee, Charles Fosseneuve, Peter Tompkins, Cliff Hessdorfer, Marcel Giraud, Charles Umperville, Frank Tompkins, Harold Lagimodiere, Roy Fosseneuve, and Ronald Collins. Left to right in the front row are: Norman Henderson, Max Lucier, Stanley Durocher, Alex Dreaver, Solomon Goulet, Roderick Bear, and Edward King* (GDI Archives). **Page 145**: *Edith Hilda Merrifield*; *Joseph George Merasty*; *Lawrence Sayese*; *Len Desjarlais* (GDI Archives). **Page 146**: *Leo Belanger*; *Max Lucier*; *Norm Henderson*; *Ora Madden* (GDI Archives). **Page 148**: *Frank Tomkins, Leon Ferguson, Claude Petit, Cliff Hessdorfer, Vital Morin, Joseph Fayant, Leo Belanger, Charles Umpherville, and Edward King* (GDI Archives). **Page 149**: *Métis Veterans Colour Guard, Prince Albert Métis Rendezvous, 1995*; *Métis Veterans Colour Guard, Prince Albert Métis Fall Festival, 1997* (GDI Archives). **Pagc 150**: *Claude Petit (Left) and Unknown Veteran*

(Claude Petit); *Frank Tomkins, Armand Fisher, Harold Ross, Peter Pelletier, Edith Merrifield, Charlie Fosseneuve, and Maurice Blondeau* (GDI Archives). **Page 151**: *Canada 125 Service Medal (Back and Front), Joseph Alexander Fayant* (GDI Archives). **Page 154**: *Sanctuary Woods—Hill 62. Iepers Belgium in the background* (Rob Waywood) **Page 155**: *Close Up, Poppy, Northern France* (Cathy Littlejohn); *Menin Gate, Western Entrance* (Rob Waywood). **Page 156**: *Menin Gate Memorial* (Cathy Littlejohn); *Tyne Cot Memorial to the Missing, Passchendaele* (Rob Waywood). **Page 157**: *Vimy Ridge Memorial, Viewed from the Northeast*; *Vimy Ridge Memorial, Viewed from the Southeast*; *Vimy Ridge Memorial, Mother of Canada Statue*; *Vimy Ridge Memorial, Breaking the Swords Statue* (Rob Waywood); *Vimy Ridge Memorial, Mourning Parents, the Female*; *Vimy Ridge Memorial, Mourning Parents, the Male* (Cathy Littlejohn). **Page 158**: *Vimy Ridge Memorial, Fallen Soldiers Names* (Cathy Littlejohn). **Page 159**: *Deville Wood Memorial, Cross of Sacrifice, Somme* (Cathy Littlejohn); *Adanac Cemetery, Somme; Vimy Ridge, Givenchy Road Canadian Cemetery* (Rob Waywood). **Page 162**: *L. H. (Lloyd) Adams, Bény-Sur-Mer Canadian War Cemetery, France* (Cathy Littlejohn). **Page 163***: Juno Beach Centre; Juno Beach Centre Statue* (Juno Beach Centre/G. Wait*); Juno Beach, Ranville Cemetery*; *Juno Beach, Ranville Cemetery* (Cathy Littlejohn). **Page 165**: *Rows of graves, Bény-Sur-Mer Canadian War Cemetery, France*; *Bény-Sur-Mer Canadian War Cemetery, France* (Cathy Littlejohn). **Page 166**: *Pte. Matthew Desjarlais*. Regina *Leader-Post*, August 24, 1944. "Killed: Pte. Matthew Joseph Desjarlais, Lebret, has been killed in France. He was born at Lebret 22 years ago, educated there and enlisted in the Regina Rifles in 1940, going overseas in 1941 … there is a brother overseas, Freddie, who has been reported wounded … ."; *M. J. (Matthew Joseph) Desjarlais, Bény-Sur-Mer Canadian War Cemetery, France*; *B. A. (Bill Andrew)Daniels, Bény-Sur-Mer Canadian War Cemetery, France*; R. R. *(Russell Rudolph) Isbister, Bény-Sur-Mer Canadian War Cemetery, France*; *J. (Joseph) Flammand, Bény-Sur-Mer Canadian War Cemetery, France*; *J. B (John Baptiste) Delorme, Bény-Sur-Mer Canadian War Cemetery, France* (Cathy Littlejohn). **Page 167**: E. *V. (Elie Victor) Sinclair, Bény-Sur-Mer Canadian War Cemetery, France*; *Sgt. Elie Victor Sinclair*. Regina *Leader-Post*, July 4, 1944. "Killed: Sgt. Elie Victor Sinclair, son of Mr. and Mrs. Louis Sinclair, Lebret, has been reported killed in action in France June 9, according to official notification received by his wife at Star City, Sask. Sgt. Sinclair, 31, was born at Lebret, and educated there. He joined the Regina Rifles four years ago, and went overseas three years ago. He leaves besides his wife and parents and two brothers and four sisters, residing at Lebret. A memorial requiem mass was celebrated by Fr. Jalbert, O.M.I., in Sacred Heart Church, June 26"; A. *W. (Anthony William) Blondeau, Bény-Sur-Mer Canadian War Cemetery, France* (Cathy Littlejohn); *James Blondeau* (GDI Archives); *S. (Solomon) Kline, Bény-Sur-Mer Canadian War Cemetery, France*; *G. C. (George Charles) Boyer, Bény-Sur-Mer Canadian War Cemetery, France* (Cathy Littlejohn). **Page 168**: *N. J. (Norman Joseph) Morin, Bény-Sur-Mer Canadian War Cemetery, France*; *P. L. (Patrick Louie) Anderson, Bény-Sur-Mer Canadian War Cemetery, France*; *J. D. (John Donald) Dumont, Bény-Sur-Mer Canadian War Cemetery, France*; *D. (Daniel) Fulton, Bény-Sur-Mer Canadian War Cemetery, France* (Cathy Littlejohn).

Author Biography

Cathy Littlejohn, Ph.D. is a historian, teacher, and writer based in Saskatoon. With Ron Rivard, she co-authored *The History of the Metis of Willow Bunch*, which won the Publishing in Education award for the 2004 *Saskatchewan Book Awards*. Since first working with the Association of Métis and Non-Status Indians of Saskatchewan in 1977, Cathy has worked on research projects and conducted policy development for the Métis at the local, provincial, and federal levels. For the last ten years, she has sought to identify Métis soldiers to document their contributions as well as that of their families and communities. Her research has taken her from family documents, to local libraries, and finally, to Europe's battlefields and war cemeteries. Through her travels and research, she has uncovered incredible stories of courage and perseverance. Her new book, *Métis Soldiers of Saskatchewan: 1914-1953* is the culmination of these efforts. Cathy is presently a board member for the Saskatchewan Archives Board.